NETSCAPE
TIME

NETSCAPE TIME

The Making of the

Billion-Dollar Start-Up

That Took On Microsoft

JIM CLARK
WITH OWEN EDWARDS

ST. MARTIN'S PRESS ⋈ NEW YORK

Book design by Diane Hobbing of Snap-Haus Graphics

Library of Congress Cataloging-in-Publication Data

Clark, Jim.
    Netscape time : the making of the billion-dollar start-up that
took on Microsoft / Jim Clark with Owen Edwards.
      p.   cm.
    ISBN 0-312-19934-1
    1. Netscape Communications Corporation—History. 2. Internet
software industry—United States—History. I. Edwards, Owen.
II. Title.
HD9696.65.U64N472   1999
338.4'7004678'0973—DC21   98-51609
                                                CIP

First Edition: June 1999

10 9 8 7 6 5 4 3 2 1

This book is dedicated to two people. First, to my wife, Nancy, who encouraged (insisted) that I leave Silicon Graphics after many years of my bitching about the situation there. Without her encouragement, I might not have left, Netscape would not have been started, and the Internet might not have developed as it has.

And to Jim Barksdale. Jim had been second in command at both Federal Express and McCaw Cellular, and I knew he wouldn't be interested in a third similar stint. But I also knew that Netscape would ultimately grow uncontrollably and that Microsoft would go after the company. I simply didn't want the responsibility of running things, and I felt I would not be able to do the job. In fact, I wasn't sure anyone could. So I lured Jim into becoming the CEO by making him an offer he couldn't refuse. Some years later, in the heat of Microsoft's incendiary tactics, he confessed that he had never had a harder job, keeping employee morale high and turnover low, while fighting perhaps the most powerful enemy in the history of business. All of the shareholders were lucky to have him leading the battle. Without Jim, Netscape would definitely never have made the difference it did.

ACKNOWLEDGMENTS

My co-author and I would like to thank all of the people who helped build Netscape for their cooperation in writing this book. My memory was enhanced via conversations with them, and they stood to gain nothing for helping me put this bit of history down accurately.

I especially thank the managers and other employees who stayed with the company during the most difficult times of their business lives.

CONTENTS

PART FOUR

RUN TO DAYLIGHT

Spring/Summer 1995

"It is the business of the future to be dangerous."

—ALFRED NORTH WHITEHEAD

PART ONE

WE HAVE LIFTOFF
Summer 1995

1 The Offering

On August 9, 1995, I woke up at my usual time. The weather at seven A.M. was typical for a summer morning in the semi-mythical part of California known as Silicon Valley: While the rest of the country sweltered, in my neighborhood thirty miles south of San Francisco the clouds lay so low they verged on fog. The temperature hovered in the mid-fifties. Had this been almost anywhere else, the dull light coming through the bedroom windows would have suggested a day of rain, but I knew that within two hours the sun would burn away the clouds and the temperature would climb into the nineties. Rain still was months away.

Despite the typically overcast weather, everything else about this particular Tuesday was full of expectation. It was as different as it could possibly be from just another day. Nothing about what would come could be predicted *except* the weather. At nine-thirty New York time, half an hour before my clock radio had blinked on in the middle of a traffic report, the first shares of Netscape were to have been offered to the public on the NASDAQ exchange. Netscape, a software company I had formed only a little over a year before in partnership with Marc Andreessen, a recent graduate of the University of Illinois, was the second technology company I had founded. On this day, the first company, Silicon Graphics, was worth $2.2 billion, but that was no longer my passion. Netscape would give me the chance at a second billion-dollar company—a rare opportunity in American business—but everything depended on the mood of an uncertain stock market.

Though Wall Street had been enthusiastic about high technology launches in the mid-1990s, some analysts were saying that this market, in the words of the old Cole Porter song, was too hot not to cool down. Little did they know that the forthcoming Netscape IPO would spark an Internet boom that would give at least five more years of life to the bull market, which was already fairly old. By the time the NASDAQ market would close, about six hours later, many people at Netscape could be wealthier than they could ever have imagined. But if we'd miscalculated in going public so early in the game, with no profits and only modest revenues, the flop would be dramatic.

As I got ready to go to work, I went over in my mind various reasons for optimism. Market share counted far more than profits in the early stages of a company's development. What Netscape had produced was Navigator, a browser "device" to give people an easy-to-use doorway into the rapidly expanding new world of the Internet and the World Wide Web. Most of the major players in the business, those who were thought to know everything, including Bill Gates, were sure there was no money to be made on the Internet. Gates had intimated at a Networked Economy conference in Washington, D.C., before Netscape released its first "beta" of the browser—in essence, a public test—that no one except operation systems vendors would make money on browsers. I knew that his mission at the time was still to put America Online (AOL) out of business by building an online service that leveraged his monopoly in the operating system; he was still in denial that this online service business model, as well as AOL's, was going to be dramatically transformed by a standard Internet network run by the communications companies of the world and accessible to all, not just those he would choose.

We had come up with something, to borrow a phrase from Steve Jobs, "insanely great," and we knew that a solid potential customer base was already using the Net. So our response to Gates's smug assumption that any territory he didn't already own wasn't worth owning was to make our product so that it could be quickly and easily distributed over the Internet. We did this by offering an early beta version of Navigator on the Internet in October of 1994, just six months after we had formed the company. In what the Army Airborne might call a "vertical envelopment," we used the Web, the very medium we hoped to support (and be supported by), to outflank the crowded shelves of the software stores and go directly to the user.

The gambit worked. By spring, more than 6 million copies had been downloaded by users all over the world. I figured that if you could get enough people to use something, you couldn't not make money with it eventually. If, as I suspected, the majority of people who had sucked our software out over the Net were inside companies, sooner or later chief information officers were going to realize that many of their employees were using Netscape and decide it was necessary to license the software for everyone. This was the biggest single bet I had ever made—not being paid for the product before it's put to use—but it was already beginning to pay off, and the company was enjoying rapidly expanding revenues. Now I was about to find out how many people in the investment community agreed with me about our competitive chances.

However the events of the day went, Marc and I, a few ex-SGI engineers, and our children's crusade of overworked young programmers—the handful of recent college graduates who had swapped having a life for months of long days creating Navigator— were convinced that somehow today would make the world aware of the huge commercial potential of the Web and the Internet. We felt certain we were in the right place at precisely the right time, poised to catch the crest of the information revolution's next big wave.

Even the man who would be king has to brush his teeth and go about the ordinary little rituals of everyday life. As I ate breakfast, I thought about an "all-hands" meeting the company's CEO, Jim Barksdale, had held a few days before. "The worst thing in the world," he sternly stressed to the four hundred or so employees who by now made up the company, "is to pay attention to the stock price. Once we are public, I don't want people to discuss Netscape's stock price at work."

A veteran telecommunications executive who had been with the company since January, Barksdale knew it was unprecedented to go public so early, and initially hadn't been enthusiastic about the brash move. He would have preferred to hold off until the spring of 1996, when the company would be two years old with a one-year-old product on the market, five or six quarters of revenue, and at least a bit of profitability. On this August day, only nine months had passed since our first browser had gone out over the Net and we'd had only two quarters with money coming in—with no profits. Even given the aura of glamor surrounding technology stocks and quite a lot of press interest, we were decidedly a dark horse.

Barksdale, a canny, hands-on leader, also was worried about the impact a liquid stock might have on the employees of the company. Since the beginning of the Silicon Valley gold rush, early employees of companies that successfully went public, like the first prospectors on a rich claim, suddenly became wealthy, while latecomers didn't. In a situation where all animals are equal, but some are more equal than others, camaraderie can unravel fast.

"I worry what it will do to our employees," Barksdale said. "There's a certain excitement at being a pre-IPO company. Anything can happen, and it's all still ahead. Once you go public, old hands and recent hires are sometimes in different classes due to the vagaries of the market."

Walk through a Silicon Valley company's parking lot in the weeks following an IPO and you'll see the proof of a new caste system; side by side stand beat-up Toyota Tercels and glittering Porsche Carreras, rusty old Volvo station wagons and sleek BMWs. The fact that the owners of such dramatically different cars may be doing very similar jobs can impact company morale.

Yet somewhere in this process of equity sharing and technology IPOs is the basis for a new economy that distributes wealth far more diversely than at any other time in the history of business, giving rise to what might be called a "new age capitalistic socialism." Contrast the distribution of wealth in the Information Age with that of the Industrial Revolution. The Carnegies and Rockefellers were downright stingy compared to the founders of modern companies. Even the biggest "robber baron" of our time, Bill Gates, has enabled thousands of millionaires by causing Microsoft to award generous stock options. Despite Barksdale's reservation, the IPO was a necessary part of this process. Most of the money made in successful companies is made after the IPO, and employees who come afterward can also make enormous wealth if they learn to compete.

Barksdale's worry was not only the sudden appearance of "class" differences but also the potential loss of focus the stock sale might cause, since at this point weariness in the company was at epidemic levels and focus was everything. The date for the release of Netscape's second product, Navigator 2.0, was approaching quickly. The nucleus of young programmers that had got us this far this fast was still putting in long hours. As Aleks Totic, a young immigrant from what used to

be Yugoslavia and one of the original University of Illinois group, described the situation in a telegraphic note to himself: "Development
was in full swing: Work all day, night, have late-night breakfast at
Denny's." In a business where success never brings rest, that wasn't
likely to change anytime soon (and in fact it hasn't). The release of
2.0 was crucial for the company's momentum, and the idea that even
one day's progress might be lost while people followed the rise or fall
of the stock price was worrisome.

I could understand and share Barksdale's concerns—I wasn't so sure
I could keep my own mind on business during our first public offering.
Not only was I a cofounder of Netscape, I had also functioned as the
primary venture capitalist, buying all the Series A stock with $3 million
of my own money (about 30 percent of the small fortune I had made
at Silicon Graphics). I'd learned a lot about the ins and outs of start-
ups since founding Silicon Graphics, where, as the technology visionary, business leader, organizer, and founder, I'd ended up with only
about 3 percent of the company—and then had to watch even that
minor share steadily diluted as more capital was raised and other expensive executives were recruited. This time, I'd been determined not
to let my equity bleed away as other investors came in. If I could have
kept the wheels on the start-up all by myself, I would have. From April
until September of 1994 I was the monarch at Netscape, at least in its
business functions. I'd really liked that brief period, because I could
make instant decisions without consulting anyone but Marc, and then
because I wanted to, not had to. But high-tech companies have a way
of becoming very expensive very fast. With no money coming in and
expenses growing exponentially, I'd known the time had come to bring
in the velociraptors—the venture capitalists.

My experience with venture capitalists at SGI had cost me plenty,
both financially and emotionally, so this was a decision made with
some trepidation. But at least I'd been around long enough to balance
the risk with talent. So for the second stage of financing, the Series B
offering, I'd approached John Doerr at Kleiner Perkins Caufield and
Byers, without question the star at the most successful and influential
venture capital firm in this phenomenal era. Doerr had an extraordinary gift for selling ideas, and for recognizing good ideas when he heard
them. And he acted on them—he's a "doer." If he was on your side

in any conflict, you were better off. Unlike many venture capitalists, Doerr was technologically savvy, and if he believed in the future of your company, he had the ability to help make that future work out well. He was as pragmatic as he was prescient, which is to say he could be very tough on management if he thought KPCB's investors' money might be endangered. His response to a reporter's question about whether his close involvement in many competing companies constituted a conflict of interest was legendary: "No conflict, no interest."

As long as Doerr was on our side, I trusted him. But I'd insisted that Kleiner Perkins pay three times as much per share for their stock as I had for mine. A couple of other venture companies had heard this demand from me and quickly backed off, but Doerr and his partners had sensed a winner and agreed. By the day of the IPO, despite several infusions of cash during the past year, I still owned 19 percent of Netscape. I was about to find out how good an investment I had made in my own company.

Just before eight, California time, I made another espresso and called Bruce Pate, my broker at Morgan Stanley, the investment bank in New York that was handling the offering. I got through right away, and asked how the stock was doing.

"It hasn't opened yet," he said. "I'm not sure why. This is strange . . ."

I felt a nagging concern. We'd had a problem deciding what the offering price ought to be. The trick is to keep the price low enough so that buyers find the stock attractive, but not so low that if it rises substantially the company itself will have left too much money on the table. Barksdale and I both felt that an IPO was as much a marketing event as a financial event, so it was just as important to price the stock where it would express the quality of the company, sell well, and create buzz as it was to reward the new shareholders with something that went up, showing that they had made the right decision.

The price had remained in flux up to the last minute, and the need for constant conferences among the executives at the company had lent an air of almost surreal comedy to a scene a day or two before the offering. Barksdale and Marc Andreessen were still on the East Coast with the Netscape road show, which included various investment bankers and tech support people, drumming up interest among institutional investors. While driving toward Baltimore in a small squadron of limousines, everyone constantly talking back and forth across the country on their cell phones, they found themselves in a dead spot where their phones didn't work. Out of touch for ten minutes at a moment like this? Unthinkable! So at a truck stop, the flotilla of black Lincoln Town Cars pulled up to a bank of pay telephones, and almost the entire team poured out to use the phones. "It looked like a Mafia convention," Barksdale told me later. The irony of top executives at a revolutionary new communications company lining up impatiently to feed quarters into roadside pay phones was not, I suspect, lost on anyone in the group.

Eventually we had settled on $28 a share, but now, with the delay in the opening of trading, we couldn't know how good a number that was. I wondered yet again whether the timing of the offering was right. In a May board of directors meeting, when I first raised the subject of going public, the Morgan Stanley bankers had said that the earliest we could be ready was August. Someone remarked drily, "But nobody goes public in August." I was against waiting, however. Earlier that month Spyglass had gone public with a market capitalization of $200 million! Spyglass—a small company in Illinois to which the University of Illinois had licensed Mosaic (spitefully, I believe), a pre-Navigator browser originally developed by Marc and his colleagues—was a company with no engineering or management talent in comparison to us.

In fact, Morgan Stanley's marketing of Netscape Series B equities had spurred Spyglass to go public; in turn, their offering made me realize the time had come to make our move. Spyglass was not a particularly formidable foe. Douglas Colbeth, who had joined the company in 1991 as CEO a year after it was founded, had previously been a salesman at Data General, whereas I had started Silicon Graphics. In my interactions with him, I had found him to be inexperienced as a technology CEO, and everything they were doing seemed small-time to me. Before being named the master licensor for Mosaic, the company was struggling to survive by marketing 3-D software tools for use in government-funded research. What infuriated Marc and me was that Colbeth and others at Spyglass were bad-mouthing us, telling our customers that we were trying to build our business around a program we had stolen from the National Center for Supercomputer Applications at the University of Illinois. The thing I understood—and Colbeth evidently didn't—was that high technology isn't about software or hardware, but about brains and people. Spyglass had Mosaic, but Netscape had imagination and IQ in the form of the people who had written the program they were selling. In trying to leverage the "Mosaic problem" against us, he was drastically overestimating the value of proprietary implementations. I knew we were going to kick their ass.

Besides the fact that we were all determined to beat Spyglass, and by extension the University of Illinois, with whom they were allied, we had been driving ourselves to make a better product, a major leap beyond Mosaic, and were already doing as much business in a week as they were in a quarter. Before the Spyglass IPO, Barksdale, Andreessen, and I had agreed that if they did badly, we'd hold off until the spring of 1996. But a market that would give a rich reward to a company we considered our inferior in every way couldn't be ignored. "If these guys can do this," I told the board, "we'd better get going."

After breakfast, I called Pate again, only to learn that the stock still had not started trading. At around eight-thirty A.M.—eleven-thirty Wall Street time—I finally drove the five miles from my Atherton home to Netscape's headquarters in Mountain View, an undistinguished two-story building typical of the no-frills anti-architecture that high-tech start-ups move into and out of like so many hermit crabs. Morning fog had burned away to a thin veil through which the sun was beginning to warm the day. In the company parking lot, start-up democracy was still symbolically evident in the gaggle of cars as nondescript as the building. I walked past the long line of cubicles occupied by programmers, saying hello to those who were already in. Some of the workspaces were decorated, if that's the word for it, like generic dorm rooms; some were individualized with a vengeance in what was a standard-issue start-up crash pad. In almost all of the cubicles, sleeping bags and pillows or beat-up couches offered evidence of life and work inextricably mixed, of catnaps grabbed during three- and four-day stints of code writing. In an excerpt from a stream-of-consciousness log kept by one of the brilliant programmers who was not from Illinois, Jamie Zawinski, the life he and his colleagues led in the long days before the IPO is perfectly described:

Thursday, 28 July, 1994, 11 P.M.

*I slept at work again last night; two and a half hours curled up
in a quilt underneath my desk. . . . On Friday, which is when I most
recently woke up, I got to work at around three, and had a ton of
e-mail waiting, all work-related. And we had an all-hands meeting
at 4 P.M., and everyone wanted to come talk to me at once before
then, so I was feeling really overwhelmed and behind. I mean, I had
only been away from the office for like seven hours! The meeting
was another mindblower; apparently we closed some kind of OEM
deal (I forget with whom) for like six hundred thousand seats of
the client. Gag. I actually get the feeling that our sales and
marketing people know what they're doing! I've never gotten that
feeling from them at any previous job. This is wild. Six hundred
thousand people is more than any software I've ever worked on has
come anywhere near. I'm completely terrified.*

At this time, of course, many of the core group of programmers hadn't
started their day yet. The elite troops who write code for software companies are notoriously peculiar about working hours, carrying over eccentric biorhythms from their college days. Nine-to-five shifts may do the job
on automotive assembly lines and at insurance firms, but the standard
workday has never had much meaning in Silicon Valley. Programmers are
the shock troops of a software start-up. Abundant energy, a reckless disregard for their own well-being, and an underdeveloped notion of what it
is to live a full life are considerable strengths. As a result, many
programmers simply go on living and working the way they had as computer science students, pulling all-nighters, cramming, and letting off
steam with pranks, obsessive hobbies, or, in Netscape's case, wild games
of indoor "chair football" or roller hockey in the parking lot. At one
point late in July, when the pressure seemed even more intense than
usual, a couple of the programmers spent an entire day building remote-
control cars, annoying the hell out of their colleagues.

But in this way, Netscape wasn't much different from many other
high-tech start-ups, which have a free-for-all quality that doesn't respond to normal management techniques; a certain level of insanity—

often a pretty high level—went with the territory. Despite the craziness, or perhaps because of it, we had accomplished a tremendous amount in very little time. We had set a new standard for the future of American industry. This defined the idea of "Netscape time," which also became known as "Internet time."

I said hello to those of the "old gang" who were at their computers, checking e-mail, drinking their morning round of coffees and Jolt colas. We had all come a long way in a short time, but somehow I doubted they had any real idea of what could happen for them today. At the moment they didn't look like young men excited at the possibility of becoming rich, but rather like very tired kids.

Approaching my office, I saw that not everyone was heeding Barksdale's decree. Our shared executive assistant, D'Anne Schjerning, who had worked for me at SGI before signing on as Netscape employee number three, had put up an electronic ticker tape on the partition that separated her desk from the corridor. Anyone looking toward my office or Barksdale's wouldn't be able to miss a running tally of our stock price in bright red lights. I knew what Barksdale would do when he saw it, but I walked on without telling her to take it down. I've been known to be a difficult, testy boss, but today I wasn't about to play the heavy. Like everyone at Netscape that day, D'Anne was a stockholder; I had promised that if she took the chance to leave a rock-solid job to work for me, I'd make her a million dollars. I didn't want to throw cold water on her anticipation. Or on my own.

What I couldn't help noticing was that the numbers on D'Anne's ticker tape read "28," our opening price. Again, I called Pate at Morgan Stanley. "Nothing yet. There is a trade imbalance," he said, though I thought I detected a note of concern in his voice.

"This is nuts," I said, and hung up.

I thought about dropping by to talk with Marc. When he and I had first flown to Urbana to recruit the programmers who had helped him create Mosaic, I'd watched them react to him and I'd known he was their natural leader as well as a brilliant technical thinker. Without him, there would be no Netscape, and he richly deserved whatever good fortune came his way. But I decided to stay in my office. All we'd be able to do, with the stock stuck in limbo, would be to talk about how the work was going. And at the moment I couldn't imagine a more artificial conversation. As it happened, Marc had worked late the night before and didn't even get to the office until later in the day.

At around eleven-thirty, the phone rang. D'Anne announced that Pate was on the line.

"The stock just opened," he said.

"At what?"

"Seventy-one," he said. "Unbelievable! Congratulations!"

To say the least. In a matter of hours, before actual public trading had begun, Netscape stock had more than doubled in value. We were making Wall Street history. It didn't take complicated math for me to know I had now helped create a second company with a market capitalization over a billion dollars. Or to understand that I owned stock suddenly worth $663 million. Although as the original investor, I wouldn't be able to sell anything for another nine months, that symbolic gestation period didn't figure into my daydreaming calculations just then. I had once joked to a friend that if the stock ever reached 140, I'd be a billionaire after taxes. On Day One I was well on my way.

Now, to some people, this discussion of wealth is considered immodest. I spent many years in an academic setting, as a professor at various universities like Stanford and the University of California, where the idea of money and wealth was considered somewhat "dirty." In other words, the pure pursuit of knowledge was considered more important than money. While this viewpoint has some merit if the objective is simply the pursuit of knowledge, I also observe that a successful business has little room for anyone without an economic motive, especially the business managers. Although a personal financial obsession will lead to problems, the ultimate goal of a business is to become self-sustaining, which means that it must make sufficient money to keep its employees paid and remain competitive. The entrepreneur without a financial motive will not be successful. On with the story.

The rocket-propelled stock ride seemed to astonish the press, even though their attention and anticipation had played a part in building the buzz that pushed up the price. On August 11, under the headline WITH INTERNET CACHET, NOT PROFIT, A NEW STOCK IS WALL ST.'S DARLING, *The New York Times*'s Laurence Zuckerman reported (more or less accurately):

A fifteen-month-old company that has never made a dime of profit had one of the most stunning debuts in Wall Street history yesterday as investors rushed to pour their money into cyberspace.

The Netscape Communications Corporation became the latest—and hottest—company in the Internet business to list shares on the nation's stock exchanges. Shares of Netscape, which had been priced at $28 before trading began at 11 A.M., opened far higher—at $71. The shares soon surged to as high as $74.75. By noon, money managers at big mutual funds and other institutional investors fortunate enough to be in on the ground floor could have cashed in a profit of more than 150 percent and gone to lunch. . . .

At the close of trading, the share price was $58.25. In the days, months, and years that followed, the price of the stock has split, it's risen higher, and it's fallen lower. It has dived and spiked. On August 10, 1998, it rose 24 percent in one day. Barksdale told an interviewer long after the IPO, "When we issued Netscape stock, we gave out neck braces and seat belts." In the same way, the company's fortunes have risen and fallen—it has ridden the crest of a self-generated wave, and sometimes struggled to keep from drowning, finally forming a partnership with an Internet giant. But the frenzy that started that day for Internet stocks has not subsided. Literally and figuratively, it has floated a lot of boats.

But that's getting ahead of the story. Day One wasn't over; the market was just beginning to test the stock. We were getting a hell of a start, but in an increasingly brutal, fast-changing business, where seemingly small missteps can hurt in the short run and kill in the long run, Netscape's future was far from secure. Jim Barksdale would later wonder if we shouldn't have let Microsoft sleep a while longer, and indeed the record-setting performance of our stock was the beginning of a change in Microsoft's thinking about the viability of Internet businesses. (Revisionist historians at the Redmond giant now claim that they were deep in thought about the Web before we came along, but if that's true, one wonders how they could have let a mere upstart like Netscape bite off the lion's share of the browser market—about which more in later chapters.) For all his nerdy ways and offbeat charm for the press, I feel Bill Gates is happiest when he is crushing the life out of companies that dare establish territory on the borders of Microsoft's sprawling dominion. He's like Fafnir, the Wagnerian dragon, jealously guarding a vast hoard of gold. At this moment, however, we had a jump on him, and it was paying off.

I stepped out of my office and leaned into D'Anne's cubicle. She seemed mildly stunned. Her phone was ringing. All at once, it seemed as if everyone's phone was ringing. I reached out and shook her hand.

"Well, I told you I'd make you a millionaire," I said. "And I have."

PART TWO

Trajectories
Winter 1994

2 One Billion Is the Best Revenge

I can't pretend to know what was in the minds of the four hundred or so hard-pressed people who on that day made up Netscape Communications, many of whom were suddenly much wealthier than they'd been when they woke up that morning. But it's not difficult to imagine. Some must have been astonished, others elated, still others simply stunned. The core programmers, a dedicated few who had been with the company—who had been the company—since the earliest days, were probably too wrapped up in the relentless demands of their jobs to be more than bemused (some of them, even today, still rent their apartments and drive the mundane cars of their pre-IPO days). For these engineers, the big moment had come months before when they'd launched a beta version of Netscape Navigator and watched through the night while people all over the world plucked it out of cyberspace into their computers. The idea that they now had, on paper at least, several million dollars must have been beyond surreal to young men who probably didn't own three suits and ties among them, much less dress shirts.

For others, those who had left solid, safe jobs to take a chance in a venture so ill-defined in its first days that I couldn't tell them exactly how we would make money, the success of the offering must have been a vast relief. Risks rarely pay off like Netscape did, even in high tech's magic kingdom. And a few people (such as Barksdale and I) knew that this was only the beginning of a new phase of what would be a long, hard fight to build a company. The amazing run-up on Wall Street had produced forty millionaires that day, but their fortunes, whether expected or not, whether entirely understood, depended on how we did from now on. We would alter millions of lives, but one company with unprecedented power would now be gunning for us.

For me, the day had brought an amount of money I had never imagined. Just the California state taxes alone on such wealth would be more than I had ever hoped to make in my life. I had had every intention of getting rich, but this was incomprehensible.

*   *   *

There are very few second acts in the world of high technology. The history of the Information Age is filled with the names of people who did something wonderful, rose meteorically, then fell just as suddenly. The pace of the tech business is fast enough to blister the skin and incinerate one's hopes. Someone ought to put up a monument in Mountain View, the center of Silicon Valley, to the casualties of the Thirty Years' War (and counting) that has pitted ideas and companies against one another in a life-or-death struggle.

The names carved on that stone would include a disproportionately large number of company founders. These are people who had the inspiration to change the way we think and do things, and the guts, zeal, initiative, and stamina to build a business on the foundation of that idea. But the pace of technological development in the later part of the twentieth century has been merciless and exponentially fast. The business plays favorites only as long as they can keep up. Not many have.

Half a century ago, the late British philosopher Isaiah Berlin came up with the fox-and-hedgehog theory of thinkers. Foxes, he wrote, know a lot of things. Hedgehogs know one big thing. (Berlin favored foxes, being one himself.) Most of the founders of high-tech companies belong in the hedgehog category; they get one idea, sometimes a truly big idea, and on the strength of it they launch a company. If the company is a success, the founder, in true hedgehog style, usually holds on to his big idea tenaciously. What the hell, he figures, it works, why not stick with it? In the Industrial Age, this often worked well; a couple generations of the Ford family saw very little reason to change the founder's fundamental idea, and did just fine until Japanese automakers turned things upside down. But in high tech, change is the only constant. Knowing one big thing is good for starters, but it can't keep you in the game anymore. Harry Stonecipher, a tough-minded CEO at McDonnell Douglas, once told an interviewer, "There's no percentage in getting attached to your product," and what's true in the world of military aircraft is doubly true in the dogfight of high tech. While founders get attached to their seminal ideas, the world they helped change goes right on changing, and in no time they're a drag on their own companies and find themselves on the outside, angrily looking in.

This doesn't invariably happen, of course. Some founders are well-suited to lead their companies through a shifting landscape. Gordon Moore of Intel, Bill Gates of Microsoft, and Scott McNealy and Bill Joy of Sun Microsystems are stellar examples. But as often as not, the founder's role is ultimately doomed.

Sometimes there's an ironic reverse twist to this classic scenario, in which a founder is able to figure out more than one big thing and advocates change, but is blocked by a recalcitrant board and management who have grown attached to the status quo. Then, just as if he were someone who hasn't been able to keep up, the forward-looking founder ends up hung out to dry. This is what I had experienced in the years immediately before the launch of Netscape, and the anger I carried with me was a powerful motivator. I wanted a second act and I wanted it to prove that the first act was no fluke.

In the early eighties, I was an associate professor of electrical engineering at Stanford, working in the computers systems laboratory. Even for distinguished academics, Stanford represents a high mark, but to a thirty-six-year-old former high-school dropout from a small town in Texas who'd had the good luck to discover electronics in the navy and to stumble on a gift for mathematics, the great university in Palo Alto represented nothing less than Mecca. After four years in the navy and a return to school, I had graduated from the University of New Orleans with a master's in physics, followed by a Ph.D. in computer science from the University of Utah, all in preparation for an academic career. Yet I had arrived at Stanford with the feeling that my future probably didn't lie in academia. I'd been at enough colleges and universities to know that a profession in which success is often solely based on the opinions of competing colleagues wasn't the right place for me. In the navy, I'd started a small loan business to augment my $280 per month salary, so perhaps one could say I had a certain instinct for business, even if the navy didn't officially approve. Certainly, the time and place were right. For someone with any ambition to get in on the business of technology, Stanford was then, as it is now, one of the best places on earth to be.

When Forest Baskett, my colleague at Stanford who caused me to be hired, went on a leave of absence, I inherited responsibility for a contract the university had with the Department of Defense, a fairly open-ended arrangement to develop integrated circuits and tools for computer-aided design. This was only one of a few research contracts between the Defense Department's Advanced Research Project Agency (ARPA) and four major universities, but it turned out to be an ideal proving ground for me. I hired one former student, Mark Grossman, and one close friend, Tom Davis, who had just received his Ph.D. in math from Stanford, to help with the contract. With them plus my top Ph.D. student, Marc Hannah, I eventually had a core group of seven people, all ready to form a company around the Geometry Engine, a 3-D graphics integrated circuit chip I'd created with the help of Hannah. The university's attitude about this sort of undertaking was wonderfully generous: If you did the thinking, you deserved the credit. If you started a company, you deserved the profit. The gratitude this philosophy has generated over the years has resulted in millions of dollars in gifts from successful graduates, and is one of the reasons the Palo Alto campus represents the heart of Silicon Valley and a powerful magnet for talent.

As a longtime academic, I didn't have a big idea about getting started. Then an article about the Geometry Engine appeared in the Stanford newspaper, attracting the attention of venture capitalists always on the lookout for start-up opportunities. A perceptive friend of mine, Ronnie Goldfield, said to me at dinner one night, "You're not an academic, you're an entrepreneur. You ought to be starting a company." She was right, but I'd thought of that myself. What made her particularly convincing, however, was that she offered me $25,000 to get started—an offer I gladly accepted. Even more important, Ronnie introduced me to a friend of hers, Glenn Mueller, who was a partner in a venture capital firm called Mayfield Fund. Glenn and Grant Heidrich, his partner, were looking at the Stanford paper when I called him. Glenn and I eventually hit it off, and Mayfield became the first and major investor in Silicon Graphics.

That $25,000, and the connection with Mayfield, ended my academic career and began my business career. Eventually the company I formed with my group from Stanford would be worth billions. But at the time, I made the move from a very comfortable place to a very unknown territory without much in the way of a map, much less the goal of getting rich. One didn't go into something like that in those days realistically expecting to make a billion-dollar company out of nothing. But when you're running a race, you're not thinking about what it's going to feel like crossing the finish line. You think about putting one foot in front of the other. And that's all it is; you're trying to keep moving, and to see far enough down the road to make sure you're not going to make a wrong turn.

This book, however, tells the story of Netscape, not Silicon Graphics, so I won't try to detail the entire early history of my first company. It's enough to say that the company grew quickly and prospered by making revolutionary 3-D graphics workstations (computers that gained their greatest fame as the tools that helped create the dinosaurs for the movie *Jurassic Park*). My later years at SGI, however, were in many ways a preamble to Netscape, and helped determine my approach to shaping that company. Those increasingly frustrating years represent a classic example of how petty politics can run a good company onto a reef. SGI, perhaps now destined for minor status in the computer business, was a fine company that fell victim to a management attached to a comfortable, profitable niche that seemed secure if one didn't look too far into the future. In this case, the attachment was not my sin.

I have never been a gifted manager. Not many entrepreneurs are, though not all will admit it. We sometimes bore easily, and, as in my case, don't have the right temperament or patience for the day-to-day management issues that a good CEO must deal with. Technology was what I knew, and I preferred to concentrate on trying to figure out where technology was going. So in 1984, I hired Ed McCracken, a division manager at Hewlett Packard, as chief executive officer. When I first met Ed, I had the impression that he was good, even though he seemed a bit remote. He had built a billion-dollar business computer division at HP, so obviously he had the management experience we needed. As an enticement, I offered him as much stock as I had retained as founder and chairman, even though he arrived two years after the company was formed.

In the beginning, Ed showed me a lot of respect, and we worked together pretty well. Immediately, he felt the need to assert himself, but I didn't mind because we were a wreck waiting to happen. Having just raised a third-round financing of $16 million, we had used $6 million to repay debt, and we were burning cash at the rate of $2 million per month because we had over two hundred people working for us. We needed strong management. Ed almost completely lacked a sense of humor, however, which is a quirk I've always considered enough of a handicap to justify special parking places. Business magazines have termed him "introspective," which is a diplomatic way of describing someone you couldn't see yourself having a few beers with. The easy rapport typical of young technology companies, staffed largely with people just out of college, was not natural for him. In his first few weeks as CEO my adolescent daughter called him Ed McMuffin out of confusion, which I thought was awfully funny. As a joke, I asked the assistant who worked for both of us to have the name tag on his door changed to that name. She had a new tag made up, and we all laughed about it for the three days it took Ed to notice. Suddenly the joke tag disappeared, and Ed never said anything about it—until about five years later, when I happened to mention it during a staff meeting. Ed's face flushed crimson and he said, "Some people don't like it if you make fun of their names."

Despite this shortcoming, he tackled the first task at hand, which was to get a vice president of sales—someone who could start making and meeting a revenue plan. In addition, he immediately hit the road to raise another $10 million in investment money. Ed wasn't a technology man, which is why we should have made good partners. But over the ten years he and I were in the company together, he grew more powerful and influential, and increasingly, he would leave me out of major decisions. Eventually I was ignored completely, and I stopped going to any of his meetings. In 1989 when the executive staff moved to a new building, I discovered that no office had been provided for me.

By 1991, McCracken had begun to block my salary and stock increases. When I confronted him about this after a board meeting (at which he'd received a raise but I hadn't), Ed replied, "I don't recommend increases for people who don't work for me." Until then, I think he figured he'd have a hard time keeping the company on track without me. Clearly, that no longer worried him. It was obvious he wanted to be chairman as well as CEO and was trying to force me either to resign or work for him.

In larger companies, this kind of political maneuvering is not unusual. Stupid, but common. It can seem so trivial that you don't take it entirely seriously until things reach a crisis, and then it's too late. When partners stop communicating, calamity follows. The doomed charge of the Light Brigade in the Crimean War, in which one of England's finest cavalry units carried out a pointless and suicidal frontal assault on Turkish artillery, occurred when two generals, Lord Cardigan and Lord Raglan, refused to speak to each other because of a slight.

The growth of SGI, beginning in 1983, coincided almost exactly with the personal computer revolution. Moore's Law, postulated by Gordon Moore of Intel, states that computer power will double every eighteen months. If anything, that already swift rate has been accelerating in recent years. Moore's Law has driven the business of high technology like a law of nature. What has made its effect especially powerful is the fact that prices haven't risen with capacity, but instead have gone the other way. These inverse trends powerfully influence the marketplace, and no company, Silicon Graphics included, is immune to that power.

SGI had a well-deserved reputation for selling the best 3-D workstations in the business. The sophisticated engineers and designers who used these computers loved them. Even as late as 1994, one Wall Street analyst called SGI "the new Apple." (Though meant as high praise at the time, this would become a prophetic statement.) But the average price of SGI's dazzling machines was in the $40,000 to $50,000 range. In contrast, Sun Microsystems was producing graphics workstations for $15,000 to $20,000. They were inferior in graphics, but they were cheaper. And increasingly powerful PCs were selling for under $5,000.

The computers made by SGI were superior and were the animation technology of choice for Hollywood studios and for engineers doing research and design. The market doesn't invariably reward excellence when budgets are a factor, however, whether it's corporate or individual money at stake. We sold our excellent machines at high profit margins, but the actual number sold was small. By 1986, I could see that the PC was gaining a huge installed base, and it worried me. Eventually software developers choose the platform with the most distribution. The platform with the most applications in the computer business wins. The PC (and Microsoft) was getting the most installed base. Despite our high profit margins and great reputation, we were never, with our strategy at the time, going to achieve significant volume. As PCs grew more powerful, our secure niche would inevitably be eroded. For years, Rolls-Royce made one of the best cars in the world. Now Rolls-Royce, the chariot of the gods, has been bought by Volkswagen, maker of "the people's car."

I wanted SGI to use its huge advantage in 3-D hardware and software to penetrate lower-end markets. We had created proprietary chips that gave our workstations immense power compared to other computers, but the chips represented a small percentage of the total cost of the system. We had to make our added value a larger part of the cost of the system by trimming the amount of memory and other components in our systems. Admittedly, at the time this seemed a significant risk. And an expensive one. We would have to go on producing our top-end computers while making an investment of around $20 million to develop a new product. Had we made that move then, producing something for under $5,000 that was modular, like the PC, I'm convinced we could have blown into the lower end of the market. But the company had already grown loose in its mentality. Fatally loose.

It was clear that the PC market was exploding, but Ed and the SGI management team didn't feel any sense of urgency. Their thinking was, "That's the personal computer business; we're in the workstation business." They couldn't see that the two markets were colliding as PCs became increasingly powerful, and in the end the bigger market would devour the smaller. The technology business may be famously unpredictable, but that much was certain.

Stylistically, Ed McCracken was the kind of manager who'd say, "Let's work the system" rather than make a bold move. Not that he didn't have conventional logic on his side. At the time, SGI was an increasingly successful computer company that rivaled the size of the business Ed had left to run SGI. We had momentum in a niche market, which guaranteed a big payoff for a while. But niche market momentum was short-term good and long-term bad. Before PCs changed the balance of power, IBM had dominated the business for decades with its supercomputers when only a few young oddballs imagined that any other technology could compete. By the time Big Blue figured out what was happening, it was almost too late. This and other object lessons stood out as stark warnings against getting comfortable with a niche, but McCracken and the board couldn't, or wouldn't, see them.

My approach was, "God damn it, listen. We don't have time to debate this shit for a year. Let's move quickly!" Accurate, although sometimes strident. Not terribly mature, I must have been increasingly annoying to Ed and some of his complacent lieutenants at the company: half crank, half Cassandra. But I knew that the PC was on a course to kill us. Microsoft had gone public the same year SGI did, but the two companies were growing at dramatically different rates. In the end, software developers rule, and they go where the volume is. To make software for the smaller market just because a given machine is technologically superior is a kind of romanticism, an emotional, illogical decision that no smart developer would make.

When things are going well, no one likes a person walking around saying the sky is falling. Looking far down the road in the technology business can be really frightening, which is why so many companies don't make changes until they're in deep trouble. But it's the harsh nature of business, particularly for high technology, that a company may be heading for the abyss long before anyone knows it. When Apple was the star of the computer world in the mid- to late 1980s, few would have predicted that its self-satisfied refusal to license its operating system would prove to be a screwup so huge that the once-great company, for all the revivalist spirit of its current management, hardly matters at all now except to its cult of loyal users. McCracken was now sliding into the same kind of error.

It wasn't just McCracken who didn't want to hear my predictions of doom. The sales force liked having large-ticket items to sell. No, "like" isn't strong enough. They loved them. And why not? You had a great product to sell, and even though the customer base wasn't large, the commissions were. For the salespeople, at the time, SGI was a great place to be. "Not for long," I'd tell them, "because you're going to be eaten alive someday. We can't count on being better than everyone else at 3-D graphics for the rest of eternity."

The typical response was "Look, Jim, I can't predict what's going to happen in five years' time, and you can't either. So get out of my face." Even my family of founding engineers seemed to prefer listening to the reassurances of top managers who were telling them that SGI had no problem. (For the record, the company eventually did introduce an entry-level workstation starting at $6,000. In October of 1996! Far too late to be a player in a field dominated by Hewlett Packard, Sun Microsystems, and high-end PCs. Not coincidentally, that same month, after riding high for years, SGI announced lower-than-expected revenues for the first fiscal quarter. There were a lot of reasons for the drop, but the company's glory days were over.)

Boxed in, left out, I grew increasingly frustrated, and began to realize that I was becoming disruptive to the company. Ed and I had several confrontations, culminating in an open argument in front of the entire management team about Ed's proposed promotion of one of his managers to vice president of marketing. I can't even remember the specific bone of contention, but the fight was the inevitable result of our behind-the-scenes antagonism. By this time I was really tiring of my situation, but I had plenty of ideas about other things SGI ought to be doing. Instead, I just dropped out for a while and went sailing.

Fate, in the form of a motorcycle accident, had given me time to think about the future of computing. In the fall of 1990, while heading home one afternoon from a ride on my BMW, a car turned into my lane. I dropped the machine into a ditch and went over the handlebars. Luckily I hadn't been going very fast, but I'm a bit tall for the bike, so as I went off my foot caught on the bars. I broke my knee, which put me in a rigid cast from foot to thigh and left me housebound for several weeks. My wife of six weeks, Nancy Rutter, claims she lost nine pounds taking care of me. (One task she adamantly refused was washing the foot I couldn't reach. "I'm waiting on you hand and foot," she said, "but I draw the line at washing your feet!")

The ironic upside of the accident was that while I was laid up, I was able to stay clear of Ed McCracken. For the first time since the company had started, I was out of the action and there was nothing I could do about it—McCracken's fondest dream, my nightmare, but with a motorcycle as the villain. Since I'd been effectively blocked in my attempts to get SGI to reassess its hardware and software priorities,

I began thinking about other ways to get the company into larger-volume markets. One of the most interesting areas of development at the time was digital communications, digital television and networking, in various forms. Clearly, the key to expanding the use of computers was to make them attractive to people for uses other than work. No one knew with any certainty how to do this, but that uncertainty made things more interesting. The way to succeed in the technology business is to get into some area that isn't yet crowded. God knows these areas were more promising than the carved-up turf of the workstation business.

I did some writing about what the future might bring, loosely connected ideas about merging computer systems with fast networks, video on demand, and interactive television. This was an early, tentative blueprint for what I called a "telecomputer" that would provide the next big step in market penetration for personal computers. As a result of the explosion of the Internet, an ongoing, dramatic growth in which I ended up playing a big part, this convergence is taking place, and is even bigger than what I anticipated. A few years back, I stated that someday everyone on earth would have his or her own Web page. Now, because of the blending of entertainment, information, and digital commerce, that doesn't seem so unlikely. Consider this: Domain names, the names affixed to Internet sites, have become, as a reporter at the *San Francisco Chronicle* put it, "the cyber equivalent of vanity license plates." In the four years between July 1993 and July 1997, the number of names registered jumped from 26,000 to 1.3 million. It was this possibility I perhaps envisioned, though—as is often the case in new technologies—I wasn't clear on how it might actually come about.

Coincidentally, early in 1991 I bought an oceangoing sailboat, and though still on crutches I spent a month of that winter at sea, mostly sitting on a sofa trying to imagine the direction technology might take in the next few years. When my leg had healed enough for me to regain some mobility, I gave a few speeches on my ideas. Out of this came a series of meetings with other companies whose markets, or potential markets, could help shift SGI off its collision course with the PC. I succeeded in getting Nintendo to build our graphics technology into their most popular game machine. I also set up a division of the company to work with Time Warner on their interactive television trials in Orlando, Florida.

But these efforts didn't counterbalance my disenchantment with SGI. Without the support of Ed and the board, new alliances in leading-edge media weren't going to change the fundamental direction of the company. And with my stock and salary compensations blocked, my position as chairman, so coveted by McCracken, was increasingly meaningless. Ed's fixation with my role in the company had reached the point where the public relations department, aware of how agitated he got whenever I appeared in a newspaper or magazine, only called when a reporter specifically asked for me. I don't know whether Ed ever told anyone that I shouldn't be made available, but his annoyance was an effective form of censorship. Obviously, if I wanted to get back into the vanguard of the technology business, I'd have to do it somewhere else.

Patience may be a virtue, but it's no virtue in high tech. When McCracken had said he didn't okay increases for "people who don't work for me," my gut reaction was to say, "Screw this! I'm out of here." Clearly, if I'd agreed to give Ed the chairman's title and put myself under him as vice-chairman, my reward would have been more money and stock. A simple enough trade-off with a comfortable outcome, but it would be a cold day in hell before that happened. I had started the company, after all, not McCracken. However, I'd been around long enough by this time to have some tactical savvy. When I left, I'd do it on my terms and there'd be no outburst that might hurt the company to which I'd devoted so much of my life. On a less lofty plane, I also didn't want to damage my own reputation; second acts are tough enough without bad press during the intermission.

My wife, Nancy, had spent too many evenings listening to me sound off about what was going on at SGI. She knew the time had come for me to move on. In her own invariably direct way, she put it very simply.

"You know, Jim," she said, "you're bitching and unhappy all the time. You should just get out."

I had met Nancy a few years before when she arrived to interview a venture capitalist whose office I happened to be in. As a business journalist, she had a reputation as a quick study and a solid analyst, and I've always trusted her judgment. She had seen enough high-level corporate disenchantment to know the importance of a carefully or-chestrated exit strategy. In the fall of 1993, she suggested that I go see Craig Johnson, a lawyer she knew, to get some advice on how to deal with the highly charged issue of how to quit my own company.

"What do you want out of this?" was Craig's first question.

"I'd like to get a new company started," I replied. "But I'd ideally like for some SGI engineers to go with me."

Johnson shook his head, then quickly ticked off a list of dos and don'ts.

"You're not going to be able to take any engineers unless they call you. You should spend the next four to six months getting things ready for a simple, smooth departure. First, you don't tell anyone your plans. And you don't go around bad-mouthing Ed and the company. You can't tell even your best friends at SGI how screwed up you think management is. Then, after the right amount of time has passed, you calmly call a board meeting and announce you're going to leave. Here's what you say: 'I'm going to leave. I don't want to stay on the board. I don't intend to be competitive with the company, and I don't intend to actively recruit from the company.' That's all you say, and nothing else. It's your mantra."

Then Johnson laid out for me how he figured it would go.

"Ed will be delighted that you're going to name some terms and become an outside director of the company. He's going to want you to be on the board, because that will give the appearance of an orderly transfer of power. But if you want any engineers to approach you from the company, you can't stay on the board. The company would never let you do that. You've got to be willing to walk away from your un-vested stock. When you quit, they're going to try to turn you around for three or four days. And you're going to have to listen to them. Because if you just resign cold turkey, that would be a little too abrupt for the Street. So let them try for a few days, and that'll give them time to get the PR organized and do some kind of orderly announce-ment for the company."

I did what Johnson advised, though holding myself back from crit-icizing the way SGI was run was new for me, and not easy. At least a few people must have wondered if I was all right. For the next four months I played the good soldier in a badly led army. And I kept my plans to myself, telling only one person at the company, Marc Hannah, a trusted old friend and the original cofounder of SGI, and I only told him two weeks before leaving.

As the first board meeting of 1994 approached, I decided I couldn't stand to sit through another of Ed McCracken's infuriating rituals. The week before, I arranged a board meeting by telephone and calmly repeated my mantra. As Johnson had predicted, I was asked to reconsider (though I could almost hear McCracken's barely disguised delight), and I said I'd think about it for a few days. But from that moment on, my career at Silicon Graphics was over. In the end, I left behind stock options worth about $10 million. I had about $20 million, which, though far from shabby, actually was relatively little to show for a dozen years of creativity, leadership, risk, and hard work in an industry that has produced vast personal wealth.

As I had told Craig Johnson, I wanted to start a new company. But I found myself at ground zero, with a few vague ideas about the future of information technology, and with just one employee—myself. At least my vow of secrecy was lifted.

As I was packing my personal belongings at the end of January 1994 while the board meeting was taking place in the conference room next to my office, I talked about my situation with Bill Foss, an old friend at the company who often traveled with me to provide multimedia support for speeches and presentations. Bill managed a customer relations center at SGI where he created mind- and eye-boggling presentations to impress those doing business, or thinking of doing business, with the company.

"I'm really stymied by this situation," I told him. "I don't know how to start a company without engineers, but every good engineer I've ever known, I've recruited here. And I can't take them with me."

"Well, what about Marc Andreessen? He just moved to Palo Alto from Illinois," he said. By Bill's tone I could tell he assumed this was a name I would obviously recognize. I riffled through my memory and came up empty.

"Who's Marc Andreessen?" I asked.

I n David Lean's classic movie *Lawrence of Arabia*, there is a pivotal scene in which Lawrence, played by Peter O'Toole, back in Cairo from his improbable conquest of Akaba, meets General Allenby, played by Jack Hawkins. As the two sit in the garden of the officers club, Allenby agrees to provide Lawrence and his Bedouin irregulars with an impressive list of weapons and equipment. But as a price for the ordnance, Allenby convinces the exhausted Lawrence that he should go back into the desert to lead the guerrillas. Finally Lawrence says, "You're a clever man, General." To which Allenby replies, "I don't know about that. But it's fair to say that I do know a good thing when I see it."

That's the way I felt about Marc Andreessen. I'd love to be able to claim that it was my cleverness that created Netscape, but I can't. What I can claim, and it's by no means a modest claim, is that I knew a good thing when I saw it.

Packing up the things in my SGI office was a melancholy act, even though the decision to leave had been mine. Bill Foss's visit and the chance to talk about the future was a relief. To my question, "Who's Marc Andreessen?" Bill responded, "He wrote Mosaic. He's out here now, working for some small company in the Valley." Foss said this, again assuming I'd know about Mosaic, but I didn't have a clue. Keeping up to date with the warp-speed changes in the technology business is tough in the best of circumstances, and for the past year or so I'd either been preoccupied by the internecine grappling at SGI, theorizing future convergence, or working on possible deals with Time Warner or Nintendo. When Foss realized I didn't know what Mosaic was, he sat down at my computer, downloaded the browser from a central server, started it up, and walked out of my office. "You'll figure it out," he said.

Despite my long involvement with computer software, I have little patience. I'm happy to spend hours working out the minute details of a program, but I hate wasting time with overly complicated applications other people have written. I'll talk more about Mosaic later in this chapter, but what matters here is that I did work it out, quickly, without any strain on my patience. Pretty impressive stuff. Significantly, in light of what eventually took place, the first time I used Mosaic was to reach its chief architect. After clicking around for a few minutes, I ended up on Andreessen's home page. I sent the following note to his e-mail address:

> Marc:
>
> You may not know me, but I'm the founder and former chairman of Silicon Graphics. As you may have read in the press lately, I'm leaving SGI. I plan to form a new company. I would like to discuss the possibility of your joining me.
> Jim Clark

I went on packing, musing ruefully at the amount of personal junk that accumulates after years at a company, bits and pieces of a career that become invisible through familiarity until, in one of the rituals of departure, you pick them up and put them into a carton. At my age of fifty, I found this process far more daunting than I might have if I'd left the offices a decade or so earlier. After about ten minutes, a reply came through from Marc:

> Jim:
>
> Sure. When would you like to meet?
> Marc

I'll let history judge whether this exchange rates a place alongside Alexander Graham Bell's famous "Watson, come in here. I need you." Assuming it will never find its way into the history books, we were nevertheless using a medium, like the telephone, that had the capacity to alter the way people communicate and do business. And though neither Marc nor I had invented that medium, we would, before too long, create a company that would bring it to a new, far more popular level.

As it turned out, Marc knew very well who I was. He had used a Silicon Graphics workstation at the National Center for Super-computer Applications (NCSA) on the University of Illinois's Urbana-Champaign campus, and had been hugely impressed (imagine Michael Schumacher's first rides in a Ferrari Formula One car). Apparently, the arrival of those supercharged computers with their state-of-the-art 3-D graphics had caused tremendous excitement among the young programmers at NCSA. To the extent that Marc associated me with that machine, he and I were off to a good start. In another exchange of messages, we decided to meet at seven-thirty the next morning at Cafe Verona in Palo Alto.

Cafe Verona is one of a number of quietly decorated bistros in the area where, on any given day, at any number of tables, conversations are going on that can create companies or bring them down, give birth to amazing technologies or major flops. These places aren't as glam-orous or famous as Los Angeles and New York restaurants like Spago or the Four Seasons, where film and publishing business gets done, and the people at the tables don't attract paparazzi. Nor would you be fooled into thinking you were sitting in a place on Verona's Piazza del Erbe (too many waitresses for Italian tastes, I suspect, and the ingre-dients in the individual pizzas are too untraditional). But the deals made at the Cafe Verona, Il Fornaio, and other such breakfast and lunch hangouts in the Valley, have created a wave of wealth that has dazzled financial markets in a way that even the movies never have. To some extent, there's a "usual suspects" quality to the people who gather at the Verona, and on that particular morning I recognized many of the faces at the other tables. Since I had just resigned from SGI, I knew I'd be bound to stir up lots of speculation, and it was fun to think that almost no one was likely to know who Marc was. Just by sitting down with me, he was a mystery man.

The world of high technology is, usually, a meritocracy. You get points for the quality of the work you do and the ability to do a lot of that work without worrying about quitting time. You do not get points for style, which is why so many Silicon Valley engineers are infamous for dressing with total disregard for how they look (the latter-day Steve Jobs notwithstanding). So as I waited for Marc, I had no idea what to expect. What I saw when he arrived was a slightly over-

weight young man well over six feet four inches tall in entirely forget-
table clothes (that I have forgotten entirely). He might easily have
been cast in the role of a young farmer in his hometown of New Lis-
bon, Wisconsin, population one thousand five hundred or so. In the
months that followed, more than a few people remarked that Marc
and I bore a kind of family resemblance, but when we met I don't
think either of us noted any similarity. About his real family, Marc was
reticent. His mother worked for Lands' End, the catalog clothing re-
tailer, and his father had retired as a sales manager for an agricultural
supply company called Pioneer Hi-Bred International. I've often wondered in the years since whether Marc's seeming distance from his
family was a residue of the stress of the chronic economic difficulties
of life among America's farmers.

My first impression was that Marc was very quiet. I now realize that
his subdued style that morning had more to do with sleep deprivation
than personality. The fact is, seven-thirty must have seemed far earlier
than the crack of dawn for him. I discovered later that it was Marc's
habit to work late into the night, then sleep late the next day. This is
a typical pattern for programmers, probably established in the days
when accessing university computers was almost impossible during the
day, and carried into the PC age because there was less distraction
after midnight. If caffeine-boosted Jolt cola didn't exist, some bleary-
eyed programmer would have invented it.

The computer revolution, like most revolutions, has been driven
forward by an army of the very young, visionaries and hackers who take
as a given endless nights in front of a screen and don't know they're
missing out on life because they don't yet have lives. So when Marc
told me he was only twenty-three, I wasn't surprised. What did surprise
me was what a veteran he was already. While at Illinois, he had worked
on 3-D visualization code for big IBM and Cray supercomputers. He'd
taken a couple of semesters off from his undergraduate studies in the
fall of 1990 to spend time with IBM in Austin, Texas, doing performance analysis and operating system work on Big Blue's highly touted
(but ultimately unsuccessful) attempt to outdo SGI in the 3-D field.
Then he'd headed back to Illinois to work again at NCSA—for $6.85
an hour—and to finish his studies. When he graduated, he headed

west to Silicon Valley, which was as logical a direction for a young programmer as it had been almost a century and a half earlier for would-be gold miners hoping that their futures would, literally, pan out. Marc was currently working on Internet security for a company in the area called Enterprise Integration Technologies (EIT), but I got the feeling that this job was more a matter of convenience than commitment. He wanted to be where the action was, and he had to pay the rent.

The purpose of this breakfast was to get acquainted; it wasn't a job interview. I needed engineers for whatever venture I wanted to try, and between what Bill Foss had told me and what I'd seen of Mosaic—a wonderfully simple, user-friendly way of using what had previously been the balky tool of those who were tech-savvy—I already knew Marc would be an asset. But talking to him gave me a chance to continue the speculation I'd begun years before on the direction technology would take in the future.

For me, at that point, Marc represented a transitional figure. At NCSA and IBM, he had been involved with the kinds of large, high-priced computers and workstations that had once reigned supreme, before PCs rose to replace them. Using those machines, he had taken a text-heavy, difficult medium, mostly the province of scientists and the computer elite, and made it modern and relatively easy to use by people whose entire computer arsenal cost a few thousand dollars.

What we now commonly call the Internet evolved from a series of communications links created by the Defense Department in the late sixties. It's a highly decentralized system that breaks information into small segments (packets), then moves them from computer to computer until they arrive at their intended destination, where they are reassembled into the original message. Called ARPAnet (from ARPA, the Advanced Research Projects Agency), this "deconstructed" system was meant to be far more resistant to nuclear destruction than the telephone, which funnels thousands of messages through a central switch. As more and more academics and scientists began to use the system, it grew into what's often called a "network of networks," a distributed architecture that allows a theoretically infinite number of computers to connect up in a kind of vast cyber democracy. Never let it be said that paranoia doesn't sometimes pay off. As a by-product of the Cold War, the Internet has already had, and will continue to have, a greater effect on the planet's inhabitants than the Sputnik-inspired conquest of the moon. And it will challenge the Industrial Revolution in its ultimate importance.

In the early nineties, after years as a more-or-less private party line for scientists, computer experts, and savvy graduate students, the Internet underwent a major change. Tim Berners-Lee, a researcher at the CERN atomic research center in Switzerland, created the first browser, and with it the World Wide Web. Using Berners-Lee's system of protocols, anyone with a networked computer could move with relative ease through the growing banks of data on the Net, accessing documents or pieces of documents using the concept of interlinks known as hypertext, conceived of years before by Theodor Nelson, visionary son of actress Celeste Holm.

The Web software, which Berners-Lee gave free to anyone who wanted to use it, transformed the Internet almost instantly. Even sophisticated computer users, it seemed, had found the old pre-browser Net a pain, so use of the Web grew at a phenomenal rate. But as user-friendly as the new software made the Internet, it was still a rather forbidding, text-only medium. The next great leap came from the tall young man sitting across from me at the Cafe Verona.

At the end of 1992, at another cafe, the Espresso Royale in Urbana-Champaign, Marc and a slightly older colleague and gifted NCSA programmer, Eric Bina, had decided they could improve on Berners-Lee's creation in the time-honored way publishers once made newspapers more inviting, or Apple energized computers almost a decade before: They added graphics and tools to turn a text-only medium into a kind of vid populi, and thus made the Web simple, intuitive, and entertaining.

In deciding to try pushing evolution in this direction, the two were doing just what many of the people using the Web at the time didn't want done: They were demystifying the medium and opening the doors to Everyman, with all the potential for wrecking the clubby, academic atmosphere that had prevailed on the Internet and the Web until then. As many others have pointed out, the effect of many of the significant breakthroughs of the Information Technology Age has been to shift power from the center to the periphery, while those at the center protest vigorously that the world as they know and love it is coming to an end. As a graduate student already chafing under the restrictions of NCSA's hidebound atmosphere, however, Marc was not worried about causing a little havoc in the establishment. He might even have taken a moment or two to revel in the tsunami he and Eric kicked up.

Extraordinary ideas need someone with the skills and focus to sweat the details. It was one thing for King Gillette, for instance, to figure out that a replaceable blade could revolutionize the daily drudgery of shaving and create a limitless new market. But without an engineer named William Nickerson, who had the technical ability to devise a complicated machine for making and sharpening those blades, we might still be using straight razors today. Eric Bina was Andreessen's detail man, and the two made a perfect pair, kind of a binary genius. In an August 1995 article in *Forbes ASAP*, writer George Gilder described the pair this way: "Every Gates has to have his Paul Allen (or Jobs, his Steve Wozniak). Andreessen's is Bina—short and wiry where Andreessen is ursine, cautious where he is cosmic, focused where he is expansive, apprehensive where he is evangelical, bitwise where he is prodigal with bandwidth, ready to stay home and write the code where Andreessen is moving on to conquer the globe."

In a marathon of code writing during a three-month period in 1993, the two friends rewrote the CERN code to make it run more quickly, then built Mosaic, with its graphics capability, on top of that, like a new cathedral rising on the site of an ancient temple. But this cathedral was constructed with an astonishing economy of means. The finished prototype required only nine thousand lines of code; by comparison, Windows 95 represents 11 million lines. In a 1997 article in GQ magazine, business writer Alan Deutschman claimed that Marc had done very little of the actual programming, but the two collaborated closely and pretty much split the work. In fact, as Bina would later recall, "We each did the job that most appealed to us, so each of us thinks the other did the hard stuff."

As the work progressed, Marc and Eric assembled a small band of Illinois computer science students to adapt the system to Windows and Macintosh machines. When the browser was up and working, or at least working well enough for a tryout, Marc and his small group of programmers put Mosaic up on the Web for downloading by anyone interested in giving it a test ride. The program was free, consistent with the prevailing Web ethic that innovations should be done for the common good, no matter how much work may have gone into creating them. One of the programmers, the young Yugoslavian transplant Aleks Totic, would later describe how it was that students would gladly devote days and nights to a project for slightly more than minimum-wage pay: "We figured if we did cool stuff, we'd get better jobs after school."

At that point, there couldn't have been anything cooler than shaking up the good gray Internet. The response to Mosaic indicated just how cool others thought the program was. Within six months, more than a million users had downloaded Mosaic, with more putting it into their computers every day. If Marc and Bina had been magazine publishers, they would have been a legend already, Citizen Kanes for the nineties. But since the Web in 1993 was not the household word—or household device—it is today, their breakthrough was known and admired mostly by a relatively small percentage of folks who spent their days at net-worked computers.

In fact, Mosaic was such a quiet breakthrough, a miracle to a small minority, that Larry Smarr, the man in charge of the NCSA at the University of Illinois, wasn't aware of it until a friend showed him the browser during a visit to Washington, D.C., just as Bill Foss had shown it to me at SGI. Smarr, a computational astrophysicist, was no different from many others at the time: He was still stuck in a world where supercomputers ruled, and sheer, awe-inspiring power was the standard of success. Though he had been using the Internet for years, like most computer scientists, he probably never thought that any change in the medium was needed. After all, the computer high-priesthood, of which I was a part, too, wasn't looking for ways to let in the vandals and visigoths of the outside world. It was bright young students with no status at risk who naturally thought that the democratization process Berners-Lee had started ought to be pushed further—that people might just as well have a little fun while astrophysicists were exchanging impenetrable theories on the origin of matter.

Smarr, like me, knew a good thing when he saw it. He, however, thought the good thing was the technology rather than the people who had created it. That's a common mistake in the technology business—maybe in all businesses—but it has led to a remarkable catalog of bad moves in a world where Moore's Law drives progress. So Smarr reacted in exactly the wrong way to the discovery. Rather than acknowledge the accomplishment of his young staffers and encourage them to take their product to market, as most department heads at Stanford would have done, Smarr decided to co-opt Mosaic. Because Marc and most of his programming team were temporary workers at NCSA, earning $6.85 an hour, and Eric was an employee, Smarr felt that the University of Illinois owned the program and should mobilize to develop it. This was an arguable legal point, but it might have remained irrelevant had he not made a crucial blunder.

When Marc graduated in December of 1993, he was asked to stay on at NCSA, a logical enough job offer considering what he'd already accomplished. But an odd proviso came with the offer: Marc had to give up his involvement with the Mosaic project. In a sense, this was a typical corporate-style decision: Break up internal elites, defray any leverage employees might have because of their accomplishments, and make sure the company gets the credit rather than the individual. The justification for having Marc work on some other project was that a lot of people had worked on Mosaic, and it was time for him to share some of the credit.

Marc may have been just a kid (though I'm not sure he was ever just a kid), but he was seriously allergic to that kind of organizational smoke. He, like me, would have a natural dislike of corporate hierarchy charts. He was the first to give credit to the few people who really did help write and adapt Mosaic software, but he wasn't about to stick with any outfit, no matter how powerful and distinguished, that was so ready to edit reality for its own advantage. Marc needed a job, and he needed to make at least enough money to support himself, so sliding right into a ready-made job might have been tempting. But after hearing that he'd be moved to other projects for transparently bogus reasons, it didn't take him more than a few seconds to decide the time had come for him to head for where the great new stuff was happening.

Without realizing it, Smarr, NCSA, and the University of Illinois had lost one of their most formidable potential assets, and in the process had killed off a loyalty that would eventually cost them a fortune. In the world of technology, products like Mosaic can be outpaced in a phenomenally short time, and an unprecedented competitive fever pretty much guarantees that any advantage based on any one break-through is short-lived. But good, creative brains will keep producing new and better things. To own something is almost meaningless in the long run (except for Microsoft, which now owns an entire indus-try). It's the ability to recruit, inspire, and hold on to smart people that offers the key to ongoing success. Call me a hedgehog, but that's one big thing I know.

At the moment Marc and I sat across from each other at breakfast, we were both disenfranchised entrepreneurs, men who under different circumstances had been cut off from their creations. Whether or not either of us was thinking about that at the time, the similarity of our recent experiences was moving us in the same direction. If I was angry while he was alienated, we were still powerfully motivated by the im-mediate past.

I liked Marc intuitively, and sensed that he was the kind of person needed for another start-up. Without any ceremony, as we finished our last coffee, we decided that we'd begin to meet at my house with a kind of "kitchen cabinet" I'd form to try to figure out what our new company would actually do. Marc had only one condition, not about what we ought to do, but what he adamantly didn't want to do:

"I'm finished with all that Mosaic shit."

4 Getting to Go

Most of the world probably thinks I had some great master plan that, meticulously followed, created Netscape, changed the nature of business, and made a bunch of us rich. After all, I was presumably a seasoned businessman. The temptation to claim a personal relationship with the muse of business is powerful. But there were other people there from the beginning, witnesses to those early days, so I have to confess that the company Marc and I agreed to form that morning at the Cafe Verona had no name, no mission, no business plan, and definitely no business. In May of 1994, the *San Jose Mercury News* quoted Allan Schiffman, chief technical officer at Enterprise Integration Technologies, where Marc had been working, saying that Andreessen was "eager to build upon his success with Mosaic." If only it had been that clear.

Whereas Marc said he didn't want to have anything to do with Mosaic, I was more ambivalent—I simply didn't care one way or the other. I was impressed with what Mosaic represented, and I knew the kind of work it had taken, but what interested me was Marc's strength as a thinker and organizer. The point was not what he had done, but that he'd had the ability and ambition to do it. If he felt that he was done with Mosaic, that was fine with me. My vague plan at the time was to continue moving in the direction I'd tried to get McCracken and SGI to go. I wanted to get something on track as quickly as possible, so it made sense to leverage the relationships I'd developed with Nintendo and Time Warner. It didn't make strategic sense to start from scratch, trying to come up with something entirely novel and then fund it on my own. By the mid-1990s, things were moving faster than ever in high tech (though not quite as fast as they're moving today)—the brushfire speed at which Mosaic had caught on was just one particularly dramatic illustration of that. In the time that had passed since I launched SGI, the number of start-ups had risen dramatically, there were venture capitalists behind every tree, and product development had shifted to warp speed. Business cycles that once had taken a year or two now were crammed into a couple of hectic months.

The year and a half postulated by Moore's Law had already begun to seem almost leisurely. I wasn't going to be able to putter around.

Another time factor was the academic calendar. Marc and I had talked about hiring his Mosaic team for whatever we might end up doing, and most of them would be graduating that spring. Before they all ended up working for Microsoft, which had a way of sucking up the top talent in university computer science departments, we had to come up with a reason to offer them jobs.

After that initial breakfast, Marc began coming over to my house in Atherton several evenings a week. In the large, two-story Mediterranean-style house that I had bought after I'd made enough money at SGI to begin behaving like the town's other Silicon *seigneurs*, Marc would have dinner with Nancy and me in the rather formal dining room, then we'd open a second bottle of burgundy and adjourn to a breakfast room that connected the kitchen with a comfortable family room. Sitting at a round table, with a mockingbird working on its repertoire just outside, we'd kick around whatever ideas occurred to us, listening to hear if anything had even the faintest echo of "Eureka!" about it. Jeff Bezos, founder of the online bookseller Amazon.com, tells about starting his business in an office in his garage in Seattle to give Amazon "garage start-up legitimacy." Netscape must have kitchen-table legitimacy, because we never once had a conversation in the garage.

We were often joined by Bill Foss and Kipp Hickman, one of SGI's best engineers. In 1983, Hickman had singlehandedly ported the UNIX system to the computer we were using at SGI, so I'd always considered him responsible for getting us into the UNIX workstation business. But his personality had always been a little too direct (a trait of my own) for the executives at SGI, so despite his contribution to the company, he'd never been given the title of principal engineer or the kind of stock options he deserved. Because I'd always made it a point to give him credit in public for his work, Kipp had told me shortly after I left SGI that he'd be interested in joining me in a new venture. Some of the others at those early meetings, at various times, were Michael Toy and Tom Paquin, both still at SGI. Ironically, none of the original members of the founding group of SGI had contacted me, despite our long trek together. They must have still believed the company was immune to any future threat. Whatever sense of adventure they'd felt when we set sail thirteen years before had obviously atro-phied, or maybe they were just tired.

By this time I had hired D'Anne as an all-purpose assistant and majordomo, an absolutely essential employee number three. We weren't really a company yet, just a group of people sitting around a table floating ideas, but we already had the beginnings of company problems: schedules, phone calls, food, and so forth. D'Anne had worked for the controller of SGI before becoming my assistant (after a fifteen-minute interview that she has described as "ten minutes of talk, five minutes of work"). She was in her forties and unusually fash-ionable for someone in the ranks of a technology company in Silicon Valley. Why she was interested in tossing over a safe and sane job for the uncertain, animal-house scramble of a mystery start-up is some-thing I've never figured out, and I'm not sure even she knows. Maybe she had a self-destructive urge, or a pent-up sense of adventure that the predictable days at SGI hadn't satisfied. With considerable diplo-macy, D'Anne has described me as "difficult," but that obviously wasn't enough to dissuade her. When she called to say she'd like to sign on, I was delighted. That was on March 1, 1994; eight days later, D'Anne tripped on the front steps of my house and tore all the liga-ments in her left foot, putting her into a cast and temporarily out of the action. Amazingly, given my mercurial moods in those days, I didn't see this as a bad omen.

On the other hand (or foot), we weren't seeing much in the way of good omens. We had so little sense of where we were headed we might not have known an omen if it had jumped up and shouted. About all we assumed at that point was that whatever Company X did, it would involve the Internet in some way. Though still an emerging phenom-enon, the Net was clearly the next big thing (even if, incredibly, the industry's eight-hundred-pound gorilla, Microsoft, had not yet paid much attention to the phenomenon). For Microsoft and others, the big question remained unanswered: How could anyone make money on the Internet? I didn't have a specific answer to that yet, but I figured that with the Web- and Mosaic-enabled Internet already growing ex-ponentially, you couldn't help but make money. It was just the law of large numbers at work—even a small amount of money per user would yield a big business.

Lurking like a shadow at the edge of my plan to make a connection with either Time Warner or Nintendo was the fact that my previous work with both those companies had been as chairman of Silicon Graphics. Thus, though the top management at both companies knew me, they had relationships with SGI that they wanted to maintain and protect. The fact that I was no longer with the company inevitably made me a lot less interesting to them. This was nothing personal, just an unwritten rule of business. You're either in a position to do something for people, or you're knocking on the door hoping they'll do something for you. Big difference. And they wouldn't have had to do much probing to discover that Ed McCracken hated my guts, further dampening their enthusiasm. I doubt that Marc realized my loss of clout at the time, but I knew that though I could get a hearing, I no longer had any real leverage.

Nevertheless, Time Warner and Nintendo were the obvious places for us to start, and Marc and I talked our way through several bottles of burgundy trying to pin down exactly what we might approach them with. My discussions with Time Warner had involved that company's pilot program for interactive television in the Orlando, Florida, market. This was logical enough for an established technology company trying to branch out, but as the foundation for a start-up, it didn't make a lot of sense.

Nintendo was more logical. Computer games had been, and continued to be, one of the "killer apps" in the business. Nintendo of America, which both rode and drove this phenomenal market, was still the biggest company in Redmond, Washington, and had been the subject of a popular, recently published book, *Game Over*, by David Sheff. Like many young programmers, Marc liked computer games, and agreed with me that there might be a future for a company that put Nintendo games on the Internet, a kind of AOL for teenage boys bent on virtual mayhem.

A week before, at the end of February, I had gone to New York for a meeting with Time Warner. I didn't have much hope that anything would come from this meeting, but I felt I had to go, if only to prove to myself that interactive TV was a dead end for us. When I got back a few days later, suitably convinced, Marc handed me a twenty-page paper he'd written about how we could create an online service for

Nintendo. For me, the significance of this memo was twofold: First, the ideas it contained, though I won't attempt to paraphrase them here, were innovative and realistic; second, the paper, detailed and carefully thought out, indicated an analytical mind missing in many young engineers. As I read it, I was tremendously impressed, both with the quality of his thinking and the clarity of his writing. I'd been working for years to perfect my writing, but at the age of twenty-three Marc, an engineer with only the required minimum of liberal arts courses, had produced a document I admired. I had become more taken with Marc each time we'd met, but this memo made me realize he had dimensions that set him apart.

Every start-up has about it the quality of a friendly intramural competition; there's no room for slacking off, and nobody wants to contribute less than anyone else (which is why start-ups are so much more exciting and productive than established companies). I felt I had to respond to Marc's effort, so over the next few days I put together a Nintendo online business plan to match his technology plan. In a real sense, this was the beginning of a true partnership between a battle-scarred Silicon Valley insider and a brilliant young outsider. Later in the spring, I described the relationship exactly as I saw it to the *Internet Business Report:* "I look at this as Jim Clark investing in Marc Andreessen." (At this point, we gave the company the tentative name of Electric Media, which lasted a couple of months until another company's use of the name forced us to come up with something else.) The fact that we were headed down a blind alley, or at least in a direction that wouldn't pan out, didn't matter as much as this unspoken, mutual commitment to match each other's efforts.

By mid-March, we had worked out the details of a plan—Marc's comprehensive description of how Nintendo Online would work with my business wrapper around it. We both agreed the plan sounded like something that could work, and I headed for Seattle to meet with Howard Lincoln, the president of Nintendo of America. It's usually not easy to measure the success of a business meeting early in the process of trying to sell an idea. Howard Lincoln is a nice guy, and whatever concerns he might have had about Nintendo's relationship with SGI, he gave me an attentive hearing. But like many executives in the technology business, Lincoln was not a technology man, and I had the feeling as I flew back to San Francisco that though he'd seemed interested, he hadn't quite known what to think of the plan.

I was feeling increasingly frustrated. The clock was ticking, and my impatience to get something going was rising. Marc and I and the others continued talking about Nintendo, but the longer I thought about it, the less workable the idea seemed. At best, given the size of the game company and the number of people who'd have to sign on to our plan, and adding the fact that they weren't likely to see an online function as a major part of their business, I couldn't imagine their making a decision in less than nine months. And in the end, even if we went ahead with Nintendo, we would have only one contract and one customer—not the formula for a good night's sleep. A change of CEO, a failure to turn a profit soon enough for Nintendo's taste, and we'd be dead. Or bought by Nintendo for a low price.

Another clock was ticking, too. Spring break had already come and gone. Marc reminded me after I got back about an impending deadline: "You know, all my friends at Illinois are about to graduate. One of them has already taken a job. The others are interviewing. If we want to hire these guys, we've got to come up with something soon."

Since I'd met Marc, the main objective had always been that we bring together the core group that had developed Mosaic. People who have worked well together in the past make all the difference in a start-up, where time can't be wasted getting people acquainted, integrating dissimilar personalities into a team. I didn't know how many engineers would come over from SGI, but no mass migration was likely; I had legal constraints on hiring, first of all, and I hadn't exactly left behind a seething mass of people who agreed that SGI was in trouble. Whether people liked me or not, or felt a certain loyalty to me as a founder of the company, there weren't many as disenchanted as Kipp Hickman. If I wanted to get going with any kind of momentum, I needed to keep the boys from Illinois together as a team.

I felt that the situation was bleak. We'd exhausted my two original ideas, and yet we had to get off our tails fast. We were still talking and talking, when what we needed was action.

Then, at about one in the morning on a Thursday late in March, as we sat in my living room working our way through yet another bottle of burgundy, out of frustration I said to Marc, "You come up with something to do and I'll invest in it." Marc leaned back in his chair, thought for a few minutes, then said—as if all he'd every really needed was a kind of friendly ultimatum—"Well, we could always build a Mosaic killer."

"A what?" I asked.

"You know," he said, "build a browser that's better than Mosaic, put it out there, let it take over instead of Mosaic. Right now, the university is spreading a copy of this program that my friends and I worked our butts off writing, and they're trying to make a business of it. We need to take it over. We gotta kill it."

Maybe it was the wine—and if so, God bless it—or the late hour and our increasing desperation. After all, Marc had said when we first met that he didn't want anything more to do with Mosaic. But now the proverbial light dawned. The idea seemed instantly right: We could jump-start the company by improving on what Marc and his friends had invented, then make money by going head-to-head with the people who had taken the invention away from its inventors. In reality, and symbolically, a Mosaic killer was a great way to go. Suddenly I felt energized. As I later told John Markoff of *The New York Times* when we announced formation of the company, "I know there are a bunch of people looking for gold in the Internet. These guys have already been there and found it."

"If you can hire the entire Mosaic team to do this," I told Marc excitedly, "I'll invest in it. Screw the business plan and conventional investors."

Just like that, we knew what we had to do.

5 Operation Pied Piper

Throughout history the key workers in most industries, those who make the difference between success and failure, have been people with years of experience in a given business, or at least in the world of work. Of course, Henry Ford couldn't have built cars without assembly-line workers, and Ma Bell couldn't have grown so fat and happy (and complacent) without the legions of switchboard operators who were the front line of communications in the early days. But the people doing the creative jobs that advanced design and technology were rarely young, and unless they had the uncommon foresight to be the boss's sons, they usually moved up in the hierarchy at a predetermined pace, fighting harder and harder for the diminishing number of jobs toward the top of the pyramid.

The computer business has turned that tradition on its head, with the glory and often the power going to kids whose brains and innate skills matter far more than the length of time they've been at the game. There have been other times when age and experience didn't matter, as when the lust for adventure and sheer bravado led young men to sail off to discover new worlds (and new trade routes), or when a sense of boom-or-bust ambition sent wildcatters in their twenties out into the heat and dust to drill for oil. The past decade has seen a similar passing of the economic torch to the young. These days, even formal education matters less than it did not very long ago. By the time the company that became Netscape employed twenty-five engineers, six of them wouldn't even have undergraduate degrees, and Marc would tell a *Fortune* reporter that computer science courses had as much relevance to commercial computer science as business school courses had to do with real business. It's not without some symbolic significance that Alan Turing, the brilliant English mathematician who came up with the concept of the digital computer more than sixty years ago, wrote his revolutionary paper "On Computable Numbers" when he was twenty-three years old. In an industry that reinvents itself constantly, experience is measured in months, not years. Not many "old-timers" in Silicon Valley have gray hair (though more than a few have very little hair of any shade).

There's a particular kind of person who seems genetically disposed to do the programming work that produces successful new software, just as there are certain athletes genetically favored to be Olympic rowers (high on strength, long on willingness to suffer). A programmer is someone who can sit in front of computer monitors for hours, focusing on putting into arcane code the thousands of commands necessary to make a program work, then go back and do it all again chasing bugs—and, in the thick of all this drudgery, can still be creative. This kind of concentration—which can be so total that those who practice it may seem almost like simpletons in their lives away from computers—comes easiest to the young, which is why chess geniuses, mathematics prodigies, and theoretical physicists so often lose their edge before middle age. It is also why the computer revolution has produced so many very young moguls. And why Silicon Valley, Seattle, and all the other front lines of the new economy are manned by armies of the young. As I write this, there's a lot of commotion about the demographics of the business, with complaints that middle-aged programmers have a tougher time getting jobs (in a low-unemployment business) than kids just out of college. Fair or not, there's a perception that younger programmers are more current in a world of constant change than those in their thirties and forties. To throw a gratuitous bone to the older of us who still practice the art of computer programming, at least musicians and composers seem to continue to improve with age, and computer programming shares some characteristics with music. But this world still belongs to the young. Young programmers have incredible stamina and a certain kind of craziness that lets them work punishing hours, maintain a sense of emergency, and stay fixed on the target until a project is finished. Marine Corps drill instructors will tell you that the ideal combat marine is nineteen years old, too young to know that there's anything they can't do. I'd say that the ideal programmer is about twenty-two, and getting younger all the time.

I started SGI with graduate students, so I knew the kind of near-trancelike focus determined young men could bring to bear on a problem. And I knew that if I could hire a group of young engineers who had already worked together to create a successful product, I'd have a tremendous head start.

Our first tentative recruiting foray wasn't very encouraging. Eric Bina, a couple of years older than Marc and married to a tenured professor of database technology at the University of Illinois, responded negatively to an e-mail invitation from Marc to meet with us in California. Besides not wanting to tempt himself with a job so far from home, Bina probably thought that this approach was not really any different from any of the other recruiting efforts that were a routine part of life for elite young programmers. Marc, visibly disappointed, sent back an e-mail saying how sorry he was that he and Eric wouldn't be working together again.

An alarm began flashing in my head. After losing a couple of months figuring out what we were going to do, I wasn't about to let one setback slow us down. But I also knew that we had to get moving. These Mosaic programmers were like figures on the frieze of some Greek temple: Once they were whisked off to this place and that, reassembling them was going to be impossible—especially given the tightening time frame we had to stay within if we were going to get a jump on competitors and potential competitors. So in the last week of March, I told Marc to send the whole group an e-mail to let them know we wanted to meet with them in Urbana-Champaign in the next few days. Bina's hesitation was based on geography, not personal strategy. Though he wasn't looking for a move, he was clearly ready for a change. For him and the other programmers, the fun had gone out of Mosaic, which had become increasingly bureaucratized as Larry Smarr and others at NCSA began to realize they had something they could license. Hearing that Marc was coming back, and bringing me along, created the most excitement the group had felt since they'd been working on the original Mosaic months before.

Marc was vague about what we might be proposing. He even tossed in a red herring, telling a couple of his friends to read *Game Over*. We weren't thinking about Nintendo anymore, but he figured it wouldn't hurt to use the game company as a temporary smoke screen. With the world of software engineers closely connected by the instant electronic grapevine of e-mail, we weren't about to let our plans leak over the Net. This time, the response was enthusiastic, so three days later, Marc and I got on a plane at San Francisco Airport and headed east. Besides Bina, we were scheduled to meet with Aleks Totic, Jon Mittelhauser, Chris Houck, Rob McCool, plus Lou Montulli, who had developed a text-only browser called Lynx while he was an undergraduate at the University of Kansas. Montulli, whose browser actually had more users at the time than Mosaic, knew Marc, Aleks, and Rob from previous meetings at Web conferences. While everyone else was in Illinois, Lou had to get to our gathering in Urbana-Champaign by a rather round-about route. When D'Anne called him in Lawrence, Kansas, to invite him to Illinois, he was at a racquetball tournament in Kansas City. When he heard the message on his answering machine, he changed clothes, turned around, and drove the seventy-five miles back to the airport in Kansas City.

Marc and I were booked at the University Inn, a place aptly described by its generic name. By the time we arrived, delayed by bad weather over Chicago, everyone was hanging around wondering where we were, and what was up. As is usually the case when I'm starting to feel enthusiastic about an idea, I was in a good mood, and in a hurry to recruit this group of young guns. Timing may be everything in show business, but hitting the ground running is everything in the tech business. We ended up arriving late in the evening, and I went to bed while Marc got together with the team. As a founder of SGI, I was known to the group, but as a person, I was just somebody who might have been a friend of their fathers. Marc revealed that our idea was to produce a Mosaic killer.

The next morning, it was raining hard and felt almost cold enough for snow. I talked about the way things were in Silicon Valley, how it was to start a business, and tried to plant what Bina later described to writer George Gilder as "a contagion of entrepreneurial excitement." Like a circuit preacher, I can be evangelical when I'm selling my own optimism—anybody who lacks that tendency has a tough time as an entrepreneur in high tech—and I had no problem making a convincing case that the future lay in Northern California, not in Seattle, and definitely not in Urbana-Champaign. I was only fifty at the time, but to them I might as well have been an ancient visitor from some legendary tribe. In fact, some air of a gray-bearded wise man must have impressed at least a few of the Mosaic group, because Montulli would later compare my effect to that of Alec Guinness turning away searching Empire stormtroopers with the hypnotic incantation "These are not the droids you're looking for."

The fact that I'd left SGI in a fairly undramatic way probably paid off here. I think if I had come away from that situation with a reputation for rashness, or shooting off my mouth (which I easily might have had it not been for some good advice), these young men might have been wary. After all, if adults are nothing else, they're expected to be stable and dependable. These guys weren't worried about getting jobs—Mosaic was a hell of a thing to have on your résumé, and, at this writing, it's estimated that more than three hundred thousand positions in high tech are unfilled. So they wouldn't be about to get on board a ship with Captain Ahab at the helm. I didn't let myself get into any talk about my anger about what had gone on at SGI, so I must have seemed about as solid, and stolid, as a banker. They had no reason not to trust me. Anyway, one of them later told me that I could have sold him his own liver, which I took to be a compliment.

We moved on to a pizza joint near the university campus for more talk and some typically mediocre Midwestern Italian food. This was definitely not the kind of place where Time Warner executives would have considered doing business, which is a pretty good illustration of the difference between the old world and the new. (By this time in my life, I had developed a taste for good burgundy, and this place was strictly Chianti-in-a-basket, but what mattered was that this was familiar turf for Marc and the group.)

It was clear to me that the Mosaic veterans were excited to have Marc back among them. They all focused on him, even Eric Bina, who is a brilliant programmer and had been an equal partner in writing the original software. (Eric, older than the others and married, seemed noticeably different. He was the only one of the group who asked about health care, for instance.) I had been impressed by Marc's thinking from our first meeting at the Cafe Verona, but now I saw that he was a natural leader, too. I don't mean the person with the best ideas, but the leader of the pack, the "silverback," as Dian Fossey called the top male in her colony of mountain gorillas. He was what I had been at the beginning of SGI, the one who could say, "This is what we've got to do," and have everyone do it. I realized I'd definitely bet on the right horse.

Marc and I had arrived with our snapshot of the future at a time that could not have been more opportune. Not just because graduation was looming for several of the programmers and they were feeling naturally restless, but more important because all of them (with the exception of newcomer Montulli) had been living through the kidnapping of their creation.

Larry Smarr, the physicist and researcher who drove the University of Illinois to set up the National Center for Supercomputer Applications, had wanted to form the world's most advanced computing environment for physics, and in many ways he succeeded. I had been so impressed with what he was doing there that while I was at SGI, I had given $1 million worth of computer equipment to the center. In the process, Smarr had created an atmosphere that attracted gifted students of computer science in much the same way the Yale drama department attracts talented acting students, or the UCLA film school draws ambitious young moviemakers. But, perhaps influenced by his never-ending need to raise money, Smarr couldn't resist taking over Mosaic once he became aware of its extraordinary popularity. Though a Web browser was far from the kind of thing NCSA was established to do, Mosaic glinted like gold in the stream at Urbana's very own Sutter's Mill.

Well, it glinted for me, too, so I can't very well fault Smarr for hoping to make money on Mosaic. The difference was that he wanted the profit to go to the university and to fund NCSA, not to the best and brightest of the university's students who had done the work, and were continuing to do it. To make sure that happened, he (or someone) had diluted the credit for the innovation, to make it vague and general, as if somehow the NCSA had created this amazing software, not a few young men who happened to be working there, most of them at just over six dollars an hour. What Smarr failed to realize was that projects with true commercial potential can't possibly be maintained by a university, because the basic business of a university is education, not profitable products and services. Stanford knew this, and as a result had spun off hundreds of start-ups; Illinois had yet to learn.

It could be that Smarr's viewpoint was unavoidable in a public school like the University of Illinois. Private universities such as Stanford are not beholden to the public for funding, and as a result perhaps they feel more flexible in their attitude toward freedom of business. Whatever the case, the university and NCSA increasingly began to shift the balance of work and power. This was why Marc was asked to stay on, then told he couldn't work on Mosaic. And why NCSA management brought in more layers of staff to run development. I've already mentioned Smarr's fundamental error in thinking that software was more valuable than talent. Another mistake—if it was a mistake rather than a disingenuous policy—was to think that the new features that inevitably would have to be added to the original browser to make it commercial couldn't possibly be determined by Marc and the original group of undergraduates.

With NCSA management's staffers increasingly encroaching on what had been the territory of a small band of friends and spreading the word that Mosaic had been done by a large group of students and staff, the original programmers were totally disenchanted by the time Marc and I arrived. In a series of conversations I had with Smarr in late 1994, he repeatedly talked about the forty or so people working at NCSA who had created Mosaic, so he may have actually convinced himself that this revisionism was the truth. But once I talked with this motley crew, I knew that they alone were the prime movers of Mosaic at NCSA.

We spent the rest of the day talking about how Mosaic could be surpassed, and where a better browser would fit on the as-yet-undefined Web business landscape. Everybody was tremendously enthusiastic, in part, I think, because the idea appealed to their need to say a resounding "Screw you!" to the university that had so totally undervalued them. It's amazing what you can gain merely by recognizing talent, and how much you can lose by taking it for granted. I had a really good feeling about this reunion, and my place in it. I hadn't made any job offers, but my "magnificent seven" were assembled and, I was pretty sure, ready to go.

That afternoon, I invited each programmer individually to my suite to make formal offers. We had talked about what kind of deal we should offer, and Marc had advised that we give all of them the same salary: $65,000 a year. They might have done a little better had they been young lawyers starting out at a large corporate firm, but the big difference was that the offer included one hundred thousand shares of stock, in effect making them partners from the first day. At this point, I had kept things simple. I'd worked up a rough budget for the next year, worked out a dilution plan for the stock, and decided how much I would buy. One of the key ways to keep it simple was my decision not to bring traditional venture capital into the initial development phase.

Of course, I could have raised all the money from outside investors, meaning I wouldn't have to put any of my own money up while getting someone else's at a pretty high valuation. But I also knew that I would then be an employee and employees receive "common stock," which has a vesting structure conditioned on continued employment that usually lasts four or five years before the stock actually all becomes the recipient's. In short, none of it belongs to the employee in the beginning, and the unvested portion can be taken away. Even at this time, I had planned to get someone else to eventually run the business, and I did not intend to remain a long-term employee. I had had enough trouble with SGI doing this, and this experience wasn't going to be repeated. Whoever I eventually recruited to run the company was going to run it without my interference, which meant that I did not want to be an employee. So I created a very rational equity structure in which I was the only investor. Starting out, I valued what the Mosaic team had already done at $3 million—one year's worth of software work by seven students was valued at this. I put in $3 million and took 50 percent of the company; of course, both their and my part of the deal eventually would be diluted as we brought on other employees. In contrast, at the beginning of SGI, ten years of my experience plus three years of hard work by seven students, and a business plan with three senior executives in place, was valued by the Mayfield Fund at $1.2 million; they took 40 percent of the company for $800,000. I was intent on giving these young men and the future employees of Netscape a fair shake, precisely because I had become so bitter about my early experiences at SGI.

As each of Marc's group came into my University Inn room, a standard-issue, chocolates-on-the-pillow overnighter, they sat down with varying degrees of self-consciousness. Up to this point, this had all been lots of evangelical talk and heady optimism. Now we'd come to the point where it was going to mean something or it wasn't. I explained the deal, offered the salary and the stock, and told them what I thought that stock might eventually mean. "I am pretty sure that your holdings will be worth more than a million dollars," I said, wondering if they believed what I was saying, "but within five years, if things go the way I hope they will, it is my objective that you make over ten million." These were numbers out of a hat, but I felt they could happen. Little did I know that they would exceed this in less than a year and a half.

From time to time after that night, I've tried to imagine what it would have been like when I was in my early twenties to have a successful older businessman hold out to me the possibility that in the foreseeable future I'd be a millionaire. Certainly, it must have been easier for me to envision what I was saying than it was for them. Aleks Totic told me later that they felt like rock stars, which, in the world of software, they definitely were. But I doubt very much that anyone promised the Beatles a fortune the day before they formed the band.

One by one, they came aboard. When the meetings were over they headed for a college hangout called Gully's while I wrote seven agreement letters, differing only in the addressee, on my laptop and sent them to the hotel fax machine, which served as a printer. Marc took the letters over to Gully's, handed them around like diplomas, everyone signed, and just like that we were in business. Before heading back to the airport, I told the suddenly employed programmers to get out to California just as soon as they could. "We've got a hell of a lot to do."

On April 4, 1994, I incorporated the company. Robert H. Reid notes in his book *Architects of the Web* that at about the same time, Microsoft was holding an offsite retreat to discuss their future involvement with the Internet (about which more later). The revisionists in Seattle like to say I formed the company on April 7, in response to this meeting, but that is complete bullshit. I was not aware of this meeting. But I knew without a doubt that Microsoft would be the long-term enemy, because this thing was going to get big. What they didn't know was

that a bunch of tough young commandos had just parachuted in behind their lines, and we were going to upset their plans to own and
control the digital electronic future. What I didn't know was that they
would eventually feel so threatened by us that they would try desperately and—I am convinced—illegally to kill us. At that time, I never
expected them to be so flagrant in their behavior as to precipitate a
Department of Justice lawsuit against them. If so, I probably would
have gone with the Nintendo idea, and the Internet phenomenon
might not have happened as it did, or even at all. Because on April 4,
1994, Microsoft was hell-bent to own the Microsoft Network much as
AOL owned their network. Microsoft and Bill Gates did not believe in
the commercial potential of the Internet, and Gates was eventually
reported to have said, "If I could push a button and blow up the
Internet, I would do it, because I don't know how to control it." I hope
he never does figure it out.

An axiom of motorcycle racing applies precisely to the technology business: Stability is a function of momentum. In other words, move fast, keep going—or end up on your butt. Slow down, give in to indecision, use the brakes when you ought to be rolling on the throttle, and you'll be off the road and into the trees. In our business, stability and security come from doing things quickly—in other words, rapidly getting out products before competitors. Which, in the beginning, is everyone else with an eye on the same, untapped (you hope) market. And later, frankly, almost always means Microsoft.

I wasn't thinking precisely in those terms as I tried to stretch out in my seat on the way back to San Francisco. What preoccupied me were thoughts of time and speed. I had turned fifty a month before, and thus found myself a middle-aged man in a world where to lose a step was to lose the game. I came from Plainview, a small town in northwest Texas, seventy-eight miles south of Amarillo. In Plainview when I was a kid, the only things that happened suddenly were tornadoes. Speed had been defined by souped-up Chevys. Later, in the navy, forward momentum for most of us had been the classic military bind of "hurry up and wait." The true hurry was to reach the end of a four-year hitch and get on with life, and that seemed to take a lifetime. The academic world I ended up in later was characterized not by how fast everything changed, but how slowly.

Obviously, in the dozen years since I'd started SGI, my conception of speed had changed. This change hadn't come all at once, but it had been fairly drastic. Gordon Moore's much-cited law had observed, then institutionalized, an eighteen-month pace that came to dominate the business. Miss one product cycle at that rate and you might be forgiven; miss two and you're on your way to relic status. Moore's Law governed the world of hardware first—after all, Moore was a chip maker—and then software. One might quibble about whether eighteen months represents a realistic constant, but even in businesses with assembly-line operations, at least a year usually passed before the predicted periodic doubling of power (and/or halving of size) took place.

As I flew west, glad to be headed back to Northern California, my thoughts weren't on speed as such, however. That had been a fact of life for years. Compared to the heavy industries that had powered the American economy since early in the century, the computer business has always been fast. In fact, compared to any other business at all, the computer hardware and software industry runs at a breakneck velocity. What preoccupied me was not so much speed itself, but acceleration, in particular the quickening pace of companies' life cycles. Consider this: Hewlett Packard was founded in 1939 to manufacture electronic measurement devices. Not until eighteen years later, in 1957, did the company offer its stock to the public. Microsoft was founded by Bill Gates and Paul Allen in 1975 to market the computer language Basic, and rolled out products for eleven years before an initial public offering in 1986. In 1976, Steve Jobs and Steve Wozniak started Apple, released the Apple I computer nine months later, but waited only four and a half years before going public. A couple of years later, with a group from Stanford, I founded Silicon Graphics on the strength of the Geometry Engine, 3-D software I'd invented in 1981. We rolled out our first product, the IRIS 1000 terminal, in November of 1983, and our first workstation, the IRIS 1400, late in 1984. In 1986 we had our IPO. (Netscape's IPO was just over a year after its formation.) The pattern is inescapable: steady acceleration, with ever-decreasing time periods between the initial product going to market and the company itself going to market. This pace was driven ever faster in part by the rising importance of stock options as a major form of compensation in the Valley. If you were hoping to collect sooner or later, then most people figured sooner was better.

Also growing dramatically briefer were the periods between leadership errors and their ultimate consequences. The legendary market misreading that led Ford to introduce the Edsel in the fifties directly contributed to making Detroit vulnerable to competition from Volkswagen, Toyota, Honda, and other foreign makers of smaller, more efficient cars. But though the Edsel suffered a flop far more dramatic than usual, American automakers didn't feel the repercussions for years. Even in the computer business, for all its raised rpms (and, indeed, revolutions-per-minute often seems to describe the business perfectly), fatal errors might pass unnoticed for a long time, masked by the appearance of success. For instance, when Apple decided not to license its operating system, thus allowing Microsoft to become the almost-uncontested PC standard, hardly anyone realized until it was too late that the miscalculation was a disaster. Now, for all the bally-hooed upturn of Apple's fortunes after the return of Steve Jobs, the company's market share is so small it has to beg software developers such as Intuit and capitulate to threats from Microsoft by dropping lawsuits and allowing investment in order to get them to continue supplying applications for its system. But it took a long time for Apple to end up in such sad shape, and there are still so many loyal Apple users that even on the ropes the company has enough resilience to stay on its feet and put out new products. But it is doubtful that the odds have changed to favor its long-term survival.

When I had tried to get SGI to move in new directions, it was clear that the price for a wrong move, or even standing pat, would be paid much more quickly than had been the case only a few years before. The irony is that although fast decisions are essential, bad decisions—which may increase as a result of hurrying the process—are more quickly damaging. Errant companies don't often get to spend years on death row anymore, filing appeals. If the fruits of success came sooner, so, too, did the wages of sin. There's an old cliché in highly competitive businesses: Either eat lunch or be lunch. In more ways than one, Silicon Valley is a place famous for fast food.

But if speed had increased, the nature of speed in technology had remained pretty much the same. Intel constantly squeezes more transistors onto their chips in a kind of calculations-per-second arms race, software makers use it up like traffic quickly filling up the lanes of a new highway, then the spiral takes another turn. This led to the wry saying "Andy [Grove] giveth, and Bill [Gates] taketh away." Though computing speeds had risen meteorically, the improvements were invariably due to chip developments. The machines were phenomenal—faster, smaller, more powerful—but the rules hadn't really changed.

As Marc and I talked during the spring of 1994, we sensed something new. Not the accelerated speed of the present, but the next level, another kind of speed altogether. People weren't going to think in the eighteen-month periods of Moore's Law anymore—that was now an eon!—but in how fast light moved down a fiber optic cable. Quite literally, we were headed for a quantum leap. It made me think of that moment in *Star Wars* (the reader will pardon yet another image borrowed from George Lucas, I hope) when the *Millennium Falcon*, chased by Imperial interceptors, suddenly makes the jump to warp speed and vanishes in a blur of stars, headed for some distant part of that galaxy far, far away. Andreessen and his friends, and the many thousands who had grabbed Mosaic as it had gone out online, were children of the Internet. They lived in a world where physical barriers weren't a factor. You didn't build some physical thing, move it down an assembly line, box and shrink-wrap it, and stick it on a store shelf. You didn't have to work out relationships with distributors and beg for shelf space—always a nightmare for a new company. You conceived of it in your head, produced it in a computer, and tossed it up for grabs on the Net. In this brave and blisteringly fast new world, nothing deterred you but bad ideas or bug-infested programming. There was no balky concept of wholesale and retail, no distribution system or sales structure. You went right to the customer and let him take what he wanted for free. If he didn't like it, he dumped it. If he liked it, you were a hero.

Of course, this wasn't a business, but that gave an extra measure of freedom to these kids who could already sidestep so many tedious realities. Call it the beta-test mentality. They'd cobble something together, clean up most of the bugs, then let whoever wanted to try it out. If the program was weird, or crashed a lot, or didn't work the way it was meant to, well, maybe the de facto testers would have suggestions about fixing it. So a second version would come out, then a third. As Marc put it, "You keep kicking versions out the door, making them better. Any individual product is less important than the basic idea. If a beta turns people off, you put out a beta that turns them back on."

The romantic legend that so many high-tech companies have started in garages is appropriate; these kids were the nineties version of the boys in Plainview who spent their nights tinkering with the engines of their Chevys and Fords to get a few more horsepower, then drove for a week and started over again. The difference was that this generation of tinkerers had created not just a new machine, but a new reality that forced all of us to redefine our notions of speed and ownership. All across the Web, people would help each other just to get things right, and use whatever worked best. When Lou Montulli realized that Mosaic was a more stable system than the browser he'd developed, he simply put Lynx onto Mosaic to improve its usability. In the process, he added millions of his users to the Mosaic fold. Then, whenever he made improvements to the underlying CERN Web software, he would send it to Marc to help upgrade Mosaic. This kind of flexibility ran through everything they did. The children of the Internet didn't worry about getting things absolutely perfect before release—that was the stuffy "old" engineering paradigm—but simply thought about getting something done so they could start to improve it. As Guy Kawasaki, one of Apple's most brilliant innovators, put it not long ago, "Don't worry, be crappy."

The Mosaic group wasn't thinking about doing crap, of course, and what they'd ended up producing was a long way beyond a casual hacker's gadget tossed out without any concern for quality. But they were working within the new rules of a new paradigm. When the Edsel bombed, Ford Motors was shaken to its foundation (and God knows what reverberations were felt among engineers, stylists, and marketing executives). The approach to a product that Marc and his generation of engineers took was flexible, evolutionary, agile—a naturally developed version of what management consultants call "rapid prototyping." And it worked beautifully with what they were doing. When a software program had problems, you worked on it for a while and put out the 1.01 version, and kept doing that. If a car crashes, people die; if software crashes, hit the restart button.

An appliance company making toasters that consistently burst into flame wouldn't survive for long, but Microsoft has prospered hugely by introducing products famous for their flaws. In the early days of any technology, there's a certain grace period when the thrill of the new compensates for the pain of imperfection. To use one last car analogy, when automobiles were still called horseless carriages, drivers didn't complain that engines were started with hand cranks; it was taken for granted that driving a car was difficult. Almost a century later, most people also took it for granted that computers were difficult, so each time they became a little easier, users reacted with disproportionate gratitude. (Some of the computer elite even worried that the technology was becoming too easy, just as Catholic traditionalists had felt threatened when the Mass went from Latin to local, living languages.) Perfection takes a long time; if "pretty good and getting better" is the goal instead, acceleration increases geometrically.

Mosaic was the newest machine in the newest and fastest technology, and my sense was not only that there was a business in it, but that it had the power to change phenomenally the speed at which business itself would be done. The model was right there in front of me, in what had already been done. For the children of the Internet, taking a product to market, or going to get a product, were virtual acts, hence virtually effortless. *Netscape time* was a term we came to apply to the speed at which we developed products and, by extension, the relentlessness of the work involved. But the effortlessness of Web use is also an aspect of Netscape time, when a consumer can research a product, find the best price, and click to buy, all in the time it used to take to get the car out of the garage. The distribution channel was very close to the thing being distributed; Mosaic, which made the Web far easier to use, was delivered to its users over the same Web. When the railroads were laying track across the vast reaches of the American interior, that track was delivered to the construction sites over the track that had been laid so far. The creation of a transcontinental railway system was made possible by the very machinery that made it necessary. A perfectly integrated system, a self-fulfilling technology. From a business standpoint, the beauty of this was breathtaking.

No less wonderful, to me, was that I seemed to see what no one else had yet seen. Kipp Hickman had once told a reporter, "Jim Clark has a way of getting a glimpse of what is a business opportunity." In this case, I had more than a glimpse; a whole panoramic view was beginning to open up, though I was only seeing it in increments so far. Yet the Internet, for so many years the province of scientists and the computer literati, was as yet hardly noticed as a potential place to make money; a nice way to communicate, sure, but the decision makers in information technology were looking elsewhere for new sources of profit (as I had been with my interactive TV efforts at SGI). It was as if I had walked into a field strewn with diamonds and found those already there discussing the future of the area as an ostrich farm. There aren't many occasions in an entrepreneur's life when none of his competitors have as yet caught on to something fairly obvious. I savored the moment.

But just for a moment. Because advantages are as perishable as they are rare. And even then, I was 100 percent certain that eventually we were going to find ourselves alone in a dark alley with Microsoft. Not that I wanted to compete with them—who does?—but because Bill and Co. don't like it when anyone else has success in the software business. Sometimes it seems there isn't a single software company in the world that Microsoft isn't going after, or hasn't gone after. So the more rapidly we got out there and the faster we moved, the further we could put ourselves ahead of this behemoth that was going to try crushing us underfoot.

High-tech companies—at least those that survive—are always thinking about the future. They look ahead to stay ahead, and there's always a large amount of anxiety in their predictions, whether or not those are ever actually spoken. Sometimes companies suffer bouts of bad vision, but you'd have to be a complete idiot in this business not to know that however good your best idea is, somebody out there somewhere has a better one. So, sooner or later (and mostly sooner), your momentary one- or two-step lead is going to evaporate. In no time, today's secrets are yesterday's news.

Mosaic, by this time, was no secret. Everyone who had downloaded it knew all about it, and among that multitude of users were a lot of the more Internet-savvy engineers at potential competitors. Also intimately knowledgeable about the browser were all the people NCSA had brought onto the project to continue developing what Marc and his group had started. NCSA was pretty sure it had a lock on the winning technology, and wouldn't figure out for a while that it didn't. What still did seem to be a secret, however, was the chance that there might be money—possibly a lot of money—to be made with the invention.

This was not entirely due to some mass delusion or epidemic of narcolepsy. Sometimes you can outsmart others in the business, but that doesn't mean you're measurably smarter. To some extent, the idea wasn't on a lot of minds simply because it was close to heresy in the Internet culture. Ever since ARPA was created by the Defense Department to give scientists and the government a nuke-resistant communication medium, the Net had carried an aura of sixties altruism. Well, partly altruism and partly the presumption by users that it was a kind of perk, that with the possible exception of telephone time and access provider fees, everything that went out over the Net should be free. This perk soon evolved into some sort of God-given right. Compaq and Apple naturally charged for their hardware, Microsoft and Novell asked money for their software and got it because those companies, and most other software manufacturers, distributed their products through retail stores. No one presumed the right to go into Computer Land and simply shoplift boxes of Word or WordPerfect or Intuit off the shelf. Yet anyone who even hinted at wanting money for software sent out over the Net was accused of the worst kind of greed. Shareware was the byword. Something, let's say a funny screen saver, could be downloaded at no cost (since there was no way to collect money at the time a consumer took the product), and perhaps its creator would ask for a small amount of money if the user liked the product. I doubt anyone made a living off these voluntary contributions, but they established a kind of digital commune whose members generally considered the profit motive the work of the devil. When Tim Berners-Lee created the World Wide Web in the early nineties, he gave it away. Though any entrepreneur might wonder about his sanity (while admiring his soul), the children of the Internet took that kind of largesse for granted. They thought of the Net as a birthright.

So when Marc and his partners went the next step, leaping from the telegraph of the Web to the telephone of Mosaic, they were just doing what came naturally to them. They weren't thinking of doing business or trying to figure out how to make money. But I was. I wasn't a child of the Internet; I was a child of hardscrabble Texas, an engineer/academic who had learned how to do business by doing it. If most of the people using this incredible new medium didn't believe in making money from it, and most of the people who didn't know much about it couldn't yet imagine any way to profit from it, then I could be one happy heretic. Sometimes there's nothing more invigorating than a good dose of sacrilege.

But even while I could revel privately in the unique advantage of our newly born Mosaic Communications, the clock was ticking. Even the three-and-a-half-hour flight from Illinois to San Francisco was lost time. Next to the law of constantly increasing acceleration, Moore's Law, with its eighteen-month increments, seemed almost leisurely. In a lot less time than that, we had to make a whole new product, get it on the market, and somehow figure out how to make somebody pay for it, all the while risking that the necessity of attracting press attention would awaken a few slumbering dragons. So the hell with the commune, this was business. Many months later, as I mentioned before, I would tell an audience at the *Internet World* conference in Washington, D.C., that someday everyone on the planet would have his or her own Web page. I was only half kidding. There was a combination of amazing fluidity—the Web, once made easy to use, was almost completely free of friction—plus the kind of impersonality and any-old-time convenience that had quickly made automated bank-teller machines an essential part of our lives.

What this meant, I was convinced, was that the technology would spread fast, pushed along by the well-known forces of acceleration. (By May of 1998, only four years later, the Commerce Department reported that use of the World Wide Web was doubling every one hundred days!) With that kind of growth, its reason for being would have to expand. As Charles Van Doren points out in his book A *History of Knowledge*, within fifty years of the invention of movable type, almost every hand-copied manuscript that existed had been printed, at which point new material was needed to keep the burgeoning publishing industry growing. In a hyper-accelerated world, fifty years in the fifteenth century translated into maybe fifteen months in the late twentieth century; uses were going to be found for the Web that no one could yet imagine.

The possibilities were really huge, and the quicker we could get moving, the more of a lead we'd have when all those prospective ostrich farmers spotted the diamonds. At any second along the way, I imagined darkly, we could be too late.

In the 1960s, a legendary rowing coach at Harvard named Harry Parker fundamentally changed the nature of his sport. He did this simply by making his teams work out year-round, instead of only in the months leading up to the spring regatta season. For a while, his workaholic crews were unbeatable, given the advantage of their superior conditioning and constantly honed technique. But before long, every coach who lost to Harvard adopted Parker's approach. Soon enough, unrelenting training was standard procedure. As my flight turned south off the coast of Marin County for the gradual descent into San Francisco, I knew our company, an unknown contender in a race almost no one realized had begun, enjoyed a head start. I also knew that in order to stretch that lead, or even hold on to the advantage we had, we'd have to work as hard and unceasingly as Parker's crews. Nobody was going to be able to case off on their oar. The very nature of time was going to shift as we sped through it, and however much time we had, it could never be enough.

7 Omens, Portents, Distant Thunder

T he time had come to sweat the small stuff. After what seemed to me a long period of brainstorming sessions, tentative ideas, and blind alleys, things had suddenly coalesced and we were all at once productive. The casual gatherings at my house had hatched an idea, the idea had attracted the talent to make it happen, and now a company was becoming a reality, with the hundreds of needs any company has. Office space had to be found, computers, phones, chairs, desks, conference tables, refrigerators (bring on the Jolt!), and so forth had to be bought and set up. The specialized wiring required for a modern communications company, even a very small one, had to be installed. Every new company passes through this underbrush of details, of course; I'd gone through it before myself. It's always a peculiar combination of annoyance and excitement. I've had other entrepreneurs tell me that it's at this stage, when per-square-foot rent is settled on and cash begins to flow out for equipment, that they have their first vague anxieties about the possibility of failure. Nothing big, usually, just a hint of tarnish on the bright silver coin of optimism. But unsettling all the same: This could go wrong; I could fail.

I wasn't arrogant enough to assume that success was a given, despite my sense that Marc was a remarkable talent and the boys from Illinois were natural-born Mosaic killers. But I never think about failing. Maybe it's a genetic flaw, an optimistic lack of caution that wouldn't have been very useful to the small furry mammals that preceded us on the evolutionary ladder. Even now, anyone who refuses to take the downside into consideration in the early days of a start-up may end up looking like a fool—worse, a fool without a company. But when things work out, the trait can seem both a blessing and a virtue. I just look for the ways to win and forget there's any alternative. My approach takes its cue from the old military adage: If you take the hill, then take the next hill, and then the hill after that, you're going to end up with major territory. Silicon Valley is overpopulated with risk-takers, a veritable gene pool of roller-coaster addicts. They're drawn to the Valley because when risk pans out (an apt phrase for California in the 1990s), the payoff can be huge. If it doesn't, and you're young, you can always get a job. But not all these swashbucklers are the same. Some people take risks without much fear of the consequences, and others don't. A lot of very smart entrepreneurs are quite rational about how they take chances; they think it through, then work out contingency plans should things go wrong and they need a fallback position. I'm not good at that. My point of view has always been, Damn the torpedoes. I don't want to think about not being successful. It's a driven state, a mild form of insanity—or at the very least, a kind of selective dumbness. Maybe there was something in the water in Texas when I was growing up.

My figuring is, you're simply going to go out there and make the goddamn thing work. By not planning for failure, you don't leave yourself room for failure. I won't argue that this is necessarily a good trait. In fact, evolutionarily, this "no fear" approach would seem to lead more quickly to the tar pits than the top of the heap. I doubt *Tyrannosaurus rex* was afraid of failure, or anything else, while those little furry mammals were afraid of just about everything. We can see who won in the end, but I still think it must have been great to make the earth shake.

To discount failure is to deny a historical reality in Silicon Valley. For all the attention paid to the handful of dramatic bonanzas in high tech, a vastly larger number of companies fall apart before they make a cent than manage to go public. Yet defensive thinking is by definition slower and more cautious than charge-ahead action. If you don't look at risk as two-pronged, as a kind of bipolar succeed/fail process, then the idea of risk is diminished. With success as the only option, all the anxious "what ifs" are tossed out, and you make an absolute commitment. Eighteen-hour workdays are meaningless. From the minute I arrived back at San Francisco Airport and drove down Route 280 toward my Atherton house on that early spring afternoon in 1994, I put on blinders. For the next year and a half, I hardly thought of anything except making this newborn company a winner. I didn't know where the threats were going to come from, but I knew I was going to have to kick some tail to survive.

I had called D'Anne Schjerning from Illinois and told her we were going to need a place to set up shop. Despite her injured leg, D'Anne shopped around for space in Mountain View, a small town that, were it put on a wanted poster, would have to be described as having "no distinguishing marks." It lay in the path of the widening scope of Stanford-based start-ups, the rents were still cheap, and so with nothing in particular to recommend it (no confluence of great rivers, no convergence of cattle drives and railroads), the faceless town has become part of a chain of similar towns that exert a global influence infinitely far beyond anything appearances might suggest.

Combining the newly hired Illinois contingent, due to arrive after graduation in May, and a few bold souls who had committed to come over from SGI, we were starting out with only about a dozen people, so I didn't want to spend a lot of money for a large space we wouldn't fill for a year or more. (Though I didn't envision failure, I did manage to control my exuberance about growth.) After my trip to Urbana-Champaign, and the evening spent watching the way Marc and the others interacted, I was sure we would create a better browser than Mosaic and build a company around it. What I couldn't have predicted was the speed at which the company would expand. I almost took a three-year lease on a place so small that twenty-five people would have filled it to overflowing. We finally settled on our first site, a typical, one-size-fits-all 11,699-square-foot space on the fourth floor of a building on Castro Street in Mountain View—a place vacated so quickly by its previous occupants the previous year that the phones were still connected. The place was a typical, generic start-up hatchery, indistinguishable from hundreds more like it that house many of the three thousand hopeful new companies that spring into being every year in the Valley: temporary cubicles with chest-high movable dividers, wall-to-wall gray industrial carpeting, bland Formica work surfaces, and an air of impermanence that was exactly appropriate for any company whose fate—either success, and the move to better digs, or early death—would be decided in a matter of months. At that point, I had serious doubts we'd ever need so much space within the period of a two-year lease, and gave D'Anne a bad time about it. Within six months we had people working in the hallways.

After signing the lease, I began to think seriously about money for the first time. I had decided how much of my own money I was willing to risk, and I knew that the cash flow was going to be all negative for quite a while. But now the question of how long became palpable. The burn rate, as the initial all-spend, no-earn period is known in Silicon Valley, can get pretty spectacular, with the need for high-end computer equipment and, of course, pricey talent. At this prenatal phase in the life of many start-ups, it's not unnatural to think about how much easier the whole process would be if you let some other people put up most of the money. This is the moment venture capitalists depend on; they can seem like saviors, and, sometimes, they are saviors. But however nice they are, they're velociraptors; if an entrepreneur is determined to make something great and make a ton of money in the process, with a few exceptions, VCs are strictly in it for the money. The good ones can be a tremendous help in hiring and management, but anybody who imagines that this help is offered out of belief in a good idea is sadly misled; a good VC wants a company to succeed so that his investment doesn't go south. If the founder, the original risk-taker, starts to threaten the investment, he's gone. The VCs don't sit around a table saying, "Gee, poor Charley, it's his company and all, I really feel lousy about this, maybe we should give him another chance. . . ." What they say is "This guy's a problem; he's gotta go."

My experience at Silicon Graphics had taught me how double-edged the relationship with venture capitalists can be. By the time I left the company, I had managed to put away around $15 million. Not bad for a former college professor who'd been living from paycheck to paycheck a dozen years before. But SGI was worth billions by the early 1990s, and I'd been the founder, organizer, leader, planner, and inventor. Why wasn't I a lot richer than I was? If this sounds like the whining of somebody who, as a poor boy out of Texas, ought to be damn grateful for what he has, I'm sorry. But it's not about money as such; it's about the value of creation. We can all feel the unfairness of someone like Vincent Van Gogh dying desperately poor when his paintings would eventually sell for tens of millions at Sotheby's and Christie's (recently a twelve-by-sixteen-inch self-portrait sold for $71 million!). If a new business doesn't have the same romantic aura of *Starry Night*, the act of bringing it into being is still one of sustained creativity. And though not many entrepreneurs chop off an ear in anguish over the unfairness of it all, is an artist by definition more deserving than a man or woman who has poured both life and life savings into starting and building a company? I don't think so.

So at the point when I could begin to predict that it might cost half of my personal fortune or more to create a Web browser good enough to beat out the emerging competition in a new and untested marketplace, I had enough experience with venture capitalists to know that the money would be well spent if I could delay having to deal with VCs, and build enough leverage to cut a deal a lot better than the one I'd had at SGI. I had given up so much of my first company in the early days, taking just 15 percent for myself at the first round (an amount that is invariably diluted in later financing rounds), that I'd decided I wanted this one to be completely different. To be honest, I decided that I wanted to take a certain significant percentage out of the company, and I didn't want to share it with anyone.

There was another reason I opted not to go the venture capital route right away. I had already worked out my equity plan and determined how I was going to fund the company. Besides being the primary investor, I was going to run things for a while until I completely understood what we were up to and where we were headed. At this point, I had many more questions than answers, and this kind of ad-lib feeling doesn't go over well with VCs, who buy into confidence (or bluff) and run screaming from any sign of vagueness. Well, they don't always run from a lack of focus, or even the lack of any kind of market. Plenty of good talkers have scored with plenty of promise and no real products. But they should, and the toughest, most skeptical VCs don't get completely fooled very often.

Even though I had a track record, I didn't want to walk into a roomful of venture capitalists with some hare-brained scheme to make money with a bunch of college kids who had already given away the same kind of product I was planning to make and sell. When you ask people for millions of dollars, you have to at least rationalize what the hell you're doing, and at that point I wasn't really rational. My only rationale was a cold, gut feeling: This is going to be big. With 25 million people on the Internet already, and the number doubling every year, this is going to be very, very big. So I didn't want to go begging without much to say. The truth is, I didn't really want to talk about what I was doing to anyone who wasn't part of it. The sculptor Isamu Noguchi once said, "I find out what I'm doing by doing it." That was pretty much my situation. Of course, for whatever reason I made it, that turned out to be a very valuable decision.

The business of investing money in return for a piece of the action has always been central to capitalism, and a tremendous amount of progress has resulted from it—shall we tip our hats to Ferdinand and Isabella? But in Silicon Valley, what had started out as a rather slow-paced process when Arthur Rock, a young investment banker from New York, raised the money to help a couple of smart young engineers start something called Intel had become fast and fiercely competitive. (Rock later turned a $58,000 stake in fledgling Apple Computer into $14 million.) The best VCs, like chess masters, were always six moves ahead of the game. When someone like me left a company with unannounced intentions, the partners at venture firms paid attention. When someone known for a highly successful start-up had breakfast with someone unknown, people started asking questions, and in my business, where there's a phenomenal amount of money to be made, gossip churns more quickly than office e-mail on a Monday morning. If there is anything worse for a Silicon Valley VC than backing a loser, it's losing out on the chance to back a winner. The pressure to get in on a good thing early is huge.

So, although there hadn't been much press interest yet in what Marc and I were up to, I wasn't surprised to get a call from Glenn Mueller, an old friend and a partner at Mayfield, a venture capital firm. Glenn was a real gentleman (a slightly outdated compliment, but absolutely appropriate here), a well-known and very well-liked member of the old guard in Silicon Valley. His annual Christmas party was one of the significant events of the year, and insofar as social status matters in the business, many people including me prided themselves on being invited. Glenn had been the original founding venture investor in SGI, and we'd become quite close over the ensuing years. Though I'd had some moments when I regretted the 40 percent share of the company Mayfield had bought with its $800,000 investment, I'd made that original deal because I thought Glenn would always look after me and the others at the company. But in the end, he didn't support me in my strategy disputes with Ed McCracken. As a member of the compensation committee, he had been part of the group that gave McCracken more stock while my share was diluted. I still liked him as a friend, but I felt betrayed in my business dealings with him. The experience fortified my determination not to get involved with venture money. When the time came to raise money from the outside—and, given my own limited resources, I was already resigned to the fact that sooner or later it would—I certainly wasn't going to approach Mayfield.

I told Glenn this, though I don't think I came right out and said it directly. I could hear a tone of urgency in his voice, but the truth is, even if I hadn't felt resentment after SGI, I would have held any and all venture firms at arm's length this early in the process. If you have the money to get off the starting line and are willing to take a big chance with it, it's best to hang tough as long as possible. Frankly, that can be the difference between money and wealth if all goes well.

Glenn called again and again, trying with increasing desperation to change my mind. I think he felt genuinely bad. My response was always the same: "Glenn, I guess I just don't feel right about the way things went at SGI." The last call I remember was one he made from his car, reaching me just before I left for Illinois with Marc. He pleaded with me to let him in on what he perceptively realized could be huge. When I told him I still felt the same way, he said, "Jim, if you don't let us invest, my partners are going to kill me." Just a typical figure of speech, of course. But a week later I'd have a terrible reason to recall it. On April 4, 1994, the day I officially founded the company, I got a phone call from my wife. Glenn Mueller, on his boat in Cabo San Lucas off the coast of Baja in Mexico, had put a shotgun in his mouth and pulled the trigger.

I soon learned that Glenn had serious emotional problems. He had told his wife that the CIA was plotting against him, that people in the business were out to get him. Coinciding as it did with the launching of a company on which I'd staked everything, Glenn's suicide was as haunting to me as it was tragic for everyone involved. I felt terrible about it and couldn't shake the feeling for weeks. Whenever someone takes his or her own life, friends wonder if they should have been more perceptive, should have seen the signs of impending disaster. Then they wonder if, having suspected the worst, they might have been able to prevent it. In the first case, I think suicide is so drastic that, for those of us who have never contemplated it, the idea is difficult to grasp and thus almost impossible to anticipate. In business, too, we are so used to everyone playing their cards close to the vest that we aren't looking for clues to emotional problems. And to be brutally honest, most of us, especially men, probably don't want to know all there is to know about our associates' private torments.

Had I known that Glenn was so near the edge, would I have dealt differently with him? Naturally, I want to think so. In fact, when I eventually did raise venture capital for the company, the first people I approached were Glenn's partners (about which more later), not because I felt any differently about Mayfield, but because I felt so guilty about Glenn. (Likewise, I offered his wife, Nancy, a chance to invest $10,000 in Netscape, but when she didn't respond, I realized I was imposing on her.) And would it have made the crucial difference? Perhaps for a while. But being kept out of the initial investment phase certainly didn't kill Glenn, so I can only assume whatever drove him to despair would have done its grim work in time. I was not the instrument of Glenn's destruction, and I don't think I could have been the instrument of his salvation.

The company now existed. We had a place to work, into which we moved at the end of April. Between that moment and the arrival of the Mosaic group, we'd have furniture, machines, infrastructure—and bills. Since we wouldn't get much real work done until the programmers arrived, I didn't do much hiring; when it's your money— if you're smart—you don't start a payroll until there's a bottom-line reason to have people on the job. Start-ups hemorrhage money under the best of conditions, so shortening the time between red ink and black (if you're lucky) is an essential survival technique. Why have lots of noses when there's no grindstone?

But I did let the SGI people who'd been part of my "kitchen cabinet"—Kipp Hickman, Tom Paquin, and Bill Foss—know that the company was incorporated, and that they should give notice and be ready to start work by the end of May 1994. I could hardly wait to get some activity going, and I could see that Marc was eager as hell to have his group there. Frankly, I think he would have forged degrees for them if they'd have passed up graduation. Naturally, those who didn't yet have their degrees wanted to get what they'd been working for. And since they now had jobs, they wanted to enjoy, at least for a while, that halcyon period in life when you're essentially finished with school and not yet into the grind of making a living; a hiatus that, for most people, comes only once in life. But every day, people were downloading the original Mosaic software that we were going to go up against, building market share that we'd have to deal with. By this time, NCSA had licensed the browser software to nine companies. I'd have liked to have called up the programmers to tell them to forget their degrees for now; if we could move fast enough and get on the market before the potential of the Internet caught the attention of Microsoft and other major players, they'd be rich in ways they couldn't begin to imagine. I felt like the coach of an NBA team who wants to urge a kid with a great outside shot to drop out of college and take a multimillion-dollar contract. As in professional sports, the software business is all about talent. Credentials, so central to academia, mean nothing. These kids had learned what they knew in the most practical way, by hacking out a tremendously popular, revolutionary product. No piece of paper was going to make them any more effective, or desirable.

This relatively short period was almost more agonizing for me than the initial months when we were figuring out what the company would do. Not too far into the future, a number of journalists would be touting Marc Andreessen as "the next Bill Gates," and, though simplistic, the idea had merit. (I, for one, think Marc is a far more imaginative thinker.) Four years later a *Business Week* article by Steve Hamm in the spring of 1998 was taking another look:

> But Andreessen has a problem. Gates has already chosen the next Bill Gates, and it's . . . Bill Gates. Not content just to be king of the PC realm, Gates set out two years ago to rule the Internet, too. Indeed, his move to give away much of Microsoft Corp.'s Internet software is working so well it threatens to level Netscape. . . . "I give them an A for putting together a solid technology strategy," says

*Dan Lynch, an investor in Net start-ups. "But unfortunately you
need an A+. I don't think they appreciated the lengths to which
Microsoft would go to crush them."*

(Now, of course, because of the Department of Justice lawsuit, everyone knows.)

Lynch was dead wrong. I, for one, had no doubt about what lay
beneath Bill Gates's jolly nerd exterior—a killer instinct and sheer,
relentless aggression. I knew that when he reacted, it would be with
ferocity. Gates was like the evil Lord Sauron in J. R. R. Tolkien's Hob-
bit fable *The Fellowship of the Rings*, whose all-seeing eye searched
ceaselessly for any threat to his tyranny. At one of our early meetings,
Marc told a then-new joke: "How many Microsoft engineers does it
take to change a lightbulb? None, they just declare darkness the standard." Though we all laughed, there was a sharp edge of truth to the
punchline. Start-ups and upstarts, if they were smart and brash
enough, might establish themselves on new territory, but Microsoft
had the power and the will eventually to define that territory. With a
market of millions and growing at a Moore's Law rate, the new world
of the Internet was going to attract Microsoft's attention before too
long, and at that moment we'd begin showing up in Gates's hungry
dreams.

But I didn't make those anxious phone calls. Pied Pipers have very
dubious reputations—in fact, the original Hamlin version was probably
a mass murderer of children in the Middle Ages—and despite my sense
of urgency, I didn't want to seem so ambitious that the company mattered more to me than the people who, after all, were the company.
Aleks Totic had been approached by a Microsoft recruiter at an Internet conference not long before I met him in Illinois. The man was
wearing a shirt with the team logo "Bloodhound," and Aleks had been
completely put off by his arrogant approach: "We're going to take over
everybody, so you might as well come to work for us," he said. From
that moment on, Aleks had decided he'd work for any company except
Microsoft. You could go just so far to get these young renegades on
board, so I wasn't going to rush them at this point.

Since our recruiting swoop into the University of Illinois, I hadn't
thought much about what effect my hiring of almost the entire orig-

inal Mosaic team might be having at the NCSA. Had I been raiding another company for several key employees, I'd have observed a certain protocol, letting the CEO know, either in person or through intermediaries, what I was doing. But NCSA was part of the University of Illinois, and these were students about to get their degrees. I had done nothing more or less than any company, whether Westinghouse or the Gap, might do on any college campus. After I got back to California—after the fact of the hirings—I called Smarr and we had what seemed a friendly conversation about what I'd done, and (vaguely) what my plans were. Now, as the press began to pick up the story that I'd snatched up seven promising programmers as a group, I waited with interest to hear the reaction out of Urbana-Champaign.

On May 6, 1994, the *San Jose Mercury News*—a newspaper often closer to area high-tech news than either *The New York Times* or *The Wall Street Journal*—headlined a story on the front page of their business section: NEW FIRM IS BUILT ON VISIONS OF YOUTH. In the story, the paper reported that I was forming a software company around Marc and Eric and "five other members of the team of students who developed Mosaic at the not-for-profit National Center for Supercomputer Applications at the University of Illinois." The editor of an Internet newsletter was quoted as saying, "Clark is starting a company with people just out of the university and in their twenties. It's a risk, but it's very exciting." In the same article, NCSA was heard from for the first time. After saying that the center would continue to upgrade the Mosaic software, the project director at the university said, "You can't hold any grudges against a bunch of guys who want to participate in the start-up of a company. I can't say we were extremely pleased, but we were pleased for them."

I could almost hear this guy's jaw muscles twitching as he delivered this left-handed hail-and-farewell. There was something similarly ambiguous about a statement in *The New York Times* a day later:

> **Larry Smarr, the director of the National Center for Supercomputer Applications, said he was comfortable with the idea of having young researchers leave academic organizations to start new ventures.**

"Jim has told us that he got his first team of people from Stanford University to create Silicon Graphics," Mr. Smarr said, "and he is getting his next team from the University of Illinois." Just beneath this seemingly cordial statement I could detect a seething territorial resentment. This resentment would erupt into full-on warfare in the months to come.

8 Into the Grinder

About a week after I got back to California, I brought the Illinois contingent out for a few days in order to give them some familiarity with the area that would, in a couple of months, be their new home. These were not some isolated tribesmen from deep in the Amazon rain forest, of course. Most of them had been to California before, and as a group they had already acquired a lot of prominence in the knowing—and growing—circle of Internet insiders. But I wanted them to see, just for good measure, that this was where the action was. I wanted them to drive south on Route 101 past the Oz-like towers of Oracle, the giant software company rising out of the flats on San Francisco Bay. I wanted them to see the billboards advertising famous companies, and those that wanted to shoulder their way into the top echelon. Like a great commercial river, the freeway flows through a landscape filled with legendary fiefdoms: Intel, Apple, Sun, Silicon Graphics, Hewlett Packard, Cisco, the Xerox Palo Alto Research Center, Adobe, and all the others that had launched the revolution the boys from the Midwest would, I hoped, power up to its next stage. I also thought it might be a good idea to feed them something more inspiring than the mediocre pizza they subsisted on back in Illinois (though this latter idea was more about my preoccupation with the good life than theirs, which did not yet include thoughts of California high cuisine and wouldn't for quite some time).

Looking back on that brief, introductory trip, I can almost see it as an inadvertently cruel hoax. Because, as things turned out, the new recruits weren't going to have much contact with the fabled pleasures of what one San Francisco television newscast jingoistically calls "the best place on earth." Those few days of relaxation on their get-acquainted tour were almost the last they would see for many hard months to come.

When I started SGI, I was in my late thirties, already edging up onto the young side of that big bell curve known as middle age. I'd been around. As a kid from a poor family and a high-school dropout, I'd kicked around as a teenager, spent four years in the navy, where

I'd dabbled in starting a couple of small businesses on the side while figuring out what I didn't want to be (your tax dollars at work). As a result, I'd seen a fair amount of life early on. I hadn't been on the fast track to anywhere. For quite a while I was on no track at all. I'd discovered, more or less by accident, that I had an affinity for math, and a certain facility for the kind of abstract invention that takes place at the keyboard of a computer. (In the navy, I'd finished first in my class at electronics school in San Diego, though I'll have to admit the competition wasn't too tough.) I had also been married, had a couple of children, learned something about office politics (though I'd learn a lot more during my years at SGI) and role-playing in academia. On the other hand, the twenty-somethings of the Mosaic group were simply shifting from the grind of school to the much more intensive grind of developing a real, ready-for-prime-time product.

And a grind it would be. Even though my recruiting raid so far had aroused only ambiguous comments from Smarr and others at the University of Illinois, I was on guard. The most contentious buzzwords in information technology at the time were, and still are, "intellectual property." High-tech companies were very different from traditional heavy industries. Many long, complex physical stages separate the initial design for a machine tool, or a new tractor mower, or a Ford Taurus. In order to end up with an object that made sense economically, a lot of small compromises had to be made, and some large ones, too. Though the process of manufacture could be accelerated, there was a still a bedrock time frame between, say, the clay models of a car and the real thing on the showroom floor.

In comparison, the manufacture of software is no big deal. The idea, the design, and the engineering are all done in the same place, by the same people. The basic materials are laughably cheap. No spot-welding robots need apply. All you need is a good brain and an okay computer (though some people have managed surprisingly well by reversing those adjectives). This has made software the most phenomenally egalitarian generator of wealth in history. Even with Microsoft always on the prowl to corner markets, you can take your best shot without having to buy a howitzer.

But the fact that anybody can do it (or so it sometimes seems) has bred a high level of paranoia. If ideas can be turned into software with relative ease, ideas can also be pilfered and copied just as easily. Intellectual property lawsuits are a growth industry, and with constant questions about what is and what isn't intellectual property, the mere threat of a suit can fatally wound a start-up. Perhaps I was feeling a bit paranoid myself, but between the lines of the published statements of NCSA officials, I heard the possibility of trouble. Maybe that was a remote possibility, but Intel's Andy Grove recommends a healthy dose of paranoia for survival—even an unhealthy dose—and he and his company have survived remarkably well.

I've often thought about whether I should have handled my relationship with the NCSA differently, but under the circumstances I suspect that I would have behaved the same even if I'd had more foresight. As I've said before, I was in a hurry to get going. I'm impatient even when there's no reason to be impatient. Maybe I should have gone to Larry Smarr before doing anything and told him what I was up to, just to be polite. If he'd protested, it would have made no difference, but at least I would have made the gesture. But there was only one of the group I hired, Eric Bina, who was actually a full-time employee of the center. And I really felt, and still feel, that I didn't have time for gestures and extra steps. My life was already complicated enough, and, frankly, I wasn't thinking much about the ripple effect of what I was doing. The University of Illinois was going into business with Mosaic, and I was going into business with a Mosaic killer. We were after the same market, and a gentlemanly fifty-fifty split was not what anyone was interested in. The last time I looked, it was a rough world out there, and business leaders, with or without the benefit of ethics, weren't knocking themselves out to help their competitors. If the NCSA had left themselves vulnerable to a talent drain because they'd failed to recognize that talent sufficiently, what kind of idiot would I have been not to take advantage? I didn't want them dead, in Microsoft's style, but I certainly wanted them out of the business of producing software with public money.

But no matter how justified I felt, the ripples were unpredictable. So my first instructions to Marc and his team were that they were not to look at the source of Mosaic, the program they had written, even though the source code was posted on the Internet for everyone to see. If I could have reached into their brains with a laser scalpel, I'd have burned out any memory of the code (while carefully leaving intact the ability to write code). Should any question arise about what it was I took with me when I flew back from Urbana-Champaign—whether I had hired intellects or shoplifted intellectual property—I wanted to be absolutely clean. In effect, the team was going to have to raze the building they'd built during many long nights at their keyboards (at least down to the foundation of CERN code, which was in the public domain), and start over again. Even the CERN code was to be eliminated, I said, because who knows what intellectual property claims would be leveled in the future. And the new work had to be entirely new, not a thinly disguised reprise of what had been done before. The end result had to function similarly without any of the same machinery. For the masters of Mosaic's universe, life in California was going to be like a year below decks chained to an oar.

In an op-ed piece in *The New York Times* called "Techno-Nothings," Thomas Friedman has complained about how insular and arrogant we are in Silicon Valley. "There is a disturbing complacency here," he says, "toward Washington, government, and even the nation. There is no geography in Silicon Valley, or geopolitics. There are only stock options and electrons."

Let me suppress my urge to say simply that he's full of crap about complacency. If that were the prevailing mood, it might be expected to breed an attachment to the status quo, and in Silicon Valley there simply is no status quo. Friedman's grasp of the complex politics of the Middle East is impressive, but I think what he and many others outside the industry (often journalists living on the East Coast) don't fully understand is just how hard people work out here. New Yorkers, alas, think they're the hardest workers on the planet because New York makes the ordinary act of living such hard work. Yet I'll venture a guess that if the average *Times* columnist put in the hours of a typical start-up software programmer, a dozen of them could put out the entire newspaper. Of course, Friedman is paid to look at geopolitics; that's his job. In a new company on the Serengeti that is the technology business, the job is to survive first, then to thrive. It might have been very noble to hold seminars on NAFTA and the future of the former Soviet Union, but once the new recruits sat down at their keyboards and got to work, they'd be lucky to see a movie once in a while.

For all the hard labor to come, however, there was a big difference between their lives as students, or low-wage NCSA workers, and the lives they'd soon be leading. They were coming to a place where what they could do, and had already done, would be appreciated by programming connoisseurs. And for their long days and nights they'd be earning real money, not $6.25 an hour, with the promise of winning the lottery if things went very well. So if, on the surface, this was going to be college raised to the tenth power, it was also not going to be the same at all. Later Aleks Totic put it perfectly: "At Illinois, we were just guys without a life. People thought that was weird. In Silicon Valley, if you have no life, you're respected. People figure you're onto something."

Despite my heady talk on our first night together in Illinois, Aleks really didn't have much of a sense of the financial possibilities for our new venture, and I suspect some of the others were similarly unaware of what might happen to them. In Marc's first job on the West Coast, programming for Enterprise Integration Technologies, he was earning around $80,000 a year, which—if he shared that information with his former colleagues—must have let them imagine that they might have enough money to satisfy a few of their college dreams. Aleks figured he could buy a decent car, which he did soon after he arrived, but he later told me his horizon stopped at about $100,000. Not a bad amount of money in one lump for a kid just out of school, but in the 1990s, in the technology field, relatively small change. Aleks and the others might end up with nothing beyond whatever they'd been able to save out of their salaries if we didn't survive to get our stock to the market. Or they might make millions. But $100,000 was not a figure that had a lot of meaning in the equation of high risk and new wealth along Highway 101.

The other thing they stood a chance to make was history. There are certain times when events and inventions merge to create deep and lasting change. In some rare cases, several factors coincide in a way so astonishing that, within a short time, human lives will never be the same. In communications, one of the most unpredictable of these convergences began to take shape toward the end of the fourteenth century. When the Black Death swept through Europe, killing at least one third of the population, it struck first in Constantinople, a city where culture and learning had largely escaped the intellectual slumber of the Dark Ages. Among those who fled toward the West were scholars who were able to satisfy the reawakened yearning for knowledge that signaled the beginning of the Renaissance. The same epidemic left the surviving population with an excess of clothing belonging to those who had died, much of which was sold and eventually used to make rag paper (a process belatedly learned from the Arabs). So much paper was made that prices for the once-precious stuff dropped dramatically. What brought these two seemingly unrelated factors together was a technology, invented in the mid–fifteenth century by Johannes Gutenberg: the printing press using movable metal alloy type. When the desire to know met the material and methodology to satisfy that desire, the seeds of the Age of Information were sown. The telephone also exploited a need for instant communication brought about by the telegraph, both made possible by the availability of electricity, and made necessary by a growing public hunger for information delivered in what we now call "real time."

This constant push forward for information moved inward in 1956, when Francis H. Crick, James Watson, and the unheralded Rosalind French, aided by developments in electronic microscope technology, discovered the molecular structure of DNA and launched a new age of exploration to the innermost reaches of the human genome as astonishing as the voyages of Magellan, Drake, and Columbus.

Now we were on the edge of another major convergence no less momentous than its historical predecessors. Since the early 1980s, the introduction and constant improvement of inexpensive and easy-to-use computers had pushed the rate of computer literacy steadily upward. Fax machines, also less and less costly, had accustomed people to receiving printed information through telephone wires, and the pervasive effect of television for several generations had made visual communication a distinct form of literacy. Finally, ARPAnet, then the Internet and Berners-Lee's World Wide Web, put into place the basis for something completely new. I'm far from the first to point out this current convergence, but as someone on the scene when all the strands came together, I feel it's worth repeating the significance of what our company was about to do.

Marc, Eric, and the others had already made a "Gutenberg leap" by making the Web easy to use and graphic. What we would do during a frantic summer would take this new, digital printing press to a point where its power would reach farther and faster than ever before through commercial leverage. In 1994, 3 million people in the U.S. and the rest of the world were using the Internet; at this writing, the number is around 150 million, with the amount of data processed over the Net doubling every one hundred days. Because of Marc and his colleagues, some old and some new, plus my faithful few from SGI, digital literacy would soar.

I wanted to make sure one aspect of history was not repeated. Having given us all an incalculable gift, Johannes Gutenberg died poor. With any luck—and warp-speed work—this wasn't going to happen to us.

9   The Vulcan Mind Meld

In June the boys arrived, and at last the starter's pistol cracked in the clear Northern California air. Chris Houck, Jon Mittelhauser, Lou Montulli, Aleks Totic, and the twin brothers Rob and Mike McCool, like a rookie class of astronauts, had arrived in Mountain View to show America the way into cyberspace. (Eric Bina, true to his original resistance to California, remained behind in Illinois, but was so deeply involved in all that followed that he might as well have been there.)

D'Anne had rented a block of rooms at a residence inn on El Camino, the main drag through Mountain View and the other look-alike towns that make up the high-technology heartland. A writer who covers the companies in the area recently suggested that Silicon Valley is the new Florence, but its bland architecture is absurdly far from the inspired buildings of Brunelleschi, Michelangelo, and the other geniuses of the Renaissance. Compared to the Florence of the Medici, the towns along El Camino are at best a hard-working Flo. Mountain View, California, is a universe away from Plainview, Texas, but from downtown the view isn't a hell of a lot better. The inn was a glorified motel, a short step up from their college rooms and apartments, but it gave the boys the chance to start work without worrying about finding apartments. The need for speed ranked far above the joys of domesticity. I knew they weren't going to do much more than sleep wherever they ended up, and the rest of their time would be spent at the Castro Street offices. D'Anne, knowing that her generous nature might get the better of her, stated up front that she didn't ever want to go to their rooms and see the way they lived. (She did end up, from time to time, doing some of their laundry, out of desperation to get them into clean clothes occasionally.)

Twenty-four-hour days became the norm almost instantly. I had anticipated a certain amount of resistance to the idea of a total reinvention of Mosaic. After all, it's monkish work to write line after line of instructions in arcane computer languages day after day, month after month. The task must be something like translating the Bible from Hebrew and Greek to English (or rather, the other way around).

With the added tedium of having to retrace your steps in order to find the bugs you introduced the first time through. To completely reinvent this particular wheel had to be a demoralizing prospect. Young men fresh out of school might decide, with some justification, that they'd signed up for way too much heavy lifting and simply take off. But Marc had told me not to worry, and he was right. In fact, the group was glad to have the chance to get right what they felt they'd more or less dashed off in college. Marc and Eric's original idea was to build a browser that would make the Internet more fun, and to give it away. Their feeling was, Hey, if you do something and the program crashes your computer, don't do it again. When they put Mosaic up for grabs on the Web, they were usually dealing with people accustomed to the quirks of computers, not paying customers. The difference was vast, and they knew it.

A real passion to get things right the second time around, in addition to their shared anger at how their creation had been co-opted by layers of NCSA managers, would sustain them during their hellish work schedules. They were still young enough not to have become resigned to the fact that life and the world aren't fair, which was a lucky thing for all of us.

Back a few months, at our meetings in my house, Michael Toy, one of the SGI programmers who had expressed interest in joining me in whatever new venture might crop up, had been enthusiastic about some of the early ideas like online Nintendo and interactive TV. Perhaps he wasn't yet sure of Marc, a Valley tyro who arrived at the first couple meetings in a tie (something Toy probably found extremely odd). Whatever the reason, Toy clearly didn't think much of the concept of building the definitive Internet browser. But he remembers the way the decision to go ahead with a Mosaic killer finally galvanized the group. "Once the idea came," he says, "focus came. And focus is the thing that makes money out here."

Like Toy, I knew that from experience. Marc seemed to understand it instinctively. And he was able to rev up his group's preternatural ability to focus almost instantly. When I walked through the small section of the floor they occupied, I felt as if they'd already been at work for a long while. Though they had a lot of new problems to solve, the learning curve was something they knew they could handle. Such was the practical beauty of remaking something they'd already spent long hours making the first time.

Not more than a day or two passed after the programmers got their computers up to speed and loaded with the software they needed (like top mechanics lining up their favorite tools at a new garage) before the drab interior of our office space began to mutate. The mess that would prevail for months to come seemed to spring up overnight, like some sort of fast-growing fungus. Walls lined with bright stacks of soda cans grew as the unquenchable thirst for high-sugar, caffeine-fueled drinks consumed case after case of the stuff. Someone duct-taped one of his cubicle walls, so that it took on a dull, silvery, vaguely sinister glow. Music from different radios satisfying different tastes blended into a kind of auditory soup. Except for certain antic touches, Castro Street remained ordinary at best. As is often the case in the indistinguishable Silicon Valley offices people call "incubators," there was an air of crash-pad temporariness about the place that might prove mind-numbing to people who would hardly get a chance to leave for months. But I remembered being told of a fitting story by John Hummer, a former Princeton basketball star (now a successful venture capitalist). When his team played UCLA in Los Angeles in the early seventies, several players complained aloud about how much more luxurious the Bruins' carpeted locker room seemed in comparison with Princeton's dingy old field houses. Pete Caril, the legendary coach who always managed to get the most out of players long on brains but short on vertical leap, told them to stop whining. "Look at the Vietcong," Caril growled. "They sleep in hammocks in the jungle, and they're kicking our ass." So far, no one had complained, but I was ready with an answer if they did.

Bill Foss, who had come over from SGI, bought an air-hockey table and put it in the center of the kitchen to provide a way to vent some of the nervous energy built up by the physical inaction and mental frustration of programming—and various sources of caffeine. From a psychotherapeutic point of view, this was a great idea, but it didn't help much on the speed/anxiety/desperation front. The game was so popular I had to put it off-limits until after five o'clock. This simply forced the new masters of the universe to switch from air hockey to chair hockey, a wild melee played while seated in wheeled desk chairs.

Given the history of my motorcycle accident and D'Anne's fall down the front steps, I half expected to lose a few programmers. But everyone survived, keyboarding hands intact.

I had a small office under a staircase—far short of mogul scale, but not untypical for high-tech executives, who leave it to the venture capitalists to put on a sumptuous show. Because I was already out working the business turf, I came in and out and got to know the members of Marc's team gradually. We hadn't yet had time for much socializing, so I had no idea whether they had girlfriends, or even managed a date now and then. But, except for Eric Bina, who flew in from Illinois for one intense week every month and had a wife back in Urbana-Champaign, none of the programmers had any time to meet anyone. For the moment, at least, they were digital monks.

A kind of free-form dormitory chic took hold as it became clear Castro Street would be where everybody was going to spend almost every waking hour. And a considerable share of sleeping hours, too. Sizing up the situation, D'Anne bought several futons. All I could think of was the moment in *The Godfather* when one of the members of the Corleone family announces that until a gang war is over, they were "going to the mattresses." The comparison would prove very accurate before the summer was out. While we were hunkering down to kill Mosaic, others would be plotting to kill us.

The ex-NCSA people were assembled together in the back of the space, out of sight from the front door, giving the impression that the sole person at work was the receptionist. Open areas not yet converted to offices, unassembled cubicle walls, boxes of equipment, random groupings of unmatched chairs, and all the bits and pieces of office life added to the air of boomtown rawness and beta-test hope. The kitchen, where everyone ended up sooner or later during the day or night, was a catastrophe, its refrigerator stuffed with the anti-matter of health food. The mess, renewed daily, reached into every part of the room, with one exception: Kipp Hickman insisted that the espresso machine be treated with respect. As a result, it stayed miraculously clean. These young stars might be crucial to the future of the company, but in California, even at a Silicon Valley start-up, some things are sacred!

We began hiring new people very quickly. Marc handled the recruiting of programmers, and I took care of general managers. To the Midwestern group were added a flamboyant Finn, Ari Lutonen, and Jamie Zawinski, a brilliant and eccentric Berkeley graduate with half his head shaved, the other half uncut for years (giving him the distinction, D'Anne announced, of having both the longest and the shortest hair at the company). To my nucleus of SGI engineers, Kipp Hickman, Michael Toy, and Bill Foss, I added Tom Paquin, a man I'd known at SGI but never really worked with. Tom, short and dark with a thatch of unruly hair that gives him a slight resemblance to George Stephanopolis, had the look of a kid. This may have helped him fit in physically with the youth brigade at the company. But Tom was married and had a child, which made him a senior figure compared to most of the others. I needed Tom there to act as a manager, to keep everyone on track. I don't think it was a role he particularly relished, but one look around and he understood how important it was to bring some order to the chaos. "They were reveling in their uncivility," Tom says of the programmers, "and, like it or not, I was the only manager around." After he walked in on a chair-hockey game, one of his first official acts was to turn down a request for a dartboard; all we needed now were deadly missiles in the air.

The problem for Tom was to manage without seeming to manage. That should be the goal of the managers in any creative endeavor, of course, but in bringing together the Valley "old-timers" and the new kids in town, I had planted the seeds of a prickly culture clash. The older engineers had been around, they'd worked at successful companies, and I'm sure they'd put enough "fuck you" money aside to turn around and walk away if anybody with less experience gave them any crap.

On the other hand, the Midwest contingent were hero hackers, the "über undergrads" who had created one of the hottest software programs in years; they were buzz incarnate (at least among Internet cognoscenti and a growing number of journalists). As rock star equivalents, they didn't feel any automatic respect for their elders. This was not the military, or ordinary corporate life; seniority counted for nothing. In fact, for all I knew, to these guys seniority meant simply that you probably didn't get it. Like professional sports, software development is a game where you're old at thirty, and young contenders are only too happy to run you down from behind. Satchell Paige's famous advice, "Don't look back, somebody might be gaining on you," is impossible to heed. People are always gaining on you, but you have to look back in the faint hope that you might figure out what they are doing and pick up your pace. Kids without lives were tough competition for men who had families and were no longer thrilled by the thought of pulling all-nighters. From the first, the Mosaic group worked and slept at odd, syncopated hours. Marc, for one, tended to sleep late and then work through the night. "A lot of the interesting stuff happens here starting around eight P.M.," Kipp said one day with a tone of exasperation. He wasn't overjoyed at the thought of adapting to the soda-and-pizza-pumped hours of the classic college computer science major. And they weren't about to start living differently simply because some of their older colleagues couldn't cut it. I might be tolerated as a father figure, somebody who could provide money and a track record, but the younger "old guys" were in a tougher place.

I didn't do anything to make their situation any easier. My main concern was that everything be done to facilitate the work of the Mosaic team. I needed the experience men like Hickman, Toy, and Paquin brought to the company, but I had to keep them from inadvertently squelching the creativity of their younger colleagues. Added to the problem was a certain distrust the SGI vets may have felt toward Marc. In essence, I had bet the farm on Marc's intelligence, and his ability to provide the leadership in the company's technology. My confidence was based on instinct, and, frankly, I've always relied heavily on instinct. But those who'd left SGI had come to work for me, not for Marc. Perhaps Kipp and the others worried that Marc would lose interest in the company at some point and drift away, as they'd seen me do for a while at SGI. It was going to take time for him to prove himself to them. In the early days, I kept a close watch to see if friction was developing. Once, when something came to a head between Kipp and the young guns, my instructions to him were starkly simple: "Get out of the way and let them do their thing."

I tried to assign work to the more experienced engineers that required a high level of skill but ran in a parallel track to the development of the core program. To Kipp, for instance, I gave the vital task of creating security for the Internet, an essential capability if the Internet was ever going to be a successful commercial medium. While waiting in April for "the boys" to arrive from Illinois, I had dusted off my own knowledge of public-key security and written a short memo outlining how this could be used for our purposes. I gave this to Kipp, and he proceeded to create what became the standard, licensed by Microsoft and everyone else. This was something I didn't feel I could trust to any of the younger programmers. But security systems could be worked on as a separate project, thus cutting down on the chance that anybody—old hand or newcomer—would end up so bent out of shape that he'd decide to walk out.

Yet there was no way I could keep the two cultures separate, nor was there any reason to create firewalls between groups. We were too small a company to tolerate mutually distrusting factions. (That kind of split was very damaging for Apple when the group building the Macintosh became an elite within the company, and at that time Apple was much larger than our tiny group.) But camaraderie wasn't going to happen through some kind of spontaneous generation, with movie music rising dramatically in the background as wary tribes joined hands. I couldn't imagine holding things together without people who'd been there before—Kipp, for instance, had joined SGI years before, back when the company had only one hundred employees. But for all the experience and steadiness we might bring to the mix, the veterans and I weren't the ones with the Promethean fire. We could help make it happen, but the NCSA group understood the Web, and the Web was the far horizon we were headed for.

Marc had to lead his team, but I didn't want him burdened by the need to manage them. I knew from my own experience that you can be a successful leader and yet a lousy manager, and that the latter weakness could fatally sabotage the former strength. The dubious honor of providing what's referred to in the trade as "adult supervision" fell to Tom Paquin, and he came up with the perfect *Star Trek* metaphor for what was needed: "We had to acquire a Vulcan mind meld with thirty-five people." For the job, I couldn't have picked a better person. Tom had spent five years at IBM and five at SGI. He knew his way around, but he had his ego well in control, which allowed him to act as a combination programmer, wrangler, quartermaster, chaplain, and hall monitor. Some of his jobs were beneath him, but he went ahead and did what had to be done. Like a true engineer, Tom was a pragmatist, much more concerned with solving problems than sorting out what was appropriate for him to do and what wasn't. For instance, as we began to hold meetings with people we hoped to do business with, Tom and D'Anne would get in early in the morning and perform emergency janitorial service in our one and only conference room. During the night, this space served as the programmers' family room, a place for pizza dinners, naps, even the occasional food fight. The next day, the litter was staggering. Soda cans, pizza boxes, partially eaten slices, and dirty paper plates were everywhere, and the room had to be picked up and aired out before people arrived to hear about what an elegant solution we were going to be to their problems. And never mind that the air still hung heavy with Eau de Domino's.

Not surprisingly, given the alienation of the programmers when NCSA brought in managers to oversee (and essentially co-opt) Mosaic, Tom had to deal with a certain amount of paranoia. Had the programmers individually taken jobs at Microsoft, Oracle, or Sun, they would have expected to answer to a hierarchy of corporate management. But they weren't the kind of people attracted to big, established businesses. Hired as a group to work for a company that only existed because of them, however, they considered anyone looking over their shoulders to be a potential enemy. Michael Toy's impression was that they brought with them from the Midwest an abiding disdain for the existing culture of Silicon Valley, which (as I'd seen at SGI) was still stuck on well-worn concepts of hardware and software. In the place of respect for tradition, they carried the romance of the Web.

Every company possesses a personality. Some are dysfunctional, from mildly disturbed all the way to psychopathic. Some are so "New Age lite"—having so little substance—you can't help but enjoy when they crash and burn. These personalities are formed early in a company's life, and are a combination of the style of the founders and original workers, the product, the marketplace, the media, and (as time moves on) advertising and PR spin. As is the case with people, real personality changes are rare. People and companies can alter their style, reform themselves, and learn to overcome destructive habits and bad behavior. But in the end, they are who or what they are. It's been years since everyone at IBM wore dark suits and white shirts, but there's still an air of Big Blue power and presumption about the place. And Apple, which carefully cultivated a happy-go-lucky nonconformist image (remember the beautiful athlete heaving a sledgehammer at the image of Big Brother during the 1984 Super Bowl?), aimed for a right-brained audience and forgot that business customers, where the real money is, tend to be left-brained. When it came time to change personalities to compete for the corporate market, Apple couldn't do it. When Gil Amelio, who spent fifteen mostly fruitless months as the company's CEO, held his first general meeting to discuss the future, he had to compete with a beach ball bouncing around among his lost boys and girls.

In our funky digs on Castro Street, a personality began to emerge, one that blended angst, aggression, and speed-freak hyperactivity. The words "We're doomed," grim and funny at the same time, became a motto of sorts. Jamie Zawinski even invented a mascot named Mozilla, a genetic mix of Mosaic and Godzilla, that still inhabits browser software. I loved seeing these elements start to fill in the blanks of the new company. Though we didn't have a logo yet, or an advertising agency, or anybody handling public relations, or—of course—any semblance of business, we were already starting to feel three-dimensional. As in the early days of Silicon Graphics, I held some all-hands meetings, a tradition carried on today. Just as I wanted everyone to be in partnership through stock options, I wanted open discussions of where we were going, and how we were doing on our way to get there. We could still all fit into the conference room, so whatever suspicion one group might feel toward another, we had the look of a happy family. Well, a functioning family at least, which mattered a lot more than mere happiness.

In the last days of operating out of my house, before the gang had moved out from Illinois, a reporter from the *Internet Business Report* called me. In a conversation with Marc, he had learned that Marc and I had formed a company. After interviewing Marc and me and writing his story, on the day before the release of his publication, he informed a *San Jose Mercury News* reporter about this. The *Mercury* reporter called me on a Thursday for an interview. On Friday, the story hit the newspaper. We had just moved into our offices in Mountain View and barely even had phones connected. After the *Merc* had reported on the story, John Markoff of *The New York Times* called, and his story appeared on Saturday. Not to be outdone, a *Wall Street Journal* reporter called to get their story in the Tuesday edition of the *WSJ*. In a matter of four days, we had gotten more press than most start-ups dream of in their first three years.

As a result of these stories and the general buzz around the Internet, we began to get a few calls of interest from potential customers. Since our phone was not yet listed with directory services, some of the callers had to contact the chamber of commerce of Mountain View to find where we were located, and they came by our offices to inquire. Over the next few days, as the phone number became listed, our telephones were ringing off the hook. I couldn't believe it. At SGI, we had worked for months to get Dick Shaffer, then of *The Wall Street Journal*, to write the first-ever article on us, and here I was answering all these inquiries from customers and the press. That is when I knew we would not be able to hide from the watchful eye of Lord Gates. It is also when I knew I needed a public relations person to manage the relationships with the press.

Public relations often gets a bad reputation. And sometimes, when it's used in its most egregious, cosmetic form, disguising mistakes, flaws, chronic lack of vision, or sheer chicanery, it damn well deserves our suspicion and disdain. If the press only knew how some companies manipulate them. Microsoft is renowned for its ability to spin the press to its advantage. But let's be very clear: Anyone starting a company who doesn't try to influence the press's impression surrenders the future to fate, a tremendous mistake. In a high-technology start-up, the perception that, as playground basketballers say, "you got game" is as important as any reality. For a while, the belief of others that your company has a future is the future. On the day I'm writing these words, Entremed, a small biotech company in Maryland, has announced a drug that dramatically shrinks cancer tumors in mice. Not in humans, yet. No one knows how human tests will go, and there have been many times when what was good for mice had no effect on people. But by the end of the trading day on Wall Street, the company's stock had jumped over 400 percent. That announcement represented the possibility of something big, and that possibility alone caused a tremendous surge. To build a business from scratch, you have to create momentum any way you can (short of downright hot air). My approach was: Announce everything, every glimmer of life, every blip of interest, every letter of intent, to make reporters feel they'd better not be left behind by a hot story.

We already had a hell of a head start. I was well known in the business, the founder of a multibillion-dollar company out kicking up dust like a rogue elephant. Marc was a young newcomer with a million-dollar idea. As a result, reporters were already coming around, pressing for interviews. As a veteran trying to make lightning strike twice, and a kid who might just be the next software superhero, we were quickly becoming a celebrity tag team. But this circus needed a ringmaster. So after a couple of weeks, I picked up the phone and punched in the number of Rosanne Siino. Rosanne had called me on first hearing about the company, and she was one of the best PR managers at SGI. We had talked about her coming aboard, but I hadn't thought I'd be needing her so early in the game. I was wrong, and when she came on the line, I said, "Okay, you saw all the press, so if you're still interested, get over here. The phone is ringing nonstop."

She arrived just in time. I told her about Marc's strengths and that he was the "rock star" of the company. Of course, she knew that every company needs a person on which the press can focus. It's all well and good to recognize that a company only exists because of the whole team, and that in fact single individuals remain just that in a company, but try to get the press to focus on a group and you fail. So she was happy to have an articulate, enlightened person to promote, and Marc accepted the role.

Even a friendly press can be dangerous, not because they get at the truth, but because they may get things ass backwards. In high tech, which moves at warp speed, it isn't hard even for a good reporter to screw up. But Rosanne had a good marketing sense, and understood that for a company at our amorphous stage, PR worked on the inside, to begin to forge unity and a sense of mutual purpose, as well as on the outside. She has a tough, no-bullshit air and, unlike PR people who think PR is to shape reporters' impressions by doling out certain aspects of a story and suppressing others, Rosanne tries to make as much information available as possible. After she arrived, she spent days talking to almost everyone to get each person's take on what Mosaic Communications was doing, and wanted to do in the future. Beyond killing Mosaic, that is. She also made my all-hands meetings a regular Friday event, during which I would report business progress and she would talk about future and present news coverage.

We put Rosanne's office very close to the entrance, so she could hold press briefings without revealing our chaotic secrets. But she was smarter than that. Instead of walling reporters off from what was going on, she often took them right into the thick of it, letting them absorb the *Das Boot* feel of the place. More than a few times, reporters walked past one of the programmers sound asleep on the futon in the middle of the floor. If the Smithsonian ever wants to do a diorama of a tech start-up in the twilight of the twentieth century, the curators could do worse than to re-create behind glass our Castro Street setup. And, as Rosanne intended, most reporters found themselves caught up in the excitement.

Rosanne knew this wasn't a chance to run a finishing school (not that she ever said she wanted to), so she made a virtue of everyone's individuality. Geek chic was not, after all, something new or off-putting to experienced tech writers, who were rarely caught wearing Zegna suits themselves. And Rosanne also knew that editors had been looking for new heroes and vivid personalities ever since Apple's happy campers had fallen on glum times. Unlike political reporters, technology reporters tend to like stories driven by optimism, and though they're perfectly happy to savage those on top, they'd just as soon build up usurpers. (Witness the 1995 cover of *Forbes ASAP* showing Marc, with the blurb "This kid can topple Bill Gates," or the 1994 cover of *Red Herring* showing Gates and me as chess pieces with the headline THE ONCE AND FUTURE KINGS.) So when Marc eventually showed up on the cover of *Time* with his feet bare, Rosanne never blinked. It's wonderful to imagine what the reaction would have been if Marc had been at IBM!

The weeks between early May and late June of 1994 passed with dizzying speed, even for a frenetic industry accustomed to a constant, headlong pace. Since I wasn't directly involved with the technology development as I had been at SGI, my day-to-day contact with the Mosaic programmers was limited. I chaired the all-hands meetings and kept up with how technical things were going through Marc and Tom. D'Anne, increasingly a surrogate mother whether she wanted to be or not, also informally monitored morale and mental states (both of which could be mercurial). Everyone was working at a tremendous clip, and time off proved to be more often a shower and a full night's sleep at the residence inn than any kind of vacation, or even a full weekend away. The intramural competition to do the coolest stuff, though mostly unspoken, was so intense that the browser team members were afraid to take off for a few days because so much would be done while they were lying on the beach at Santa Cruz or hiking in the Sierras. Aleks Totic has told me that when he tried to stay away from the office for a day, all he did was think about the code he should be writing. Mozilla was proving to be a carnivore in a keyboard.

The Fourth of July seemed a natural time to break stride for at least one day, to give everyone a chance actually to go outside during the day, eat real food, drink too much, and behave like millions of other Americans. So I decided to throw a party at my house for the forty or so people who now worked at Mosaic Communications—the first official company social event. With the weather hot and sunny, we set up a barbecue grill and a bar outside in the backyard near the swimming pool. Out front, the circular gravel driveway began to fill up with the motley assortment of cars everyone had quickly bought on arriving in California. I'll never forget the sight of the Mosaic crew, one by one, stepping into the yard, pale as lab rats and squinting as if they hadn't seen the sun in weeks (which, I suspect, many of them hadn't). For one brief, guilty moment I felt like the Japanese prison camp commander played by Sessue Hawakaya in *The Bridge Over the River Kwai*, letting the British prisoners out of their punishment cells and urging them to "be happy in your work." Jamie Zawinski, with his half-shaved, half-shoulder-length black hair, black clothes, and black combat boots, was an astonishing sight; like some mythical demiurge, he seemed capable of absorbing sunlight.

The day was close to Marc's birthday, and his friends had bought him one of those joke hats with holders for beer cans and a drinking tube. They clustered around him, seeming younger than when they were at their computers, set apart from the older, more at ease guests who had attended plenty of company parties. But for me, the odd mix signaled a new force to be reckoned with. This was a quintessential scene, a celebration not of accomplishment or success, but of all that was possible; a merger of the present and the future, and the past be damned.

The good wines and regional ales and beers did their usual efficient work breaking down barriers, I was happy to see. As the afternoon wore on, inhibitions were erased. Then, since a lot of the guests were only a few weeks out of college, silliness reigned. Soon anyone wandering near the pool risked being thrown in, whether or not he or she had thought to change into a bathing suit. Beyond a certain point, not many of those who were there clearly remember what went on. To the east, the sounds of fireworks echoed like rumors of war. Near the end of the evening, while several people splashed around in the pool, our Finn Ari Lutonen peeled off his bathing suit, dropped it at the edge of the deep end, and became the first of our programmers to leave nothing to the imagination. The legend that Lutonen's bathing suit is still lying untouched by the pool years later is simply untrue—though it definitely remained there until the gardeners cleaned up the place.

As the party broke up and everyone said good night, heading out through the front door into the cool, clear night, I told them to take the next day off. They wouldn't have much time off after that if we wanted to produce our irresistible new machine before the end of the year. Back to your boxes, I thought. Let's get rich. Be happy in your work.

10 Making a Business

For the record, I never felt like a billionaire, even when I was one. During a brief, altogether pleasing period when my company's stock hit its high point and hovered there for a while, the actual amount my shares were worth was $1.4 billion. (With the recent AOL acquisition of Netscape, I'm in the running again.) But when people gush about the vast wealth the Gateses, Dells, Groves, Ellisons—and Clarks—have accumulated as successful entrepreneurs in the Information Age, what is rarely noted is that relatively little of these fortunes are real, usable money. How long would Bill Gates be worth $60 billion (and counting) if he decided to cash in all his Microsoft stock tomorrow, or even 30 percent? The supply of shares would quickly exceed demand, the price would drop accordingly, the valuation of the company would decrease, others would rush to sell their stock (further diminishing its value), and things would spiral downward quickly. And if any material discussions are under way with another company that would affect the stock price, up or down, an insider can forget about either buying or selling shares, because that is strictly forbidden. All of the restrictions combined usually leave a few months a year to do any buying or selling of shares by an insider.

Don't get me wrong. I'm not looking for sympathy here. You're not going to see me at the side of the Mountain View on ramp to 101 behind a sign, "Will start a company for food." Having even a potential worth in eight or nine figures gives you a major corner on the good life (if you have time to live it). But high-tech winners, whose wealth is largely held in stock equity, aren't likely to do a Scrooge McDuck, gleefully rolling around in a vault full of cash. Shed no tears for those of us who have done well in the vanguard of the digital revolution. Even when things go wrong, we end up with more in the bank than most of us once could have imagined (especially since, with a few notable exceptions, few of the high-tech wealthy grew up with a lot of money). We've won a lottery of sorts, but like lottery winners who are paid in twenty-year increments, we get our infusions of cash over a period of time. Add to this the almost invariable need to work like hell in order to keep stock healthy, and such attention-getting very young billionaires as Jerry Yang and David Filo, founders of Yahoo!, have very little time to spend their astonishing gains.

Even an unstinting work ethic offers no iron-clad guarantee. The only control we have over what our stock is worth at any given time is how well our companies are led; the rest is a combination of market forces, the toughness and quality of the competition, customer desire (by no means a fixed star to steer by), and luck. Between one period when stock can be sold and the next, paper profits can plummet dramatically. In any event, what we're said to be worth is always substantially more than what we actually are worth.

In general, I suspect most entrepreneurs dream about vast riches only once in a great while. What you want is to do something terrific, turn a good idea into a good company, then turn the good company into a winner in the marketplace. This happy sequence of events doesn't happen very often—as I've said, it's a Serengeti out there, and young companies are impalas among the established cheetahs and lions—but when it does, the by-product is money. It may be so much money that there's an air of fantasy about it, but it's still a by-product of success, not success itself.

But I won't be coy and try to claim that the idea of getting very rich wasn't a significant part of what drove me while I drove everyone else. My friend Matthew Moore claims that I told him early on at Netscape, "I just want to make a fucking billion dollars. Is that too much to ask?" Though I don't remember being quite so blatant about it—one billion of anything, especially dollars, is not a number easily grasped and rarely spoken of in terms of personal gain, even by an ambitious entrepreneur—I may have said it just because one billion is a Really Big Number. If you're going to set your sights implausibly high, why not go all the way?

So sure, I wanted a financial success, something substantial enough to make up for the twelve years of investment in Silicon Graphics with what was a comparatively small return. Here was a company worth more than $4 billion. Anyone else in history, I'm sure, who had ever created a company of that size ended up with a lot more money than I did. I had something less than one half of one percent, less than the CEO and less than the venture capitalists—even the individual partners of Mayfield! If Mosaic Communications wasn't successful, people would say I'd been lucky with SGI, nothing more. So I wanted a clear success, a big resounding success. And what that means in business is simple: growth, high market capitalization, high revenues, and a highly valued company. If we ended up with a success like that, I certainly wanted to have the biggest piece.

Everyone, I think, has a number. This is the amount of dollars, rubles, yen, pounds, and so forth that they believe will let them tell the world to go to hell. Commonly known as "fuck you money," this number varies drastically from person to person and place to place. What Donald Trump might think of as just getting by would be unimaginably excessive to a country doctor. In Tom Wolfe's book *Bonfire of the Vanities*, Sherman McCoy, the stockbroker who is the central character in the story, stands in the entrance hall to his Upper East Side apartment and tries to figure out why, when he makes $1 million a year, he doesn't have any extra money. After almost every entry in his mental list of expenses, he thinks about how absolutely essential are the limos and the country house, etcetera. His is the same plight of the man making $10,000, only the number of zeroes is different. The moment is funny, but fundamentally true.

A person's number can change, and usually does, as soon as it is reached. All of a sudden, what seemed a peak to be conquered is just a high base camp for an assault on a higher peak. (The number can change downward, too, but that's a process most of us prefer not to think about.) In 1960, when Robert Noyce and Gordon Moore sold their equity in Fairchild Semiconductor for a few hundred thousand each, they probably had money beyond their wildest dreams, but that was only the beginning for each of them. When I left Stanford to start Silicon Graphics, a few million dollars sounded like a lot of money. By the time I left, a dozen years later, I had several million, but compared to the multibillion-dollar value of the company, that seemed disproportionately small. Using my own money to start Mosaic Communications, I was flirting uncomfortably with the possibility that all I had built up over the years would either increase fabulously or diminish by half or more. My number had grown, not out of greed—though I agree with Pearl Bailey, who said, "I've been rich and I've been poor; rich is better"—but because the stakes were higher, and the measure of whether I'd been smart as hell the first time or just lucky was now on a different scale. Did I want the fruits of a big score? Absolutely. But what I really wanted was to be ahead of the curve again. And whatever your number is, when you're ahead of the curve in high tech, you stand to be extraordinarily well rewarded. (It's what you do after that that determines whether you'll be famous or infamous.)

To be ahead of the Internet curve, an as yet vaguely defined arc, requires two things: a technological advance and an accurate sense of how that advance can be applied. One of these two we already had. However much Marc and his group might improve on their original creation, Mosaic was already an intrinsically valuable invention. Though I'm proud of the 3-D graphics with which I'd been able to build the foundation of SGI, a user-friendly, highly visual Web browser was a far more significant breakthrough than that, one that could change everyday life for millions of people. If the invention at the heart of my first start-up was an internal combustion engine, Mosaic was fire itself.

What we didn't have yet was a clear bead on the application—the "killer app"—that could turn the elegant technology into a relevant business, the way spreadsheets had propelled personal computers. But, like the hedgehog, I had one big idea. Marc and Eric had developed Mosaic to make an elite method of communicating and retrieving information useful for a vast number of users. Their metaphor was the letter and the library, which made perfect sense, since they were students and computer scientists. But for the past several years, my life had been less about research and science than about business relationships. There was no doubt the browser we were going to produce had an important user base among individuals who were using the Web, or would when it became easier. But I doubted there was much money to be made in that market. Marc and I agreed that however enormous the impact of the browser promised to be, the personality of our company would not be like that of certain small, well-funded, self-important start-ups that talk for years about how nice it's going to be once the market sees the value of what they are doing. These places, characterized by highly evangelical and persuasive CEOs quick to let everyone know their companies were doing Very Important Work, tended in the final analysis not to be serious about having a business.

Their genius was for raising money, not making it, which is all very lovely in the short term, but never the source of sustained growth.

With his immersion in the de facto nonprofit commune of the Internet, Marc had already begun talking about giving away our browser when we were ready to send it out. In a normal business, this might have seemed a very odd idea. But for building market share and user buzz, a free download—at least of the beta—made a lot of sense. At that time, just a few years ago, asking for money for something that could be plucked out of the air was a new concept that risked alienating Net users. Honor systems don't always work well when your customer already has the product, and especially when payment required an effort (clicking a mouse was one thing, licking a stamp quite another). But even if consumer sales were unpredictable, you could clearly make money, I knew, in company-to-company sales. Corporations tend to pay their bills. Also, I believed strongly that the future was two-pronged: One related to corporate customers and the other related to consumer users of the Internet. On the corporate side, where most Internet connections were coming from for now, if we could get enough individuals at giant companies such as General Motors and AT&T using our Mosaic killer, our machine would be the de facto choice for Web communications, working its way up through the management structure. With a majority of employees already devoted to a certain technology, when the company reached the point where it was ready for Internet and intranet connections, the obvious option would be the product most of their employees were already using. Thus, we'd also be the obvious providers of the more expensive server software necessary for corporate communications both private and public.

But the consumer side was less clear. I had spent a lot of time trying to convince the leaders of *Rolling Stone*, various people at Time Warner, Times Mirror, Knight-Ridder, and numerous other publishers that this new Internet thing was their future. And I tried to convince ITT that hotel and airline reservations would best be served with this type of technology. But it was like showing a great painting to a blind man. No one believed, back in late 1994, that the Internet had any chance for commercial success, and certainly it did not represent a threat to their existing business models. The press were still pointing out that

I might be a bit crazy, because everyone knew you couldn't make money on the Internet. After all, it was "free."

These concepts were not going to be easy to swallow by many of the people who would join the company on the sales and marketing side in the next few months. In fact, I won't pretend that it didn't cause me more than a little anxiety. After all, it may be a good idea to send out a free sample of your product or service to induce someone to go out and buy it—America Online is living proof of that venerable strategy—but the effect on the bottom line of sending out the whole product is to pretty much eliminate a bottom line just when you need one the most. At this point, however, all our top-line spending was my money, so if I could handle the anxiety, I didn't have to justify the approach to anyone else. The sales staff was on the same learning curve as the rest of us; they'd either figure it out or they wouldn't.

My metaphor for what we were doing wasn't mail and the library. At least it wasn't only that. E-mail had the potential to grow, as did information retrieval. For the time being, it seemed likely that both those aspects of the Web were going to appeal most to people already familiar with computers. But the usefulness and power of the Internet would eventually reach a limit if the numbers of users remained within the circle of the existing digital class. Had the Gutenberg Bible been the only book to result from movable type, that remarkable invention might not be thought of as remarkable at all. The more computers (or TV sets) that hooked into the Net, the more any individual user could get out of it. As George Gilder wrote in *Forbes* ASAP: "Every new host computer added to the Net would not only use the Net; it would also be a new resource for it, providing a new route for the bits and new room to store them. Every new flood of megabyte bitmaps would make the Net more interesting, useful, and attractive."

The real growth of the Internet, my instinct told me, was going to be in providing a revolutionary new way of doing business. Our business was going to be in bringing the acceleration of the Net to bear on how business was done: fast, friction-free, with lower overhead leading to higher profit margins, and greater convenience raising consumer satisfaction. When you could order supper, buy a book, or sell a car through your computer, not being on the Internet would be like having your telephone disconnected. Which was why, after deciding that the original Mosaic code had to be scrapped and entirely rewritten, I put Kipp Hickman to work developing security systems so impervious that people and businesses could exchange financial information with the same level of confidence a woman feels when she hands her Visa card to a sales clerk at Neiman Marcus. Our popularity would rest on the appeal of our browser for millions of individuals; our financial success would rest on that, and on how essential we could be to business service providers and online services. If we produced a fully secure system, we'd be able to offer these companies a near-perfect medium for financial transactions. Why would anyone want to order from a catalog and lick a stamp when they could do it with a mouse click instead? And catalog shopping was a $50-billion-per-year business.

Only a few years later, in a time when people routinely order merchandise through their home computers—when Amazon.com has become a major bookstore without having a store, and a small men's clothing shop in San Francisco sells leather jackets to customers in Moscow who've never been to the States—it may be easy to imagine that Internet commerce would have been, well, easy to imagine. But evolutions in technology, any technology, often come at the expense of the status quo and are therefore invariably resisted. Mosaic, which changed the Internet fundamentally, wasn't welcomed by a lot of traditionalist users, who had no vested interest in having their turf made more accessible and entertaining. So the next step, the use of a revolutionary communication medium to grease the skids of consumerism and commerce, wasn't something simply hovering in the air waiting to happen. As is often the case, the person who wants to make money is the one willing to dream the implausible dream.

Creating a foolproof security system is a lot of work, so getting there first with the best would give us a major advantage and help make us the obvious choice of large corporate customers such as marketplaceMCI and Prodigy. Also, while the profit margin was small on a forty-nine-dollar browser, what we could make on a $50,000 secure server application certainly promised positive cash flow down the road.

Curiously, for all the brilliance of Marc and Eric Bina's original concept, there really wasn't an enormous amount of technology in what Netscape eventually accomplished. In fact, over the years, Netscape has obtained many patents, but that's beside the point. In information technology, with its premium on innovation, advantage is gained by how fast you can get new products out, so that by the time your competitor has copied what you've done, you're on to something better. (And Microsoft, the master copier, is constantly cutting the amount of time any software developer has.)

Our breakthrough was in the application of technology to a new medium and a new market. The Internet was ready to explode anyway—Mosaic had made that inevitable. In the six months following the program's initial distribution at NCSA, one million new users began logging onto the Web. Our innovation, beyond a quantum improvement to the original concept, was in the features we added to open the medium up to the needs of business, and the rate at which we added them. What I had to do, while the engineers were building the basic program in both client and server forms (simultaneously for Windows, Macintosh, and UNIX machines), was reconnect with some of the companies I'd been in contact with during my last couple of years at SGI and convince them we could take them to the promised land. How did this make me different from the heavy-breathing evangelists I mentioned a few pages ago? I could confidently promise a real product to do real work in the real world, and, unlike some of the others on the circuit, I had delivered before, in a big way.

In a couple of months, from the original nucleus of Illinois and SGI engineers, the company had already expanded to around one hundred employees. At this stage, an ambitious start-up grows geometrically, not arithmetically, as tasks go from general to specific, and departments each build up their numbers to take on bigger jobs (and secure more territory). I had begun to sign on a sales force and bring them up to speed on the unprecedented product they'd be selling. And the selling part of the process couldn't come soon enough for me.

In my hometown in Texas, as in small-town America everywhere when I was growing up, it seemed as if every dry cleaner, bar, bakery, and hardware store that launched itself into the uncertain seas of commerce put a precious icon on the wall as if to offer some kind of protection against the wolves: the first dollar the business had earned. You won't see a framed greenback on the wall behind the reception desks at successful high-tech companies, but don't be fooled into thinking that they are any more sophisticated below the surface. Every start-up—or at least every start-up that survives long enough to become a going business—experiences the same rite of passage as any mom-and-pop store. At some point, often when things look fatally grim, there comes the magic of that first sale, and with it the promise of positive cash flow. Not that dazzling moment when you're actually in the black, a moment that may not occur for years, but just some money showing up on the plus side of the ledger. In our case, where the nature of precisely how we were going to make money wasn't entirely clear, the first dollar (well, several million dollars) was a major morale boost.

By this time I had hired several good people on the business side, among them Garth Neil as vice president of business development, and Bill White to handle sales in the crucial telecom area. All of them were from SGI. White was employee number thirty-eight. Toward the end of July, Vint Cerf, a major Internet pioneer working for MCI, paid a visit to talk about the commercial possibilities of the Web. Cerf had been one of the original architects of the Net, and remains one of the most clear-sighted visionaries of what kind of universe will result from the big bang he helped create (though he admits being one of the many who underestimated the spread of personal computers). In the mid-seventies, Cerf was doing research at UCLA with Robert Kahn under the aegis of the Defense Department, and the two invented TCP/IP, the fundamental protocols that allow computers that use different computer languages to communicate with one another over phone lines. Later, at Stanford, his research lab worked out the details of the system, and Cerf earned the nickname "Father of the Internet." At MCI, Cerf had perfected MCI Mail, the company's ground-breaking e-mail system.

During his visit to our Castro Street offices, Cerf and Jim Sha, an innovative technology thinker who had been a vice president at Oracle, designed what amounted to a cyber shopping system, incorporating the security system we were developing. To have someone as experienced as Cerf show an interest in what we were doing was a tremendous boost; it wasn't cash flow, but the "interest flow" that often precedes it. Since we were going to be licensing our browser to users with no assurance that everyone would pay for it, involving a company like MCI in the server software that would make Internet shopping possible seemed, at the time, at least one guarantee for making money. So I felt tremendously hopeful when Cerf's visit was followed up a couple of weeks later by a business dinner with a couple of MCI executives in a private room at the Lion & Compass, a restaurant in Sunnyvale. Bob Harcharik and Michael Mail from MCI joined me, Marc, Bill White, and Jim Sha to discuss our development of a commercial version of Mosaic that we could license to them. Since we weren't going to be delivering any kind of server products until at least December, we were asking MCI to sign on for something that didn't yet exist. Thus, communicating our excitement about what we were doing, and getting them to share our belief in something that existed entirely as a potential, was all we had going. Given the amount of hot air blowing through the Valley at that time for what is disdainfully called "vaporware"—ideas that sound great but never turn into anything that comes to market—we had to move carefully to keep our enthusiasm down to earth. In a recent novel, the writer Ward Just describes a character who attracts people because "he wore ardor on his sleeve." At that point in the company's short history, I think Marc and I and most of our colleagues could have been described the same way. Though we weren't selling something tangible, like a car, that a potential buyer could test-drive, we had something better going for us: We were selling the key to a machine that could take individuals and companies much further down the road ahead than most of them had ever imagined going. It was as if we were building a car in 1920 and were able to describe to buyers the entire interstate highway system—with the added incentive that the whole system would come into existence within the next few years. Ardor was the easy part.

The meeting went well, and by the time coffee was served, we'd reached a tentative agreement: For a certain number of licenses, MCI would pay us $3.6 million. I could barely conceal my delight. The business was growing fast, and in high tech, growth is very expensive. Every new programmer represented not just a salary and stock options, but a workstation and all the other equipment that is the ordnance of software development. I had anticipated spending a certain amount of my personal fortune, but the "burn rate" was far faster than I'd anticipated. It's one thing to sit down with a legal pad and calculate how much you're willing to risk on a new venture, but quite another to start writing checks and watch the funds gush out. Things had reached a point where D'Anne and Tom Paquin were hiding deliveries of new equipment from me so I wouldn't start agitating about expenditures that absolutely had to be made. The fact that we were growing so fast was a function of the speed I was demanding, so it should have been something that made me feel great. But every now and then the specter arose of running out of money long before we were ready to go to market.

By the time we were in the meetings with Harcharik and company, I was eager to get a deal done. But you can't look hungry in a deal like this. I had to convey the impression that I was willing to fund this business ad nauseum, as if I had unlimited funds. But I also had to get a deal. I was almost ready to have a handshake on a $3 million deal when we took a break.

"What do you think?" I asked Bill, because he was a good read of people and their interest. "I think we can get more if we offer a bit more," he said. Offering more product was easy, since we didn't have any yet, so I said, "What the hell, it's worth a try."

I felt a rush of anxiety. I trusted White's instinct, but this was the first real business deal we were on the verge of closing. What would we be risking if we asked for more? Could we get them to double the offer? What if the gamble turned out to be double or nothing, and they turned us down? We'd be back to zero, with the money still going out at the same rate. But to be cautious now seemed like a waste. I'd risked plenty; might as well go on risking.

Back at the table, White told Harcharik and Mail that we'd give them more licenses, but that we wanted $7.2 million. They looked at each other, and I knew the whole deal could go down the tubes at this point. It was the kind of moment I've experienced in aerobatic flying, when you've committed yourself to a maneuver but suddenly get the feeling you're not going to be able to get all the way through it before you run out of altitude—and if you throw up on the canopy, you won't be able to see and will crash for sure. The two MCI executives now excused themselves from the table and took a walk. I thought about the programmers' dark mantra: We're doomed. None of us said a word. Then they were back, announcing they would take the deal. Between that day and our public offering, we would close at least twenty-five deals with major corporations, some of them substantially larger, but none would feel any better than earning that first ($7 million) dollar.

Because I had name recognition among the corporations I planned to approach first (or was planning to approach them because they knew me), I usually made the first contact, then had the sales force follow up with more detailed explanations of the technology. Since we were developing a revolutionary communication device, we kept going after major telecommunications players. Dealing with companies that were ferocious competitors required a combination of secrecy and diplomacy that sometimes made me feel like an arms dealer trying to sell heavy weapons to all sides of a war.

This memo, sent to Bill White after we'd made the MCI deal, illustrates the approach we used.

Subject: AT&T
Date: Thu, 8 Sep 94
From: jim@mcom.com (Jim Clark)
To: bwhite

I had a meeting with Kathleen Early and Erik Grimmelmann from AT&T on Wednesday morning. Erik Grimmelmann will be sending a technical evaluation team out to visit us soon. I want us to follow up and grease the skids. This must happen FAST, so Bill, please talk to him via e-mail to coordinate—you should be the lead on keeping this going, at least for now.

I'd like everyone to be aware of the importance of AT&T. Our deal with MCI is great, but imagine if Godzilla got a deal with AT&T—we'd have a hard time being successful. Thus, AT&T is a very high priority, because we aren't going to be successful if we only have MCI. To make matters worse, they are extremely competitive with each other.

In our meeting on Wednesday, AT&T was looking for a competitive position, and we'll have to dance around this carefully as we talk to them. I'm VERY worried that we will not have made much

progress with AT&T before the MCI announcement, and thus po-
larize them or make them mad. Let's do our best to make sure these
meetings do not fall between the cracks.
Jim

"Godzilla" was obviously a reference to Microsoft. Though Bill
Gates had been uncharacteristically slow to pay attention to the Internet, he hasn't become the richest man in America by dumb luck,
or by surrounding himself with unimaginative yes-men. Gates and his
colleagues read newspapers and business magazines, so they knew that
we were getting a remarkable amount of attention for a start-up with
fewer than one hundred employees. In July, *Fortune* did a feature story
on us in their annual "25 Cool Companies" issue, which raised our
profile dramatically among both potential customers and potential
competitors. Some of the online gathering places visited frequently by
Marc, Eric, and the other programmers were also used by people at
Microsoft, so awareness of the increasing activity on the Net was sure
to percolate up at the company pretty quickly. Toward the end of
September, Jared Sandberg, a staff reporter for *The Wall Street Journal*,
wrote an article about Mosaic and its possible commercial use. The
headline read, MOSAIC SOFTWARE HELPS TO SELL GOODS ON LINE,
followed by the subhead "It Has Become the Electronic Sales Booth."
In the piece, Vint Cerf was quoted as saying that Mosaic "has become
the single most important factor in commercialization of the Internet,"
and the editor of an Internet business trade magazine predicted that
by the end of 1995 online commerce "could easily hit more than $100
million." Not until eleven paragraphs into the story was the alliance
of Clark and Andreessen mentioned, and then only as one of several
companies working on improved versions of Mosaic. But our cover was
clearly blown.

Early in October 1994, Rosanne Siino sent the following e-mail message to all hands.

Had to let you all know that now we've TRULY made it in the press
world—not only have we hosted CNN and Fortune this week, been

covered in the Wall Street Journal and [San Jose] Mercury News, had a cover story in Microtimes, have an upcoming article in Business Week, had a zillion calls so far today about the news release [about the beta release]. . . .

But now we've also gotten a call from Vogue magazine's food editor, who is doing a story about food on the Internet, and just had to find out more about this "Netscape thing."

What more can I say?

Rosanne

Of course, I was glad to get press attention while I was out making calls on corporate CEOs, and constantly urged Rosanne to shovel the pizza cartons out of the conference room and bring in the reporters. But I had my moments of missing our brief stealth period. I could almost feel the all-seeing eye from Redmond, Washington, scanning the horizon, trying to decide which cool new companies might dare to claim a new piece of profitable turf.

Jumping ahead to an intriguing act of historic revisionism, I can't resist pointing out Microsoft's claim to have been Internet-intensive before we even came along. In a story on August 6, 1998, in *The New York Times* headlined MICROSOFT SAYS CHICKEN (WINDOWS) HATCHED BEFORE EGG (NETSCAPE), Redmond executives indulged in recovered memory syndrome about a retreat in April 1994 for twenty top Microsoft executives called by Gates at which he announced (as recalled by one of the attendees), "We're going to make a big bet on the Internet." That such a retreat was held I have no doubt; modern companies typically engage in more retreats than the Italian army. And it's possible that the Internet was one of the subjects that came up. But a few factors make me wonder if Gates ever sounded the charge at that early date. For one, given its heavy spending on a proprietary, non-Internet system called Microsoft Network, this new direction would have been at cross-purposes to an ongoing strategy. For another, Microsoft—always more inclined to buy technology than develop it from scratch—didn't take a license for the browser software on which it has built Internet Explorer until December of 1994, by which time we had already been in the news for nine months. And finally, with

Gates's renowned determination to vanquish all contenders and win wherever he chooses to compete—and Microsoft's vast cash reserves available for research and development—if Gates and company saw the Internet coming way back in April of 1994, why were they so uncharacteristically slow getting off the mark? Microsoft is capable of screwing up, of course, but their mistakes are usually strategic; once they've targeted a particular market, they're formidable. So to believe Microsoft made plans to create a browser in the early spring of 1994, you have to conclude that they were hopelessly inept to take so long, and that would be a characterization both naive and potentially dangerous.

11 The Deal

In astrophysics, there's an ominous term called the "event horizon," which refers to the theoretical point in space-time where light, an unfortunate astronaut, a celestial body, or for that matter, all matter begins the fatal descent into a black hole and can't escape. It's the cosmological equivalent of aviation's "point of no return," where a pilot has enough fuel to reach his destination but not enough to turn back and make it home. If you happen to be aboard a craft drawn toward the black hole, one of the odd characteristics of the experience is that, though you're in big trouble, nothing around you seems different.

Event horizons, in one form or another, lie in wait for all business start-ups. Like the gravitational pull of a black hole, these disaster thresholds draw entreprenuers onward until they're in too deep to save themselves and their businesses. Various things can cause catastrophe, but the most common is simple financial miscalculation: Too much is spent too quickly, leaving no resources to adjust to changing circumstances. Of course, if circumstances don't change, disaster may never occur. But that almost never happens. Buoyed by optimism, people starting a business tend to underestimate what they'll need to spend and overestimate the amount of money that will flow in, as well as when that elusive cash will begin to appear. Black holes aren't a danger only for start-ups—Apple, at the height of its success, made some crucial mistakes with regard to licensing and product development and passed through, or at least very close to, an event horizon without anybody being aware of it at the time. But for a start-up, the danger of mistaken calculations is much greater because the money is tighter.

By mid-summer of 1994, the burn rate of my money was faster and fiercer than I'd anticipated. I'd managed to get a pretty good start as the sole Series A, or first phase, investor. But it was clear that if we were to avoid our own black hole, the time for the next stage had arrived. The last thing I wanted to do was go out hat-in-hand looking for money. As I've indicated already, inferior venture capitalists like nothing better than a promising young company on the verge of going broke, since they can get far more for their money than they could from a start-up not yet in desperate straits. At such moments, perfectly nice men in well-cut suits make hyenas look good. But the really good ones, such as John Doerr and his partners, think about how to retain employees and build a future after a company has gone public—they know some reward has to be left for the people who tirelessly work to make a business happen. The others are sometimes pennywise and pound-foolish.

At this point, things were going extremely well. Publicity was plentiful and positive. What we had was a marketing dream: young guys, a young team, the world's most popular software, a seasoned Silicon Valley veteran—must be wise, must know something, he built SGI—and the reassurance for other customers of a contract with MCI. Though I was beginning to wonder if we might be hiring too fast in certain areas, our growth was only slightly out of control. And we were starting to generate real interest among companies that would be our customers, both in the U.S. and Japan. We looked good, I figured, and not at all needy. But I could sense the inevitable event horizon some- where just ahead.

I was still feeling a certain amount of guilt over Glenn Mueller's su- icide. Whether or not I had played any part in his personal despair, I couldn't forget his saying to me, "If you don't let Mayfield invest, my partners will kill me." So when the time came for a second phase of money-raising—bringing in Series B investors—I felt I had to give Mayfield the first chance, despite my resentment about having let them talk me into taking a small percentage of SGI in 1982 while they got 40 percent, and their failing to support me in my face-off with McCracken. But my understanding of venture capitalists had gotten a lot more sophisticated during the past dozen years, and my ability to play hardball with them had increased, too. My guess was that we were a hot ticket, and that this time around I would set the terms.

So I met with Gib Meyers and Grant Heidrich, two of Glenn's senior partners at Mayfield. (Grant was one of the young partners who twelve years earlier at the start of Silicon Graphics had convinced me that I was worth only 15 percent of $1.2 million, or about $150,000. He was young then, and not at all malicious, but this always stuck in my craw.)

I filled them in briefly on how we were doing, then laid out my terms. The deal I offered was simple: I wanted them to pay three times as much for their shares as I had for mine. (Given our progress, this was a good deal, except that we still didn't have a firm business plan.) My rationale was equally simple: My money was worth that much more than theirs because it came with me as a full-time employee, while theirs was only money and they would be working full time elsewhere. This may sound arrogant, but it's really just good business sense; experience is one of the most valuable currencies, and I would be there full time, while they would sleep normally. When I stated my requirements, neither of the two men said a word. I think they must have thought I was completely out of my mind. After all, by this time in the rapid evolution of Silicon Valley financing, venture capitalists had grown immensely powerful, taking on a formidable aura in the eyes of novice entrepreneurs. They were (and still are) accustomed to having entrepreneurs come in with their hands out, ready to agree to any terms the VCs laid out. Money bought time for a start-up, and time, which was usually running out when the new company went begging, was the most precious commodity. So the price for venture funding was, at the very least, a pound of flesh, which is to say a sizable chunk of a company.

Frankly, I had been thoroughly enjoying my time as the lone Daddy Warbucks of Mosaic Communications. For all the anxiety about where we were going and how fast we could get there, I had spent years dealing with the Byzantine politics of corporate hierarchies and boards of directors, so the rare purity of being able to make business decisions without having to lobby anyone else was a real pleasure. I was the CEO and chairman, major owner, and, except for Bob Gunderson, my lawyer, the entire board of directors. Since I had enough money to go on bankrolling the company for a while, I might gladly have basked in the divine right of sole investor right through the year. But I'd already spent (or committed to spend) $3 million, and the rate of spending was rising. Like life itself, the funding of a new venture resembles an hourglass. At first, there seems to be an unlimited supply of sand (or time, or money), and though there's a steady trickle, you can't really see the whole amount changing. Then, when you get down to about one fourth of that amount, the outflow seems to be going at an incredible rate. We weren't at that point, of course, but I didn't want to get there. But I wasn't about to cave in because Mayfield didn't jump at my unusual deal. In fact, they never even stirred. I met with them one more time, but I never heard back from them after that. I sometimes wonder whether things would have gone differently if Glenn had been at that meeting, but I have the satisfaction of knowing how much their silence cost them.

My approach to Mayfield had been dutiful, not enthusiastic. I like to tell myself that I don't spend a lot of energy holding grudges, but that's only really true when the grudge isn't worth holding. Most grudges aren't, so they don't last long. But a few have the half life of radioactive waste, and one of those was the grudge I held against Mayfield because I felt they'd betrayed me twice. So had we reestablished a relationship, it would have been strictly financial.

The next stop on the venture capital circuit was New Enterprise Associates. NEA had been the other major funder of SGI, and managing partner Dick Kramlich is an old friend. In fact, I'd met my wife, Nancy, at NEA when I stopped by his office and she was interviewing him for a magazine article. Dick had been on the SGI compensation committee along with Glenn, and as such had approved Ed McCracken's increases while my package remained unchanged. But Dick had always trusted my instincts and even had me as a special partner for his firm for my last five years at SGI. Plus he and his partners at NEA had asked me to become a general partner, sharing a pro rata part of the carried interest, which was a great gesture I will never forget, because I was not feeling too well in my last days at SGI. I'd turned down the offer because I knew I make a better entrepreneur than a venture capitalist. The partners there also figured I was crazy to ask for a richer deal than I'm sure they'd ever given anyone else, but at least they hedged their bet a little. "We've been a little too close to you, and would rather not set a precedent. If you get someone else to agree to this price," they told me, "let us know. Otherwise, we think two times your price is more fair."

In other words, they were ready to pay twice what I paid for each share, but were still asking for the right of first refusal should I get a better offer. Not exactly a major vote of confidence. I can't help but feel that the expression "Familiarity breeds contempt" applies here.

Had neither firm known me so well, they might have listened more carefully, but they had intimate knowledge of all my problems over the years with McCracken. Those who had not known me looked at me as a smart guy who had been the creator of SGI. I made up my mind that if some other venture firm wanted the whole deal, they would get it.

At this point, I was not worried. Two strikes is a long way from out in the game of raising money in Silicon Valley. Arthur Rock, the man who really invented high-tech venture investing, went through more than thirty turn-downs when he was looking for money in the late 1960s to launch what became Fairchild Semiconductor (when Fairchild Instruments finally invested). His tenacity paid off, making the first fortunes for Robert Noyce and Gordon Moore and leading to the founding of Intel. Now, with venture firms crowding Palo Alto's Sand Hill Road like so many souvenir shops on the Via Doloroso, money is given far more quickly, often to companies that are 95 percent smile and 5 percent content. I had something worth investing in.

In fact, the unresponsiveness of Mayfield and caution of NEA set me free to establish a connection that would give Mosaic Communications both an infusion of capital and a strategic ally. That last was far more important than the cash. I placed the call to John Doerr at Kleiner Perkins Caufield and Byers on Sand Hill, just west of the sprawling Stanford campus.

Doerr is a quintessential creature of the Information Age. He possesses a genius for deeply understanding both the technology and the business of this era, as well as the personalities that make that business happen. Doerr is among the handful of venture capitalists who have had a disproportionately large effect on the success and direction of leading-edge start-ups. Unlike his smooth, stylish senior partner Tom Perkins, an ocean sailor and car collector now married to Danielle Steele, there's nothing elegant or physically impressive about Doerr. *New Yorker* writer John Heilemann described him as "a highly caffeinated Clark Kent," but it's hard to imagine John emerging from a phone booth as the Man of Steel. He is, nevertheless, the Nerd of Steel, and he's capable of a lot more than simply leaping tall buildings. Compaq, Lotus, Sun Microsystems, Intuit—he's had some blockbuster successes during his eighteen years at KP, yet he looks just a few notches above the kind of guy who wears a pocket protector to keep his pens from staining a wash-and-wear shirt. He has a master's in electrical engineering and an MBA from the Harvard Business School (not an unusual combination of degrees these days, but rare when John was in college). He holds patents for computer memory inventions, and because he's totally in love with technology, he sometimes walks around festooned with pagers, cellular phones, hand-held organizers, and e-mail devices. And an ordinary snapshot camera, with which he tries to bring his hectic pace to a stop once in a while. Doerr has been described as a one-man beta site, and he can appear slightly mad with all the stuff and his hair looking like he just got out of bed, but he probably understands the state of the art in high technology better than any other money man at the end of the twentieth century. Far earlier than I, he understood that the desktop computer was destined to revolutionize the computer business. If he has a weakness, which I doubt he does, it's that he can be seduced by technology, and his most notable flops, like GO Corporation, a company that made pen-based computers, have been those where the technology was impressive but didn't really make much sense in the market. (One good outcome of the GO debacle was Doerr's recruiting of Mike Homer from Apple as vice president of marketing, a connection that brought Homer to us in the same crucial role that fall.) In fairness, the best venture lenders bat around .100, but when they hit home runs, the ball tends to leave the stadium. John's failures didn't worry me, however, since I was as sure of our technology as I'd ever been of anything before. With great stuff, this guy would be a great asset. Besides, I had always respected the way Sun Microsystems beat SGI in getting market share, and I felt it was because of the good management by Scott McNealy and the good advice of John Doerr.

Doerr represented a second or third stage in the evolution of venture capitalists. Sometimes I feel that this evolution is simply from carnivore to smart carnivore, but John is one of those VCs who brings far more than money to the party. He doesn't just roll the dice and hope for the best, but gets actively involved with the staffing and management of a company to make sure he and KPCB get amply paid for their risk. I mentioned earlier Doerr's response to a question about whether an activist VC didn't somehow risk a conflict of interest: "No conflict, no interest." In my optimistic moments, I think what he means by this is that if he can't get into the give-and-take struggle that characterizes a new company's growth, he doesn't want to take a chance with his fund's cash. Almost by definition, entrepreneurs should hate this kind of interloping attitude. In any number of highly publicized cases, proactive venture capitalists have forced entrepreneurs out of their own companies. Some particularly ferocious examples of the species probably would have had the founders dragged outside and shot if they'd thought they could get away with it. Neater that way. Dealing with the mob may be more dangerous than dealing with the velociraptors, but only a little. If Doerr weren't so knowledgeable, his determination to be involved with the running of a company might be annoying at best, destructive at worst, but getting his input along with his company's investment is like getting a really fine prize in a box of Cracker Jacks. Money wasn't hard to get, even for a company with a notably vague business plan; getting a top consigliere and a bona fide CEO magnet made KPCB's dollars worth more than other dollars. A couple of other KPCB partners, Doug McKenzie and Kevin Compton, brought me together with Todd Rulon-Miller, whom I hired as vice president of sales at Mosaic Communications. Both he and Mike Homer were absolutely essential to the company's fate in the months and years to come.

I'd known John Doerr since my early days at Stanford, when he was new at KPCB (having gone there from Intel) and looking around for some way to make his mark. He hung around the engineering building on the campus, asking questions and checking out who was doing what, a first-hand curiosity that would give him an inside track on some great companies. We had met at a Caltech conference, and he was very impressive from the first moment we talked—brilliant, articulate, persuasive. I had introduced him to Andy Bechtolsheim, who worked on my project at Stanford. Later, Andy formed Sun Microsystems, with John as an early investor. I ended up competing with Sun for years, and I always found myself wishing that John had been on my board. I could see that he remained good friends with Andy and cofounder Bill Joy, and while I was finding myself increasingly isolated at SGI, it seemed to me that in the same kind of situation he would have backed me. That's pure speculation, of course, and probably wish-

ful thinking, since venture capitalists are known more for cold calculations than warm hearts.

Two things made John precisely the right man to add to the Mosaic
mix, however. First, he had often said that he no longer wanted just
to start companies, but to start "whole new industries." I knew that
what Marc and his crew were doing on Castro Street amounted to
mining the ore for an industry as new as personal computers had been
a decade or so before—the Internet industry. That was just the kind
of thing John would throw all his brains and energy into, as well as a
fair chunk of his firm's money. Second, Doerr had evolved into one of
the most perceptive and effective recruiters in the business, with a
great ability to help find the right managers for the companies he got
involved with. I'll have more to say about CEOs in the next chapter,
but getting someone who fits into the culture of a start-up is both
vital and extremely difficult. In that area, Doerr was a fixer of the first
order. Phone booth or not, sometimes the S on Doerr's chest seemed
to glow through his wash-and-wear shirt.

Despite all that, I still didn't entirely trust John. My wariness came
from a time in the early 1980s when I had introduced him to Martin
Newell, one of my first collaborators on the Geometry Engine, around
which SGI was built. Before I could get SGI started, John lured Newell
away for another venture that ultimately didn't work out. For that
reason, I made sure not to introduce Marc to Doerr until the work at
Mosaic Communications was well along. Would John have tried to get
Marc interested in another venture had he met him earlier? And would
Marc have been tempted to do something else before the original Mosaic programmers had signed on? Probably not, but happily for me, I'll
never know.

I may be recalling more self-confidence about my ability to raise
Series B capital than I actually felt at the time. After all, the terms I
was demanding were not something VC firms were used to hearing
from entrepreneurs. To pay three times per share what a founder was
paying represented a deal so favorable to the entrepreneur that it was
nothing short of scandalous (to the venture firms, that is). Definitely
not something they wanted to hear about. Until I was willing to cut a
more customary deal, I might have bounced from door to door along
the money-green archipelago of Sand Hill Road, beginning to sweat in

the increasing heat from the burn rate of my own investment. But I had a lot to keep me going: a dozen years in the business, the energizing resentment at getting the short end of the SGI stick, a top team, and a powerful idea that was probably the best shot I was ever going to get at repeating my earlier success. So I was determined that this one would go my way no matter how much I had to spend to keep the company growing while I looked for new capital.

When you're dealing with venture capitalists, you can't count on holding an advantage forever, any more than you can make a living betting against the house at Las Vegas. Doerr and his partners had been around many blocks, many times; they knew exactly how to play a situation like this. So I wasn't at all sure how it would go when Marc and I, with no business plan but boundless confidence, went over to Sand Hill Road to meet a gathering of all the KP partners.

But I had the feeling that finally we were in the right place. They didn't balk at the idea that my shares should be worth three times theirs. For one thing, they had the foresight to understand that if we managed to win a major share of the potentially huge market for Internet browsers, there would be plenty of money for everyone. For another, going along with me at this point didn't cost them anything. They could keep me on the hook without any real risk for quite a while. Probably encouraged by John's support for the company, Kleiner Perkins made a verbal commitment to put $5 million into Series B stock, on my terms. I agreed to put $2 million more in myself to protect my stake from further dilution. We would both pay $.57 for the new shares. Technically, this was a new series and it is not unusual that the series was three times over the Series A. Even at three times my Series A rate, they got a hell of a deal. And to keep things simple, I paid the same price as they did after all. We put the lawyers to work on the paperwork for that round of investing, which would take another month to six weeks. I can imagine what might have been said after Marc and I left: "Look, we don't have to hurry on this. He doesn't need the money right now. If we're going to put in money at three times his rate, let's let a little time pass, and see how it goes." There was nothing unscrupulous about this, of course, just a measure of shrewd judgment.

In time, maybe even just in time, we closed this round of financing, and KPCB wanted all of it. According to my resolution, NEA did not get to make the investment.

Doerr joined the board, where he serves today. John's involvement with Netscape was crucial; Marc and I probably would have done it without him, and even without KPCB money. But since he played an important part in helping me recruit our CEO, without whom my life, and the company's success, would have been far more problematic, I'm grateful we didn't have to try. So here's to John Doerr, one of the few velociraptors I want on my team.

PART THREE

CREATION AND CONFRONTATIONS
Spring 1995

12 Jim Barksdale—The Right Stuff

eadership isn't a constant, like π or the rudeness of New York cab drivers. There are all kinds of leaders, and countless ways a given situation can affect and change any of them. So any calculations in which a leader is the X factor are extraordinarily tricky. Leadership is invariably significant but never simple. One kind of leadership may work brilliantly in one situation but fail disastrously in another. General George Patton is the kind of leader you want facing the enemy across the front line, while soldier-statesman General George Marshall is the sort of person you want to manage the difficult transition from war to peace. If their roles had been switched, the history of this century might have turned out very differently (try to imagine a "Patton Plan" for rebuilding Europe). In the same way, the value of classic leadership traits may change according to circumstances. Lincoln's top army commander in the early stages of the Civil War, General McClellan (yet another George), inspired tremendous loyalty among his men, and he returned this loyalty in equal measure. But when it came to sending his troops off to die in battle, he was so reluctant that Lincoln had to replace him with the tougher-minded Grant (alas, a Ulysses). In some cases, obviously, loyalty matters less than ferocity.

Ironically, but maybe not too surprisingly, the people most resistant to the idea of these differences in leadership are leaders themselves. If you can get people to follow you to hell and back, they figure, what more do you need to be a leader?

The answer is: That depends. Business isn't war, for instance. The workers of Alpha Corp. tend not to invade the factories of Omega Inc. and slaughter all the inhabitants. Though in the case of Microsoft the desire to destroy competitors veers dangerously toward reality, life and death in economic competition is usually metaphorical. If there is a wide spectrum of military leaders best suited to various tasks, then the spectrum in business is even wider, shifting and changing as a business grows, flourishes, or declines. There are small-company leaders, large-corporation leaders, start-up aces, turnaround specialists, demolition experts, and people who can come in, get a business ready to be sold, handle the merger, then ride off into the sunset with saddlebags full of money. The variations go on and on. One thing that remains unchanging, however: There are always more good companies than good leaders for them. Companies, that is, with smart ideas, quality employees, a viable market niche, and a receptive consumer base. What they often lack, and may never find, is the right person to take those advantages and maximize them.

Perhaps nowhere is this shortage of leadership more dramatic than in high technology. Added to the normal factors that complicate any business leader's existence—and militate against success—are the things I've mentioned earlier in this book: speed, acceleration, change, and a highly unusual culture of workers. The combination of abilities needed to survive is so rare and subtle that it's amazing anyone ever makes it. The surprise isn't that so many fail, but that any succeed. A man or woman who can fit in with a bunch of creative programmers determined not to be manageable may be more like a camp counselor than somebody who can do the daily heavy lifting of running a business. A really good manager maintains a delicate balance of human concern and ruthlessness—mentor and tormentor, part Mother Teresa, part "Chainsaw Al" Dunlap. You ought to care about those who work for you, but you can't take your eyes off the prize. And you can't be unwilling, like old George McClellan, to do whatever it takes to attain it.

In high tech, the military model of rigid hierarchies and absolute obedience that prevailed at corporations for generations (and never mind the various theories of new, sensitive management touted by the New Age management consultant types) has become completely irrelevant. So leaders have to find new ways to inspire people to work their asses off. Fear and insecurity, those trusty tools of autocrats of all kinds, are useless in a world where smart people can pick and choose from an abundance of jobs and a résumé with few entries is no longer anything to be proud of. Consider the difference between someone like Woody Hayes, longtime hardass coach of Ohio State's football teams, who could simply demand almost limitless sacrifice of his young, idealistic players, and Phil Jackson, Zen-practicing former coach of the Chicago Bulls, who has to be far more deft and diplomatic in dealing with highly talented, well-paid professionals. In this difference you have a perfect example of old versus modern management. Of course, I could cart out all the old clichés—leading by example, consensus building, etc.—but that leaves out the hard reality that you can only be touchy-feely up to a point, then you have to move on, make things happen, demand that people do more than they think they're capable of (bearing in mind that talented engineers think they're capable of a hell of a lot).

But before you can inspire accomplishment, you have to inspire trust—a very tricky business in today's high-tech world. If a CEO can't find a way to connect with the culture he finds in place, he's doomed. Cultures can be forced to change, but not often quickly, and not usually with a result that makes the effort worthwhile. This is especially true if the work of a company has to continue at any kind of pace at all. If someone like Gil Amelio doesn't like having to put up with a certain sophomoric streak that runs through a company like Apple (and always has), how much can he change things without going too far and messing with the fundamental nature of the organization? Even IBM, traditionalist domain of the dark suit and white shirt, finally realized that the times, and the talent, were changing (not that Big Blue hasn't always had its share of slightly wacky geniuses like John Cocke, inventor of the RISC chip, who could never remember to cash his paychecks).

Not many of the bright lights of computer science coming out of the top universities care a lot about business; they want to do cool stuff and be recognized for it by the others doing cool stuff. The ones who manage to do the coolest stuff are an elite, and they know it. They weren't about to stifle their eccentricities to make a bunch of suits feel good about how well discipline was holding up. I can just imagine what would have happened if I'd told the fiercely individualistic Jamie Zawinski that he ought to adopt a less extraterrestrial haircut, or said that our virtual mascot Mozilla—Jamie's invention—wasn't appropriate for a serious business looking for serious money. In an Internet minute he'd be working for some smart little start-up where a half-shaved head verged on being conservative. The last thing a leader in this business wants is the reputation of a stiff. (Some business consultant must have thought that Yahoo! should change its name to something more serious-sounding before going public; luckily for newly wealthy founders Yang and Filo, that old-paradigm view didn't prevail.)

After a few months of intensive work, the Castro Street offices of Mosaic Communications looked like a conceptual art exhibition at a state mental institution. If that wasn't exactly my style, so what? These were my rock 'n' roll stars. I wasn't about to make them unhappy by telling them to grow up. That was their business. Might as well tell the Beastie Boys to mind their manners. (In fact, I had absolutely no desire to provide adult supervision, being perpetually immature myself.) However dormlike the scene might be, I knew from experience that good programmers—and these guys had already earned their spurs producing extraordinarily effective software—don't need a lot of prodding and monitoring. You let them be as weird as they want, and remind them from time to time what the goal is, and they'll produce. In fact, riding herd on them is pointless; they ride herd on themselves more mercilessly than any manager could. And anyway, the off-the-wall style of the company perfectly suited the manic spirit of the work. Michael Toy, making the adjustment from the more staid halls of SGI, observed that the wildness of the young programmers was a kind of romance. These were revolutionaries, maybe even anarchists, who were about to play havoc with the ancient regime. I liked them just the way they were, and the most idiotic thing I could do would be to make the mistake of hiring managers who were uptight about the scene.

Not the least of the requirements of leadership in a place like Silicon Valley is a knowledge of technology and where your company's products fit into the larger context of a rapidly changing market. This isn't an absolute necessity; sometimes a CEO is brought in from a related field, and if he or she is a quick study, any shortage of specific savvy can be made up on the job. But the record of outsiders who come from completely nontech businesses isn't good (read "disastrous").

All in all, the kind of character who can lead hot start-ups is almost freakishly rare. Find a combination engineer, marketer, futurist, pragmatist, sociologist, visionary, gambler, circuit preacher, guerrilla fighter, Zen monk, zealot, smile-and-a-shoeshine salesman, and quick-change artist, and maybe you'll have found someone who can run a good high-tech company. In the end, the way these companies are led is so new and so demanding that no one has yet written a real job description. No executive recruiter, however effective, can describe completely the perfect individual for the job. When you find the right person, you don't always know it right away. When you find the wrong person, you may not know it until it's too late. Bringing an ace CEO into a good start-up is like signing a left-handed reliever with a 98-mph fastball to a team with pennant potential. The likelihood of winning everything goes way up.

The hardest thing to accept for most entrepreneurs is that they're not necessarily the perfect leaders for their companies. How can that be? After all, if it weren't for them, there wouldn't be a company, so doesn't it stand to reason they have a right to lead? Tell that to the velociraptors, who'll bounce a founder the second things don't suit them. There is, of course, no right to lead, just the right leader or the wrong leader. In fact, since the qualities that make a successful high-tech CEO are so many and so unusual in combination, the chances aren't good that someone with a great idea will also have what it takes to run the company created by that idea. One of the advantages of having been through all this before was that I could be a realist. And one of the advantages of not being the inventor of the technology around which Mosaic Communications had formed was that I didn't feel a deep, emotional need to protect the baby. Or rather, I didn't feel that no one else but I could do the job.

But who could?

When Marc and I had agreed to create a company to do something, I had only one answer to that question: Not me. Even when I'd started SGI, an academic with little understanding of business, I had known what kind of leader I was. I could get people going, "spread the contagion," and gather a nucleus of talent that would attract other talented people. But I don't have the temperament for the long haul, for negotiating the sprawling minefield of guiding and nurturing a company—dealing with personnel issues, keeping up morale, interacting with directors, fielding the daily decisions and putting out the constantly erupting fires—once it's had a birthday or two. One of the best compliments I've ever had was Kipp Hickman's statement that "Jim is good at knowing what he's not good at." If that's true, and I think it is, no trait can have served me better. But in the early days of Silicon Graphics it wasn't easy to get out of doing what I wasn't really good at. Back then I was the guy with the vision about what we were going to do, as well as one of the developers of the core technology the company was built around. Like it or not, I had to make decisions about endless details so the company could get on with its mission. I was an inexperienced manager who knew he needed help, which is why I hired Ed McCracken. Now I was a seasoned veteran, with an acute awareness of my limitations. I wanted to enjoy life a little more. I also had the hard lessons of a rancorous leadership struggle at SGI as a constant reminder of how not to do things.

From Day One when I started Mosaic (Netscape) Communications, I looked back on my experience at SGI and asked myself, What went wrong? What did I do that I feel most regretful about? Obviously, my strained relationship with Ed McCracken—really, the lack of a relationship—detracted immensely from the possible growth of the company. Something similar happened at Apple at around the same time. The inability of Steve Jobs to get along with John Sculley, and vice versa, led to bad decisions, or no decisions at all. It also led to a showdown. In that case, as in mine, the entrepreneur lost and the manager won, and the dynamism began to leak out of the organization. I don't mean to imply that either Jobs or I was perfect. We both needed people to run our companies, to substitute patience and methodology for our impetuosity and sometimes abrasive personalities. But somehow neither of us could make a solid, working connection with the CEOs we ended up with. As far back as Marc's and my conversation at Cafe Verona in March—which already seemed long ago by the blurred measure of Netscape time—I'd decided that I wasn't going to let that happen again.

Whenever a strong-minded company founder brings aboard someone whose institutional power is equal to his or hers, there's a potential for disaster. To be a successful entrepreneur, you have to have plenty of attitude. And a good CEO has to have plenty of attitude, too. The founder, knowing he needs a strong partner, looks for strength and ego in his CEO, but he'll still be jealous at seeing his creation in the hands of anyone else. So at best, the odds are even that things will go well. And to get to the fifty-fifty mark means making no mistake finding a perfect CEO, a creature as elusive as Sasquatch. No, make that more elusive.

For me, early on at SGI, the portents weren't particularly good. I had brought in a very able and amicable man named Vernon Anderson to be temporary CEO, and we'd already had a few disagreements when I had trouble convincing him that we ought to do certain things. His approach was "Wait, I want to think about that a while." At Netscape, I was still the way I had been at SGI: "We've already wasted too much time. Let's get this the hell done!"

Past the age of about six, I'd say, not many people change very much. After fifty, you're definitely stuck with yourself, for better or worse. So I knew I still had the deep-seated streak of impatience that gave rise to sudden displays of annoyance and, sometimes, fairly incendiary anger. I won't bother to offer tear-stained testimonials to my unpleasant moods from my assistant D'Anne, and to those who meet me socially I may seem quite laid back, but in high-stress work situations—pretty much a constant in a start-up—I can go off without warning over what seem relatively minor things. For example, when Bill White sent this innocent but misspelled e-mail to Marc (copied to me):

Mark,

Thanks for the lead. BNR/NT is in my area. I'll follow up today.
Bill

To which I responded:

Bil, you want to lose points with me and Marc, you continue to spell his name incorrectly.
Jim

Marc, on the other hand, sent a good-humored note to me and Bill (another sign of his maturity):

You kidding? I'm completely used to it. I'm just glad I don't have a dull name, like "Jim Clark" or "Bill White." Snoozeville . . .

Marc

To whatever extent my personality had been a problem in the fractious relationship I had with Ed McCracken—and certainly it was part of the problem—I was determined not to let the same thing happen this time around. There would be no power plays, no clashing egos, no strategic screwups because the CEO and I weren't able to get along. How was I going to manage this unlikely miracle? Since I wasn't going to wake up the next day as a saint, I had to be ready to back out of the management of the company as soon as the new CEO, whoever that turned out to be, took the reins. As the sole investor thus far, I felt it was important that I provide overall business guidance as Marc provided technological guidance. But I had a very simple role written for myself: big investor. Stepping back into this money-in, hands-off role, of course, required finding someone I could trust to do the job without putting me into a role no one wants: big loser.

I had been so preoccupied with the hiring of sales and marketing people that I hadn't been able to spend much time thinking specifically about filling the CEO position, so I'd hired a top recruiter named David Beirne to start the search. He quickly put together a short list of top executives he knew or knew of, and prominent on that list was the name Jim Barksdale. He had been president and chief operating officer of McCaw Cellular Communications and, after McCaw merged with AT&T, had become CEO of AT&T Wireless Services, headquartered in Seattle, where he was working at the time. Though I wasn't inclined to make the crucial decision on a CEO quickly, Barksdale's background was appealing, and Beirne, whom I trusted, thought highly of him. Around this time, I was also in discussions with John Doerr about KPCB's investment. Beirne and Doerr had a kind of mutual admiration club, and each was a highly successful judge of talent. When Beirne brought up Barksdale, Doerr seemed to know quite a bit about him already, and liked what he knew of his accomplishments.

Those accomplishments were solid and attention-getting. As president of McCaw, he had a large part in pushing the company's profits to more than $2 billion in 1993, making it attractive to AT&T. Since the merger had been announced, he'd worked to smooth the problematic meld between what was essentially a tough, independent young company and an established, powerful corporation. Even more impressive, while he was chief information officer of Federal Express from 1979 to 1983, Barksdale was responsible for developing systems to track packages and communicate with customers that have made the company one of the superstars of the service economy. Barksdale became chief operating officer of FedEx, and in an era when CIOs were often fired but rarely elevated, this was a significant vote of confidence. While he was COO, the company's revenues went from $1 billion annually to just under $8 billion. Barksdale didn't make any effort to glamorize his reputation, as is often the case with ambitious executives. As a result, he wasn't a household name in any but the most business-savvy households. But attention must be paid to anyone who can pump up revenues by a factor of eight. Clearly, Barksdale was a rising star in American business. But what I liked especially about him was that he had spent his career (he was in his early fifties) ahead of the curve in modern network communications. He would later point out to a reporter that the common connection between FedEx, McCaw, and Netscape is that "all three are network companies."

There is a belief held over from the eighties, probably foisted upon us by business school professors who've done far too little business, that a good manager can run any company, no matter what it does. This is one of those idiotic ideas that somehow become business axioms, and it has led to any number of doomed marriages. It was especially inappropriate in a field where the ability to envision technological innovation is vital, as is the skill to drive forward at speed, avoiding dead ends and staying on the right road without a map. One only has to look back at John Sculley's ill-fated tenure at Apple to see that selling cola and anticipating future markets for computers and software are vastly different things. Sculley was smart and successful; like any good marketer, he understood that new products were important (think of Diet Pepsi). But as a newcomer to high tech, his problem was in correctly judging which pieces of gee-wizardry out of R&D made good sense, and which were so cool that no one ever asked the hard question: Does anybody out there really want this thing? Even tech-savvy veterans get it wrong with embarrassing frequency, but to ask an outsider to make those difficult choices is to ratchet up the uncertainty to dangerous levels.

Late in the summer of 1994, as my work increased and my time diminished, I felt it was time to take the next step in the CEO search. After enough preliminary contact to assure us that Barksdale might be available, Doerr and I flew up to Seattle, where McCaw Cellular was headquartered. Instinctively, I liked Jim right away. He's a Mississippian, smooth as a julep, with a relaxed style and a soft-spoken accent that has probably led more than a few Yankees to underestimate his intelligence and toughness. All you had to do was look at Barksdale's record to know that underneath his affability he was determined and smart. But the fact that he was someone other people seemed to feel at ease with right away could be an essential quality for a company trying to make money playing with the big boys. I had heard he'd been approached by Microsoft to take the job of president but had turned them down. I couldn't help liking that.

This was really just an introductory trip, both for us and for Barksdale. As a result of the "Top 25 Companies" article in *Fortune*, he had already had his interest in us piqued. We weren't there to offer him a job, but rather to get a sense of how he might respond should an offer be made. And the feeling I got was that he wanted to stay on in Seattle at least until all the loose ends of the merger were tied up. That gave us all time to think things over. Though finding someone with the right stuff to run my company was a pivotal decision for me, the decision for Barksdale was just as momentous. Leaving the solid ground of a huge corporation like AT&T, where he clearly had a future and tremendous prestige, for the uncharted waters of a start-up with fewer than one hundred employees meant making a leap of faith—a life-changing, without-a-net leap—that not many executives want any part of. For me, this whole business was a deeply personal fight for the vindication and validation that could come with a dramatic success. I didn't have a choice about whether to go for it or not. But for a man like Barksdale, who seemed never to have made a wrong move professionally, the decision would have to be more rational; if he joined up and we failed, he'd end his career on a down note. You're allowed to make some mistakes in the Holy Order of Management, but not without atonement. And if you're no longer young, that atonement can be very grudgingly granted. My impression of Jim was strengthened by the fact that he wanted to see the merger through. This implied to me that he was concerned about the fate of people he'd worked with, and the last thing I wanted to do was hand over the company to someone who might not be concerned about the people who were working through the night to make a great new machine. (A financial crunch waiting just over the horizon would cast me in the villain's role soon enough, but I wanted a CEO with a heart as well as a head.)

At that first meeting, I could have grabbed him by the lapels and given him the full Henry V, band-of-brothers treatment, convincing him that what was happening down at Castro Street in Mountain View, California, was eventually going to make a lot of people wish they'd been there for the great battle.

I'm shameless when it comes to talking people into doing what I think they ought to do, but such a dramatic approach, especially with a man who knew at least as much about the pragmatic, unromantic side of business as I did, was not my style. At one time or another, I'd persuaded a happy few, and then a few more, to follow me into uncertainty. But for the very top level of the company, I couldn't make that kind of pitch. First, experienced managers are often successful because they're highly rational, more inclined to use their emotions to inspire others than to sway themselves. Anyone we offered the job to was going to weigh the pros and cons, toss in a certain amount of swashbuckling spirit, and decide. There was no point in my trying to convince and cajole a real leader into joining up. I could provide the deal, but if I had to provide the desire, then I hadn't found Mr. Right.

Barksdale wanted to honor his commitment to McCaw and to AT&T, and he wasn't ready to commit to our little band of brothers. But he was somebody I wanted involved in some way, somebody simply too good to be missed, so we convinced him to join the board of Mosaic Communications while he shepherded McCaw into the AT&T fold.

The fact is, as impressive and likable as Barksdale was, I'd had another idea about who should be the CEO. Tom Jermolak, at the time SGI's president, was the best manager I had ever known. Much of SGI's success was due to his leadership and hard work, and I felt he was capable of even greater things if he could work in the looser, make-it-up-as-you-go environment of the burgeoning Internet. I also knew he hadn't ever received a very big equity position in SGI, so he probably wouldn't feel locked in. Tall and blonder by the moment, given to wearing Teva sandals and Hawaiian shirts, Tom had real charisma, a rare quality among high-technology managers. He looked more like the bass guitar player for the Beach Boys than an executive, and his offbeat sense of humor and lanky, collegiate style inspired affection among his younger employees. Even against Silicon Valley's backdrop of informality, Tom stood out as someone who wasn't going to let business run—or ruin—his life. Since I'm that way myself, we'd always stayed close, even during my final days of disaffection at SGI. He was famous for his antics at company parties, so I could easily picture him fitting in with my ensemble of odd characters. Since we'd worked together before, I figured the chances of our ending up in an adversarial relationship were minimal. That, plus the fact that he was a known quantity to the key players at Mosaic Communications who had come from SGI, made him seem ideal. In my mind at that point, Jermolak had one advantage over Barksdale. While Barksdale had done great things at communications companies and had a more impressive résumé, Jermolak had made his bones at a technology company—a fine distinction to those not in this industry, but it put him ahead on the learning curve. It didn't make him a better leader, just someone who already knew his way around a unique territory.

Through David Beirne, I asked T J, as he's known, to come over and speak with us. Actually, given the careful choreography required in such matters, Beirne asked him to call me. As I'd anticipated, he showed up and instantly looked right at home amid the craziness on Castro Street (he was somebody we didn't have to clean out the pizza boxes for—in fact, he wanted the pizza), and we made a date to talk further. But by this time, McCracken and others on the board at SGI were getting tired of losing talent to me—men and women they tended to value more after they were gone than while they'd been there. Before T J and I had a chance to get down to cases, SGI launched preemptive negotiations. Tom let it be known that he was ready to jump—he had some major leverage now, and he was too smart not to use it. They offered him a package worth a guaranteed minimum of $10 million. Frankly, given T J's what-the-hell attitude, I thought he might turn down the sure thing for a shot at a jackpot. But $10 million is a very serious carrot, and Tom bit.

People I know have told me they can't imagine what kind of company Netscape would be if Jermolak had said yes. Tom probably has wondered about how things would have gone for him, since a couple years later, again with my prodding, he left SGI to become CEO of the successful Internet start-up @Home. Because things turned out so well, I've never really indulged in a "What if . . . ?" retrospective fantasy. But what I can say is that I can't imagine what kind of company Netscape would be today if Jim Barksdale had said no.

In fact, he might have. Between the tentative courtship with Jermolak and the time I spent running around the country putting together business partnerships, I'd let things cool off on the Barksdale front. Doerr, not being on the board at that time, had had to just go along with my instincts that Jermolak would be a better bet at that time—he didn't really know T J. But there's a certain pace to any courtship; it may be gradual or brisk, but if the pace changes, especially if it slows down, someone is going to take that as a bad sign. If a woman is used to getting a call from an admirer every third night, let's say, a five- or six-night drought may cause her to see the beginning of the end of that romance. In business recruiting, the same law of rhythmic continuity applies. If you come on strong enough to get a prospective hire interested, then slow down, your quarry may decide you're simply not serious. At the level of a top managerial talent like Barksdale, someone who clearly can get plenty of dates for the prom, the act of slowing down can lead to distrust. After Jermolak had decided to stay with SGI, Doerr and I had begun talking about Barksdale again. Realizing a little late that I'd let things slide, I said to Doerr, "Hey, let's go with it. We can't equivocate anymore or we'll lose him."

By this time it was absolutely clear to me that Barksdale was the right man for the job. I knew, however, that to get him to take the leap, the job had to be more attractive than anything else he might be thinking about, including staying put. It was obvious that being a strong CEO was important to him, so I had to make sure Barksdale understood that he would not be sharing power with me, but instead would be running the business (with Marc as the technology chief) without interference.

"Look," I told him as we talked about what he'd be doing, "you don't have to worry about me. I don't want the job of running things. Just the opposite. In fact, if you want to be chairman, you can be chairman." As far as I was concerned, he could be tsar, emperor, maximum leader, and lord high executioner, just as long as he took the reins. After all, I owned so much more of what then had become Netscape Communications than I had of SGI, even after the influx of KPCB's Series B money, that I didn't need to worry about fighting for territory. John Doerr, determined not to let Barksdale get away a second time, was doing his share of persuading.

I don't want to give the impression that Barksdale was being coy, letting us fall all over ourselves with promises and stock options. He was simply not someone who was going to jump into a new situation until he felt he'd done what needed doing in his current job. You've got to admire that. But I wanted him enough to make an offer I was sure wouldn't be easy to refuse. I was prepared to give him half as much as my percentage of the company, and to vest half of that up front. My thinking was, What the hell, what do I have to lose here? If Barksdale doesn't work out as CEO, given the tight Netscape-time frame we were working in, this thing's dead anyway. So vesting a large amount of stock for him right away was giving the sleeves to my vest. You can never know if a new business is going to be successful; it's simply never certain. All you can do is optimize things. Getting Marc to lead the technology, and getting the core team out of Illinois and dependable veterans to work with them—those were parts of the optimization. Barksdale was the next key. Operating a growing company is nothing but day-to-day innovation in every aspect of the business. If these innovations are going to be effective, you have to have smart, creative people in all top management positions, and they have to be led by someone who knows how to keep them all working together. That's what CEO recruiting is all about.

Barksdale had a lot to weigh before making a decision, and a lot to do at the job he held at the time. But in the end, the chance to lead a company that was doing something truly revolutionary, a message preached passionately by Doerr and myself, proved irresistible. It is the destiny of most managers, even very talented ones, to take on jobs that have, to a great extent, been shaped by those who filled them before. A good manager may leave his mark (a bad manager will leave his, too), but is still part of a continuum. Once in a great while, the chance comes along to do something truly new, in which inspired leadership will mold a job, and a company. Not everybody wants that kind of job, with its demands for creativity and originality. Luckily, Barksdale was the kind of manager who couldn't resist the challenge. In late August 1994, Barksdale "winked" that he'd join us as soon as he could finish his work on the merger. He was not willing to make it definite at that point, because he would have to tell AT&T, which he was unwilling to do. I was not certain that he would ever join us, but I decided then and there that I was going to make the bet. So this wasn't a done deal, but it was as close to a commitment as we were going to get for the moment.

That "moment" lasted another four months. Given what was about to happen, it would seem like forever.

B y September of 1994, just three and a half months after the programmers began work, the action at Castro Street was frantic. The summer had burned away along with the morning fogs and a lot of money. Autumn in Northern California is right up there in beauty with the fall months in Tuscany, but Marc's "happy few" programmers were lucky if they glimpsed even a few rays of sun each day through their cranked-down blinds. The local Denny's was doing an astonishing middle-of-the-night breakfast business, and the Domino's Pizza deliveries must have set some kind of franchise record. Once in a while, the group would decide to get out to eat real food at a "real" restaurant in Palo Alto, such as the Peninsula Creamery, which caters to the high-cholesterol crowd. But after three or four straight days at work, if D'Anne hadn't been able to chase them home for a shower and change of clothes, they were on the unacceptable end of the social scale—to put it kindly. Dismayed maître d's would take one look, or one whiff, and wonder, Why me? Invariably, the programmers, the brilliant pride of Mosaic Communications, would be shown to a table as near the kitchen or rest rooms as possible. From then on, "the Netscape table" was a term meaning the worst table in the house.

A sense of company identity had begun to grow during and after my raucous July Fourth bash. But the work of the programmers, the breeder reactor at the heart of our operation, was still so specialized and monkishly labor-intensive that those not directly involved in that end of things tended to steer clear of the boys. Marc led our strategic planning sessions, and I tried whenever possible to gather all hands for an update on what was going on inside and outside the offices. Though we'd grown closer as a company through daily contact, however incidental that contact might have been, the engineers were the ones who had to build a product—one that was already being energetically marketed and sold—so they had little choice but to press ahead without paying a lot of attention to what the rest of us were doing.

At a June planning meeting a few months earlier, Marc stressed something that was especially memorable to most of the people in the conference room: He argued emphatically that whatever software we created, "it's gotta be open." This was consistent with the philosophy of traditional academic and scientific Internet users. After all, the Internet itself was a gift from the government, and it was treated as a kind of family possession. Marc and his group had already given their original version of Mosaic away to anybody who wanted to download it. But I was worried at the thought of trying to make a business by opening up the safe in which the crown jewels were stored.

Nevertheless, from the beginning I'd seen Mosaic in the context of publishing, with money to be made through advertising. If we could create an Internet-based online service—what is now called a "portal"—through which people accessing the Internet would naturally pass, the chance to sell display space would provide income. The viability of the Internet as an advertising medium was unknown, but it didn't take a genius to see that whoever won the lion's share of the browser market could promise advertisers a lot of traffic passing by their billboards—and interactive billboards, at that. Then, Marc's initial desire to make the software available free made more sense, since it could expand the user base. Gannett Publishing had done this for several years with *USA Today*, and now they profitably charged for the paper. The Knight-Ridder newspapers would comment as we put out our beta software in October: "Chairman Jim Clark has adopted a very competitive price for its first product. It's free." Of course, at the time, I still didn't know what business model would develop. Seat-of-the-pants still ruled.

In September, we took a booth at the InterOp Conference in Las Vegas and announced our first product, the browser we called Netscape. At the time the company was still called Mosaic Communications, but I had insisted that the product name be different and unrelated, because I could see a potential dispute over names brewing between us and the University of Illinois, and I didn't want to waste more precious image-building on establishing a name that we would have to change.

Like someone pushing a big pile of chips into the middle of a poker table, we were marking ourselves as a serious player, prepared to show our cards. Not least, we identified ourselves as players to ourselves.

That's when most of the employees realized we were actually in business. This rite of passage—the first trade show—means a lot to any company, but in today's high technology, a product announcement, with a set date, begins to move you out of the ranks of companies that endlessly talk about vaporware. Once you put yourself on the line to deliver, you begin the transition. Build something customers can believe in and you begin believing in the company you're a part of. Virtual becomes real. Plans become Porsches, or refrigerators. The satisfaction of creation outweighs the motivation of money. This straightforward act of creation is the goal that makes good people push themselves. Too much planning, without a product that tests the marketplace, will almost inevitably bring on entropy and apathy. The knowledge that we'd be out there with our creation in a matter of weeks galvanized the team.

It also put even more pressure on the programmers. Not that they had enjoyed much of a life outside their work since arriving in California. Internally, Marc had laid out a relentless schedule—we would introduce a new product every six months, do or die. (His initial plan called for a three-month cycle, but some of the veterans had convinced him to compromise.) Before that, even a nine-month software development time was highly unusual. Of course, this was possible only because the Internet itself was the distribution system, and new versions were therefore easy to release.

The first of these products, the 0.9 beta version of Netscape, a completely reinvented, far more effective program than the original Mosaic (which had been a hard slog in the first place), required Herculean labor. For everyone writing code that summer, June, July, and August passed in an endless freight train of late nights. The group spent countless hours squinting at screens until their eyes ached, typing code and moving computer mice until their wrists ached. Ten-minute ad hoc meetings were called by anyone who encountered a problem he couldn't solve, a bug he couldn't track down and squash. The group cobbled together some way around the problem, then everyone went right back to work or curled up to sleep on the floor next to their desks. By now, what everyone had discovered about Netscape time—those who didn't already know, that is—was that the Internet is a creature that never sleeps. Since you could be in touch with people everywhere, twenty-four hours a day, seven days a week, downtime was only when you simply couldn't stay vertical for another second. Aleks Totic remembers bleakly that often when he woke up on a futon and saw the sun low in the sky through the window, he couldn't remember if it was the beginning of a workday or the end. In fact, the idea of beginning and end no longer had much meaning.

What relief there was came not with time off, which almost no one took, but in violent chair-hockey games and the radio-controlled toy car races that careened noisily down the lines of cubicles. (In later years, these steam-valve releases came in the form of roller-hockey games in the parking lot of our new headquarters. No one watching these games would ever again be able to indulge in the stereotypical notion of the nerd as a busy brain stuck onto a vestigial body.)

When people did leave the office, it was usually just to go home to take a shower, catch a few hours of uninterrupted sleep, put on a clean T-shirt and shorts, and come back to their computers. Their real home was where the code was. By this time almost everyone had found apartments and moved out of the residence inn D'Anne had put them in when they'd first arrived. But having apartments of their own didn't yet mean having lives of their own. When Aleks Totic's sister paid him a visit, she walked into a place with virtually no furniture. Aleks had hardly noticed.

We'd hired new programmers to help with the work, but at this stage in writing a program you can reach the point of diminishing returns fairly quickly. Simply throwing more talent into the mix won't necessarily make things go any faster. Nine women can't make a baby in one month. Some things can only be done by individuals, and that's especially true when software is being written for the first time; a crowd of workers creates problems, not solutions.

From the beginning, we had all been driven by a powerful sense of competition. In a sense, the Illinois programmers were competing with their younger selves, pushing hard to outdo what they'd done before as undergraduates. But I mused over the impact this would have on Spyglass, the small Illinois company that NCSA had made the master licensee of the original Mosaic. Actually, there was some confusion about this at the time: A media relations official at NCSA, which was trying to co-opt our plans, told *Internet World* magazine that October that "Spyglass is just like any other licensee." Everything Spyglass had done so far was amateurish. Probably most notably, they, too, thought the Mosaic "product" licensed from the university was the valuable thing, not the people. Had CEO Doug Colbeth been really smart, he would have recruited at least some of the members of the team before me. Netscape would never have happened if he had.

Numerous people have said we should not have made Microsoft angry at this stage, that we should have remained under their radar longer, but I submit that they would have been just as intensively trying to kill us no matter what. Given the publicity we were getting, there was no way to hide. And with the forthcoming success in the 0.9 release, we were enemy number one. As our success grew throughout 1995, their rash behavior got the best of them, and this gave the Department of Justice what they needed to indict Microsoft. More on this later.

During this time frame, we had many discussions under way with partners beyond MCI, and there was increasing interest from many geographical locations around the world. It was clear to me that once we released our product, lots of business was available. Garth Neil, who was acting as VP of sales and business development, began to construct a revenue plan based on the prospect list that was developing. We had closed the Series B financing, but I could see that even the $7 million we had just raised was going to run out sometime in early 1995. I needed a business plan, because seat-of-the-pants works only in the early stages, and no institutional investor could invest without it. Besides, it is the right way to run a business, and we had been too loose for too long. By the time the revenue plan was done, Garth estimated revenues for 1995 at $70 million. (Such a number was outrageous for a company in our stage to suggest that we would do, and although the categories of income were inaccurate, the result was almost exact: We ended up doing $75 million in 1995. Party on, Garth!)

But the engineers were not aware of the business planning; they just assumed I would somehow get this done. They were focused on the imminent product release. Within the company, a kind of intramural competition was going on. Different engineers on Marc's team were writing the browser program for various UNIX machines, PCs, and Macintosh operating systems (Jon Mittelhauser and Chris Houck on Windows; Totic on the Mac; Jamie Zawinski on UNIX; and Eric Bina and Lou Montulli on cross-platform applications). Like young hot-rodders tinkering with their cars, these guys were working through the nights to make their machines faster than the others. When Mosaic was originally built, both its makers and most of its users were working on fast computers and accessing the Net over T1 and T3 lines paid for by businesses and universities. These were the equivalent of large pipes through which information sluiced at high speeds. In comparison, the 14.4 modems in most homes were like soda straws, and if we were going to make a Mosaic killer, the program had to be refined to work well with less sophisticated equipment, at the same time handling better graphics and more complex documents. Each group, competing hard to come up with the fastest program, was forming an invisible bond with their eventual users. If members of Congress cared half as much for their constituents as the young men did about millions of potential customers on the Net, there wouldn't be many complaints about the state of government. It's always been tempting for outsiders to think of the Netscape IPO as an overnight success, but it was built overnight after overnight after overnight. In late July, when the decision to ship a product in October was made, Tom Paquin sent out a gung-ho e-mail to the engineering department that perfectly captures the spirit of the young company—and also indicates why it's so good to have people like Tom:

To: engdept
From: paquin@mcom.com
Subject: Welcome to the Silicon Valley

OK, we have decided we need to ship a product in October. This is great—it's what this "valley" is all about. If you can't tell, I'm kinda pumped by this, or, as Chouck [Chris Houck] would say, I'm all over it.

Here's the deal. We need to do a 3-platform NCSA-function–only release in October. The business case is pretty overwhelming; we can talk details tomorrow. We'll have to completely refocus our plans on this. . . . We do whatever it takes. And feel damn great about it when we pull it off.

I'll be grabbing people Friday to collect some data and responses. You can bet our Friday meeting will be about this. One thing's for sure: Busting our asses won't be enough for this; we must also focus.

Think roughly NCSA function done mid-August, everything done, including GUI [graphical user interface] end August, debugging & whatever else we need to do through September. Ship to customers for evaluation Sep 30. Release 10/14. I have some wacky ideas about testing starting mid–late August through end Sept. We can talk about this.

Start thinking. How many boxes of Nodoz should we buy?
Tom

Many people have written about the fact that Marc and the others were among the first of a new breed of "baby millionaires" created by Internet start-ups. It would be easy, then, to get the idea that money was what all the hard work was about. But at the core of their amazing drive was a belief in the Web and what it could accomplish. They knew they were part of something major and they were people with an abundance of idealism. I was keenly aware of the business possibilities and the money to be made, but I doubt any of them ever thought much about what could happen. Money was just a by-product of giving the world a phenomenal new way to communicate. Some weeks after the beta was distributed, Jamie began to notice URLs—uniform resource locators, as Web site addresses are known—showing up in places as varied as movie credits and grocery bags. "When I saw that," he says, "I knew that even though we didn't make the Web, we were having a tremendous impact on it." Their belief in the Web is what inspired me to go out and deliver my own passionate sermons about the Internet.

All the frantic action was focused on the moment when the product, the better hot rod—the beta version, Mosaic Netscape 0.9—would be sent out into cyberspace. Up to this point, all the days and nights of tinkering, brainstorming, testing, bug fixing—then chasing the new bugs the tinkering introduced—had gone on within the family. One programmer might do a test of another's work, but the two would be like boxers who had sparred together so often they didn't need to be at their sharpest. The system was so familiar to them all by this time that the word *test* didn't really apply anymore. To really know how they were doing, the only true test was the mass quality check by the core of computer jockeys already using the Internet, a group always eagerly awaiting the newest, coolest thing. Sooner or later—and in our case, the sooner the better—you had to put the machine out on the road and let people drive it. Then they'd figure out for you dozens of ways to get more out of it. And they'd tell you about them, in a remarkable feedback loop that is roughly akin to the way kids take mainstream fashion, mix it up to satisfy themselves, and end up inspiring designers to create new styles. During the prerelease phase, you might have ten or so programmers working on a piece of software; afterward, you have thousands. Most of them aren't geniuses, but some will come up with ideas that really do advance the design.

No matter how much Marc and his team wanted to see Mozilla (our internal code name for the browser, as well as our virtual mascot) pushed out the door, it was hard to make the call "Now!" Bugs are as natural to software as weevils are to cotton, and just as unwanted. Some companies are more blasé about infestations than others, but as Joe E. Brown put it at the end of the movie *Some Like It Hot*, nobody's perfect. Releases of software are notoriously late, the result of bugs being hunted down until the last moment. The group worked toward some theoretical perfection, but at some point you just have to say, Let's stop messing with this! It's good to go—or good enough. If you don't, you'll never ship a product. And somebody else sure as hell will.

As Jamie Zawinski remembers it, "We wanted something that was good enough. We knew there were bugs, but it was time to let others see the thing. After all, the choice wasn't between Perfect and Late or Imperfect and Nothing. We came to the time when we said, 'Well, we've learned what we can learn, now it's time for feedback.'"

The beta launch was scheduled for mid-October. Unlike a NASA Mars shot, where there's a finite window during which the planets line up correctly, the date was not one we absolutely couldn't miss. But, dating from when we started working, it conformed with the six-month schedule for product releases we had committed to. And as a critical way to ease the pressure (if only briefly), the debut of the almost-ready-for-prime-time Netscape needed to happen before the programmers began to implode. They had long before had T-shirts made up that carried their slogan, "We Are Doomed." Jamie, an "outsider" from Berkeley and fiercely individualistic (remember that bipolar haircut), was as good an indicator as any of how things were going in the trenches, and how the almost endless work hours were affecting the makers of Mozilla. Since he'd joined the company, Jamie had been keeping an online diary in which he'd make periodic entries, making sometimes acerbic observations on the behavior of his fellow programmers (he was definitely one of the anti–toy car group) and assaying the state of his own psyche.

Monday, 10 October 1994, 5pm.

Well today has been more than a little bit frustrating. The details don't really matter (what does!), but I've spent most of the day so stressed out that my skull is rattling from the pressure of my *teeth* grinding together. I feel like I have finally exceeded my *stress* limits and am about to blow a gasket. But I can't go home, because if I do, the world will end, right? I'm trying to work, but every few minutes I have to stop typing and make fists so tightly that my whole body shakes.

Deep breathing. In. Out. In. Out. In. Out.

BLAM BLAM BLAM!!!!! Aaaaaauuuuuugggghhhhh!!!! Cut the phone! Kill the dog!

Cubicles have no doors to slam. I've been alternately chugging Coca Cola and Pepto Bismol. It's not helping.

Some email from *Laura* says, "You are rapidly approaching meltdown. Get out now." She told me that I need to go Coot Chasing. Apparently there's an open space preserve north of Shoreline and *SGI*, and at the end of a twisty road is a lake. Around this lake are hordes of little black birds called *coots*. They run around on the mud flat on little half-webbed feet, and when you chase them, their feet make a *phup phup phup* noise. And if you get them really agitated, they *oink*, like little black feathered piggies.

"It is," she promises, "the funniest fucking thing."

Coots know how to live. I wish I were a coot.

Mr. Wizard, I think I'd rather be a coot than a hacker. Yeah, sure, every now and then a giant *pink-haired* ape would come running after me and chase me into the lake, but really, could it be that much worse? I'd have a *tiny little brain* and wouldn't be expected to worry about *anything*.

They bought us Indian food for dinner today. I hate Indian food. I think I'm getting an ulcer.

The day leading up to the download was quieter than usual. The programmers came to work later than normal, and those who kept vampire hours, sleeping into the afternoon and working through the night, showed up even later. It was as if they were afraid any last-minute fiddling might unleash a new batch of bugs, or perhaps they were just taking a figurative deep breath before going off the high board. Messages had been sent to Web newsgroups to announce the moment, so there was anticipation at both ends.

Of course, many of them had been through this once before, when Marc and Eric had led the charge of the original Mosaic release at NCSA. But the previous effort was, by comparison, almost for fun—call it a high hacker's thrill or a notable notch in the résumé. So what if the early Windows and Mac versions were prone to crashing? Nobody thought that was a major deal. The situation this time was fundamentally different. It was about quality in the real world, and maybe, peripherally, about showing the management at NCSA how much they'd lost when they'd taken the original Mosaic team for granted. I don't know whether or not this added to the intensity, but the Big Download was also about millions of dollars that could be lost if 0.9 fell short of expectations. Maybe that particular piece of the anxiety package was all mine. Marc, for whom the release had to be tremendously significant, seemed unperturbed. In typically laconic style, he'd stated his philosophy about such momentous events: "Any individual product is far less important than the basic idea." In other words, if the beta release didn't receive rave reviews, that didn't mean we weren't onto something great. We all had high hopes, and everybody was working like hell to make the prototype machine a winner, but—being purely practical—falling short of expectations was not unheard of in computer technology.

For the programmers, Netscape time was life lived in a blur, like stop-action photography speeded up to a point where individual events can't be clearly separated and understood. There were only a few times when things slowed to a near-normal pace and clarity reigned. This night was one of those times.

Appropriately for a commando raid, the launch was scheduled to begin at midnight. In the conference room (not yet named after a famous prison like the meeting rooms in our next offices), a large monitor was set up and attached to the server. Separate windows on the screen would keep track of downloading for the various configurations, wherever and whenever they happened. The intimate and precise nature of the Internet makes it possible to measure numbers of users with an exactness impossible for radio, television, and print publishing. In fact, the interactive nature of the Internet allows the measuring of a great deal about the user, which makes it the most powerful of commercial media and is why it will replace these other media as a delivery mechanism, and do so over a short time period, when compared to the evolution time of conventional broadcasting. That precision let the programmers chart how they were doing with a rare degree of immediacy. Somebody had rigged each platform with a signature sound: a cannon shot for UNIX machines, a frog croaking for Windows, and glass breaking for Macs. (There are those who remember other sounds, cows and bells. Whether it was exhaustion, or the beer—a little of which went a long way with the weary group—memories are a bit hazy on the details of that extraordinary night.)

It figured that UNIX would log the most downloads, simply because at that time the majority of Internet initiates were scientists, faculty members, and students who had access to sophisticated workstations. But the PC and Mac teams expected a tight race for a coveted second place.

Just before H-Hour, the programmers and most of the ex-SGI engineering contingent came into the conference room and found places to sit, like NASA controllers preparing to track a moon mission. Someone turned off the overhead lights, and a group of tired, anxious, excited faces reflected the glow of the monitor screen. At midnight, Pacific time, Mozilla was let out of its cage and charged into the world.

Almost immediately, a cannon shot rang out. Then another and another. The group, possibly prepared for a certain amount of slack time before the action began, sat up and started cheering. It was as if, in rooms and offices everywhere, people who'd been prepared for the release by postings to Internet user groups had been sitting at their computers, waiting breathlessly for the browser to appear, like kids with a string attached to a stick propping up a box waiting to catch a squirrel. Somebody in Japan was the first to log on, probably from his office in some Tokyo high-rise, where it was mid-afternoon. The instant the beta version of Netscape appeared on the Web, Mosaic users, primed by newsgroup announcements, couldn't wait to see if we'd built a better browser. They wouldn't be disappointed. In terms of speed alone, they could now boost the top-end horsepower of their computers on the Net by a factor of ten, and in terms of visual pleasure and features, there was really no comparison. By the time the 1.0 version launched, there would be improvements—that was the whole point of the beta— but what went out that night was already a quantum leap into the future of the World Wide Web.

The downloading started fast and quickly built to a frenzy. The cacophony of sound was almost deafening (with the UNIX cannon, as predicted, the dominant noise). Beer was flowing, and the crowded conference room looked like a Super Bowl party. The electronic connection with users out there in the wide Web world was so direct that if someone had trouble downloading the program, those in the conference room could tell, and shout their encouragement. "Come on, 129, try again! You can do it!"

After a couple of hours, and hundreds of downloads, the excitement began to wear off. Michael Toy, Tom Paquin, and some of the others who were used to keeping more normal hours congratulated all hands and began to drift away. They were terrific managers and successful engineers who had been deeply involved in the process that brought the company to this point, but I think they knew, as I did, that this moment really belonged to the young programmers who had built the browser from the ground up. All-nighters were pretty much business as usual for them. Jamie remembers feeling that "we were done, but we still couldn't go home."

I've searched for a comparison in history for what went on that night, exactly five months after the first planning for the new product began in mid-May. In a real sense, for all the ferocious competition the future has brought, at that moment little Mosaic Communications, in its funky headquarters on Castro Street in Mountain View, California, owned the Internet. It had prepared the ground for hundreds, even thousands of new businesses. Yet unlike the launching of a great ship, the event was relatively low-key and, except for the raucous sound effects and cheers, fairly quiet. Likewise, it didn't have the ritual quality of the driving of the golden spike that connected the transcontinental railroads in Utah, or the pell-mell, headlong dash for property and prosperity that accompanied the great Oklahoma land rush—though history may judge it no less important. What happened in that room was intimate—a group of imaginative young men watching as their creation was snatched up by avid consumers and enthusiasts. The closest analogy I can find to their experience goes back to Aleks and his feeling about being a rock 'n' roll star. I suspect the programmers must have felt at least a slice of the elation and astonishment that hit the Beatles when they stepped out of the airliner in New York for their first tour of America and saw thousands of fans going crazy.

14 The Plea for Reason

I had been on the road when the first release occurred, visiting Time Inc., *Rolling Stone, Playboy*, the Tribune Company, Times-Mirror, and other major magazine and newspaper companies—in line with my idea that the Internet was a new publishing medium with an early natural affinity to print media. At each stop, I spread the gospel of what I considered the Net's virtually unlimited future, and showed eye-catching demos put together by Bill Foss (who'd done the same thing for SGI) and Jeff Treuhaft and a small team back at Headquarters. The responses to the demos were always good, but they were like beautifully made Detroit concept cars that no one could actually drive. Now at last we had something people could put up on their own computer screens and begin using. For that reason, and countless others, the beta release gave everyone at the company an enormous boost. For all its intimacy, however, this scene had a cosmic scale. A machine had been built that was going to fundamentally change the computer, which had already changed everything. For the moment, however, beyond the enthusiasm of the cybernauts, not much attention was being paid. That would change soon enough.

With Rosanne Siino walking reporters through the office and sending out press releases about everything we did, there'd been a consistent low buzz about the company following the flurry of publicity when I'd hired Marc and the Mosaic crew. But the beta download had caught the attention of computer-savvy reporters; now we had actually produced something, and since we'd improved upon a browser that already had six hundred thousand users (with one hundred thousand more downloading the NCSA version in the month of September), we had earned our right to be thought of as bona fide news. Nine days after the beta went out, an article appeared in *Business Week* under the headline FROM THE MAN WHO BROUGHT YOU SILICON GRAPHICS... The obligatory "offbeat" business magazine portrait photo showed me smiling through a tank of brightly colored tropical fish. Lou Montulli had set up the tank in the office, then trained an unblinking video "fish cam" to send images out over the Internet—a funny and novel idea at the time which has led ultimately to women giving birth in living color on the Net and a Swiss farmer named Kaspar Gunthardt offering anyone who cares a twenty-four-hour pictorial record of his cows. The article described the Mosaic Communications plan to "tame cyberspace" as "wildly ambitious," and pointed out, almost as an aside, that with the right software the Web "could make the Internet a mass medium for home shopping, banking, and a host of other services." Best of all, a user of the new Mosaic Netscape browser was quoted: "It blew us all away." The nerd's ultimate compliment! Amen.

The writer also pointed out that as many as ten other companies had bought licenses to commercialize the original NCSA Mosaic. The question implicit in the article was whether we could establish Mosaic Netscape as the industry standard, in which case we "could be the Gutenberg press of cyberspace." A marketing VP from Spyglass was quoted as saying there were already hundreds of thousands of free copies in use, so "we don't think Mosaic Communications will be able to set a standard."

I assume he hadn't been one of the people who had downloaded 0.9, or he'd have known that with Mosaic Netscape we had already set the standard. But his relatively mild comment masked crosscurrents of seething resentment that had been building up under the surface since the summer. When Larry Smarr, director of NCSA at the University of Illinois, made Spyglass its master licensee, with the right to sell sublicenses for what was called Enhanced NCSA Mosaic software, I felt that the move was something more than "just business." Spyglass was an unlikely company to handle a technology that showed every sign (to those who could interpret such signs) of being a huge phenomenon. That indicated to me either that Smarr severely underestimated the potential, or that he wanted to undercut the work being done by graduates—Marc and Co.—whom he considered disloyal (or insufficiently obedient).

Over the course of the summer and into the fall, we had been getting reports that people at the university were privately complaining about Mosaic Communications planning to do business with what they considered legally the intellectual property of NCSA. This was crap, of course. Short of giving Marc and the others lobotomies, I couldn't very well erase everything from their minds that they'd ever learned about how to program a browser. But at my insistence, they had, of course, started over again completely, so totally rewriting Mosaic that not a line of code was taken from the original version. But at this point in our development, with letters of intent being written by prospective corporate customers, we were vulnerable to any kind of negative publicity. The slightest rumor that we might be facing a legal challenge could kill us, so I began to have some very bad feelings about Larry Smarr's intentions.

I knew I had to head this off before any of the private mutterings became public complaints, or even legal threats. Any belief on a potential customer's part that we were selling purloined goods and might face a protracted court fight would stop any deal dead in its tracks. MCI would pull out and everything we had in the pipeline would dry up. The effect for us could be very widespread. I had begun negotiations with several Japanese media and telecom companies—a tough market, often left until later by companies with global designs, but one that I felt at home in. The merest tremor of impropriety would bring those talks to a standstill. In other words, no deals, no cash, no customers. And the company's cash-burn rate would peel the paint off the walls.

At this point I did a little soul-searching about my relationship with Larry Smarr. I had a lot of respect for him, and considered him a friend, at least in the collegial, academic sense. As I pointed out earlier, I had been supportive of NCSA, which was unquestionably one of the most important computer science education centers in the world, and the university had given me an award. I began to wonder, and wonder still, if the looming storm might have been nothing more than a quick-moving summer squall if I'd simply been more diplomatic. I felt strongly, after meeting Marc, that the way the original Mosaic group had been shunted aside at NCSA was not the way a university organization should operate. But when Marc and I went to Urbana-Champaign to hire the programmers, I might have made one of those pro forma gestures that can, in the corporate world, turn back wrath (and lawyers). "Hey, Larry, how are you? I'm here on campus to interview some of your best and brightest. How about getting together for a drink." Or words to that effect. That kind of gesture wouldn't have changed the reality that I was spiriting off several young men who the university would eventually realize, far too late, were special talents. (NCSA's primary concerns were supercomputer applications, as its name stated, not small stuff like browsers. I'd been told that Smarr didn't know anything about Mosaic until, on a visit to Washington, a friend brought it up on a computer screen to show it to him. Apparently he was surprised to hear it had been created in his own backyard.) But some little professional nod to ceremony might have blunted the resentment that seemed to fuel what came later.

With the hope that "better late than never" would apply in this case, I sent Smarr a note toward the end of August. Rumor had it that the university might demand we pay a per-copy licensing royalty for our software just as other companies were doing through agreements with Spyglass. That wasn't about to happen, ever. We had created an entirely new program, faster and better in every way than what Marc and Eric had originally written. We'd done that without referencing or using any of the old code. Even if we hadn't, there was a big question about whether or not NCSA actually owned Mosaic. After all, Marc was an undergraduate doing part-time hourly-wage work and hadn't signed any agreement that surrendered the rights to his own work. (Eric had been an employee, but deciding who did what would prove to be a legal challenge.) Furthermore, Mosaic itself was based upon public-domain code written at CERN. Notably, in accepting an award it received for Mosaic, NCSA had ignored Marc's central role in the project. Now it seemed ready to claim he was capable of re-creating it somewhere else.

In any event, I wanted to avoid the issue if possible, because I didn't think anyone would emerge in good shape if we went to war on the confused (and increasingly bloody) battlefield of intellectual property. A certain combative tone had already been established that I was now trying to defuse. Smarr and I had already had a few e-mail exchanges, faux-friendly in the manner of people who know that it's just a matter of time before they'll be coming to blows. But I'd actually suggested to him that if we could forge some working relationship, he might chair a technology advisory board for us. I told him that when NCSA designated Spyglass as the relicenser of the original Mosaic, he'd backed the wrong horse, and said, in so many words, that really all he had accomplished was to energize my company, "with funding of $20 million plus the original team that wrote the program, plus me and the team of experienced managers I am recruiting," to kill Spyglass. In this note I also took him to task for failing to give Marc the credit he deserved. At the end of this e-mail, I mentioned for the first time the reports we'd had from other companies that "someone, either at NCSA or at Spyglass, has implied that we are doing something improper having to do with intellectual property. . . ." I stated emphatically that no one at Mosaic Communications had ever had in their possession since leaving the university any of the source code written at NCSA. I also said that I would have no option but to take legal action if we ascertained that any of Smarr's people or Spyglass were making that kind of claim.

As I read this note now, I can still feel the growing anger at what I considered an arrogant betrayal of some of the best graduates Illinois ever produced. (Within the first two months, we had hired twelve University of Illinois graduates, not all of them NCSA workers, but all of them excellent.) All in all, it was not the kind of note to forge a cozy relationship. In a side note to Marc, I said: "I believe [Smarr] is potentially in deep trouble, because I can't conceive that the University will accomplish getting ongoing revenues from Mosaic. It's just too simple a program to duplicate in functionality. If we did it in four months without using their code, another smart company can do the same. What a shame for them."

Much of the basis for my dismay toward Larry results from my own experiences while a professor at Stanford. Sun Microsystems was formed right under my nose, with me in charge of the DARPA contract that funded Sun. If I had behaved like Larry, I would have tried to inhibit them. I was, after all, forming Silicon Graphics at the same time, based in part on some of the same technology, and Sun and SGI were to be competitors.

Perhaps taken aback by my aggressive tone, Smarr responded briefly, after returning from his vacation, and seemed to want to avoid problems. Or so I thought. In late August, I sent another long e-mail, including a capsule version of my philosophy about how universities and companies ought to relate:

Date: Wed, 24 Aug 94
To: pls@ncsa.uiuc.edu (Larry Smarr)
From: jim@mcom.com (Jim Clark)
Subject: Re: Greetings
Larry:

Thanks for your response. I'm happy that you and the University do not consider what Mosaic Communications is doing to be improper. As I reflect on the start-ups of HP, Viacom, SUN, MIPS, SGI, Varian Associates, Cisco Systems, etc. out of Stanford, I realize there is no fixed model. Always, however, these companies were founded by the people who did the initial technology work at the University, and Stanford encourages the start of such businesses. The actual rewards to Stanford are not [always immediately] tangible, but they are nonetheless real—usually in the form of endowed chairs, buildings, equipment, and money. Actually, my model for interaction with you and the University of Illinois is not well formed. I initially felt that getting you to chair our technology advisory board was a good way to start, but I wonder if you'd like us to do something else. I do consider that the company owes its start to you and the environment you built there. Also, all of the employees from there do feel a sense of gratitude to the University, NCSA, and to you.

The reason for [our] not licensing NCSA Mosaic is that Marc and the team felt that there were fundamental problems with the implementation that would require a rewrite anyway. (They have achieved a factor of 10X speed improvement by rewriting, so maybe they were right.) So they didn't see the point in licensing. And I believe Marc is actually of the opinion that what he did there does not belong to the University, anyway, since he did it as an undergraduate student and did not sign an employment agreement.

This is not the point, however, because I want to keep good relations with you and the University, so we have been careful not to infringe copyrights in order to avoid specific royalties. This is the same as a company like Microsoft, which never pays royalties on any commonly used software—they just write their own. And incidentally, they would do the same with NCSA Mosaic.

Would you consider it appropriate for Mosaic Communications to donate some stock to the University, or to NCSA? Rather than money; at this point in our young life, this is easier than money. This would be done freely, but with no obligation, because as I said, we are not using any of the copyrighted technology.

I think the team here would support a gesture of this type if you were receptive—because they want to show their gratitude for what you and the University did for them. They would also welcome your public support of their company, since for the most part they currently feel that you and the University agents would rather see them fail than be successful, and they do not believe there is a rational basis for this on your part. Thus, these young guys are confused. They don't mind competition—that's not the point. It's just that they are confused by the apparent behavior of the administrators you've hired, and thus indirectly they are confused by you.

Sincerely,

Jim Clark

Though I showed Marc this letter and he didn't object (particularly), I was, of course, completely inventing this magnanimous attitude for the programmers. Aleks and some of the others have told me that, at this point, they didn't hate their alma mater—though that feeling would eventually change—but "gratitude" was certainly a quantum leap beyond the cool neutrality they felt. But whatever it took, I wanted to get past this potential roadblock.

On August 26, I got an e-mail note back that seemed friendly, if noncommittal:

Jim—thanks very much for your thoughtful and generous proposal. I, like you, am unclear on what would be the best way for NCSA or the University to officially relate to Mosaic Communications. I am not sure whether to think in terms of money (or stock) or in terms of research efforts. Let me knock these ideas around inside NCSA and with some of the top University people in the next week or two (University is just starting up this week) and see if I can come up with some ideas to send back to you.

This sounded unthreatening enough, but also unconvincing. In fact, it sounded like just what it was: a stall. And I had a business to run. Not many men can turn the other cheek convincingly. Technology reporters and columnists in various publications had begun to sense that trouble was brewing, and their articles no doubt raised the temperature. At the beginning of September, a story in the *Dallas Morning News*, in announcing the university's alliance with Spyglass, named several of the companies that had licensed Mosaic. The article went on to say, "There will also be an unlicensed super-strength Mosaic from many of the original developers." The writer pointed out that we had started from scratch on the next generation of the browser, and pointedly mentioned that we'd hired a "forensic engineer" to make sure there was no violation of NCSA code. That expert, one of a rare new breed of computer-age investigator/analysts, was Andrew Johnson-Laird, one of a team we had begun to assemble to strengthen our position against the university should worse come to worst.

At this point, though I didn't have a particularly good feeling about the adversarial circling Smarr and I had begun, I was so heavily engaged in the details of starting a business, both major and mundane, that I let myself believe this situation would resolve itself before reaching a flashpoint. There was nothing complicated about it, so with what may have been a mixture of rationality, optimism, and denial, I decided that we wouldn't have any trouble clearing things up if my approach didn't work. Perhaps I wasn't quite so sanguine. I did take the great American precaution, bringing the law firm of Brobeck, Phleger and Harrison into the loop, and here I got lucky.

Robert Barr was the lawyer most closely involved with the day-by-day overview of the growing legal problem, and he was uniquely well-suited to the task. Barr, a man with a dark beard and an intense, competitive attitude, had graduated from MIT in 1969 with a degree in electrical engineering (the degree most computer types took before computer science became a major). He then went to law school at Boston University. After finishing, he realized that a lawyer with an engineering background was more or less doomed to be a patent attorney, which is about as unglamorous as lawyers get. So he took a job teaching at Berkeley, then spent seven years as a programmer at a Silicon Valley company. At which point, the increasingly contentious subject of intellectual property and patents had taken on a new luster in the Information Age. Not many lawyers had the background to understand the complications of the new generation of software lawsuits, so Barr began practicing law again.

Nothing much happened during September, so I began to think Larry Smarr had seen the light. But in the frenetic days leading up to the beta launch, the problem resurfaced. More potential customers were telling our salespeople they'd heard we might have a legal problem. On October 3, a few weeks before our beta release, I sent a note directly to the chancellor of the University of Illinois making an offer I figured they couldn't refuse: We would give them access to the source code of our browser, allowing a review by outside experts to prove that not one line of code in our Mosaic replicated any of the code in the original version, in either structure or form, but only in function. Our forensic engineer had run both programs through his own analysis, which compared the two line by line, so I was sure that an examination of the code would end, once and for all, any intellectual property dispute.

My letter was forwarded to the chancellor of the Urbana-Champaign campus, Michael Aiken. Again, his response seemed friendly enough, and he stated a willingness to let experts examine the code. He also mentioned wanting to discuss "related areas of concern," among them the use of the Mosaic name. Since we had built an entire company around that name, this set off an alarm bell, but for the moment I let it pass. Once the issue of infringement and other problems were resolved, he would, he said, be ready to discuss my proposal to donate stock. What a guy! At the end of the letter, he said he was involving the university's vice chancellor for research, Richard C. Alkire, and a couple of other high potentates. Having spent a considerable part of my career laboring in the flinty vineyards of academia, my hopes didn't exactly soar when I saw this.

About a week later, on October 12, a letter arrived by fax from Vice Chancellor Alkire. The veneer of diplomacy had suddenly vanished; the gloves were off. The university had decided that the possibility of infringement was significant enough to "warrant a proper solution." Of course, I thought I'd already offered a proper solution, both in the form of a donation of stock (a good-faith gesture I didn't have to make) and the chance for them to look at our code. Notably, when he wrote the words "University Mosaic programs," he affixed the ™ mark, and added an accusation that we were "promulgating false and misleading information" about their browser. When people start using words like "promulgating," you know this isn't going to be the beginning of a beautiful friendship. Alkire finished with the most maddening idea of all. He urged us to get a license from Spyglass: "I have discussed such a license arrangement with Mr. Doug Colbeth, president of Spyglass, and he has assured me that Mosaic Communications would receive terms equally favorable to their other licensees."

Of course, just a few days later, we would send out the beta version of our browser, prompting people in the business to say NCSA Mosaic, ten times slower than ours, was effectively dead. But at that moment, the University of Illinois had lost the chance to make a pact with us that would have proved immensely profitable. The idea that I would approach a company like Spyglass to license a technology we had already left in the dust would have been funny if it hadn't been so infuriating. Nevertheless, I flew to Chicago and had a meeting with Colbeth in O'Hare Airport. Though we stayed cordial, we got nowhere. Colbeth asked that we change the company name, which I wasn't ready to do, so I told him we weren't likely to do so. He also asked that we join the "other licensees" to Mosaic through Spyglass. Because he insisted that we pay a minimum per-copy license of fifty cents, this was simply not going to happen because we planned to allow free downloading of the beta, and paying a per-copy royalty would cost a fortune if we generated a large market share, which in the end would mean Microsoft would ultimately win the forthcoming battle.

On the thirteenth of October *The Wall Street Journal* ran a story laying out the basics of our plan to release the beta version of our new browser for free. The article included Marc's estimate that our software would run ten times faster than any version of Mosaic then in use. These were the kinds of signals that must have driven the people at Spyglass, and NCSA—to which it paid a royalty on each sale—crazy. The companies that had so far licensed the enhanced version of the original program had been predicting sales of 12 million copies, and— in a business haunted by obsolescence—nothing could be worse than the news that what they had bought was about to be consigned to the buggy-whip bin of history.

After the beta release, the situation deteriorated further. Up until then, we'd been telling potential customers and reporters that our software would be superior to other browsers either on the market or heading for market. Naturally, we focused on our advantages over the older version of Mosaic, which was relatively well known, and emphasized that it was our team that had created the software. But without a product to show, we could be just another bunch of hucksters selling what one critic has called "Silicon snake oil." Now, overnight, Mosaic Netscape was a fact, and it lived up to and beyond our promises. Until then, Spyglass had one thing going for them, a single business argument: We have Mosaic. Now Mozilla, our Mosaic-killing Godzilla, ruled, and that self-perceived advantage evaporated, as I'd always known it would. With it went any willingness on their part to accept my offer to have independent experts compare our code to theirs. Incredible! Now they did not even want to know if we had copied their code and actually violated their intellectual property. I can only speculate, of course, but I imagine that Spyglass's feeling was "We can't compare the code, because if there's no copying and no similarities, we'll have no way to stop them from winning. And it is ten times faster than ours! Our business model is out the window!"

At the end of October, an elaborate description of the face-off surfaced in a trade publication called *WEBster*. After mentioning that University of Illinois officials had sent letters to publications insisting that editors refer to their software by its trademarked name, NCSA Mosaic, the writer referred to "potential legal moves to reinforce its software copyright and trademarks for Mosaic." Then, at last, Smarr sounded the charge: "It's very straightforward. There are twenty companies with licenses, so this family of companies thinks it very important that the University of Illinois defend its intellectual property rights." At the second annual World Wide Web Conference in Chicago, Smarr gave the keynote address, in which he said, "Web citizens are pretty unforgiving about people who take and don't give back to the community. You've got to play by the rules and you must be a part of this undertaking."

I'm still not sure who was taking and who was supposed to be giving, but when somebody says that others ought to play by the rules, you can be pretty sure the rules he means are his. I guess being part of the undertaking meant making a deal with Spyglass to license software we'd just made a joke of. The article about the keynote speech had been forwarded to one of our sales executives from a customer who said he was concerned.

It was time to unleash the lawyers.

As tensions grew in mid-October, our in-house counsel, Jennifer Persson, suggested that Robert Barr be on the premises for a couple of hours each morning to move along the effort to find a way out of the impasse. I agreed, and before long Barr was spending almost all his time at our crowded Castro Street headquarters, much of it in my small office going over tactical options with me, the increasingly agitated and pissed-off chairman. In fact, he became so much what basketball players call "my go-to guy" that he remembers many mornings, arriving around nine-thirty, seeing my face looming above the rows of cubicle partitions as I growled, "Where the hell is Barr?" I became obsessed with this problem.

I liked Barr, but my conversations with him weren't always satisfying. That is, his interpretation of the law didn't always support what I had thought of as our unassailable position. He and another copyright attorney had decided that the university probably did own Eric Bina's part of the Mosaic code, which Eric had created after signing an agreement that his output would be "work for hire." Since Eric had done everything from scratch on our program, like all the other programmers, this only meant we wouldn't be able to claim that the university couldn't defend intellectual property they'd never owned in the first place. I wasn't sure they were right about this, but that wasn't the heart of our case anyway. On the plus side, Barr and another outside lawyer, David Hayes, felt strongly that the agreement Eric and a couple of others had signed with NCSA entitled them to 50 percent of the royalties—a little club we could hide and use if things got nasty.

Jim Barksdale was not coming aboard for another three months or so. Customers were growing wary as more press reports came out about the controversy. Our business in Japan had come to a standstill—the Japanese actually have more engineers than lawyers, unlike the litigious

United States of America, so they didn't understand why a company was in a legal dispute with a prestigious university. . . . Maybe we had done something wrong? The burn rate was rising as we added staff. And though I had a hell of a lot to do in day-to-day hiring and management, I found myself totally preoccupied with the possibility of a lawsuit that—by delaying us even a crucial month or two—could end any chance we had to succeed. We would find it impossible to raise money with the specter of an intellectual property dispute with the team's alma mater.

I'm one of those men who would rather go down fighting than give in when I think I'm right (and I'll admit to thinking I'm right most of the time). Barr, however, was looking for ways to make small concessions in order to avert a major legal challenge. He was right, of course, but both Marc and I were so outraged at the university's assault on its own alumni that we would have dug in our heels on every point. One of the first clearly defined demands from the university was that we give up the name Mosaic. This was no small thing. Archie Leach may have been happy to become Cary Grant, and Bernie Schwartz may have been positively overjoyed to change his name to Tony Curtis, but Clark and Andreessen were furious at the idea of losing the company's birth name. Marc and Eric had invented that name. Pride and stubbornness aside, a name change was a major shift. The power of a brand has long been understood to be invaluable. A recent example of this came when Volkswagen and BMW competed to buy Rolls-Royce Motor Cars. After a titanic struggle, VW's bid of $780 million sealed a deal with Vickers, which owned the luxury automaker. The catch was that while Vickers owned the manufacturing plant and all the equipment for making the cars, an aerospace company called Rolls-Royce P.L.C. actually owned the rights to the name. Taking no time off to lick its wounds, BMW quickly bought the hallowed name—which was pretty much what VW wanted all along—for a mere $65 million. What Volkswagen got was an automobile company that needs fundamental change to produce a quality car able to compete in the luxury marketplace. But in a deal worked out with BMW, after the year 2002 they're not going to be able to call those cars Rolls-Royces. Clearly, BMW got the better end of the bargain.

The question of establishing a brand on the Internet is tremendously important. In the fight for Net market share in the business of selling books online, an established company like Barnes & Noble had no particular advantage over an upstart like Amazon.com because the venerable bookseller wasn't a Net brand. Though its founder, Jeff Bezos, had never sold a book before 1996, Amazon had been the first to establish an online turf and thus became the company to beat. Also, since it was a company created for the Net, Amazon understood better how to offer a superior product, but the point is the Internet is that rarest thing in American business—a whole new ballgame.

The situation was similar with Mosaic. As created (and named) by Marc, Eric, and Rob McCool (who wrote the server code), Mosaic had already become an established brand on the Web. Though we couldn't own the name exclusively, as Coca-Cola owned "Coke," it still made sense to have Mosaic in our company name—even though it was what lawyers call a "diluted mark." Despite the fact that our version was entirely new, Marc and the others, for reasons of authorship, and I, for obvious marketing reasons, hated the idea that anyone might be able to stop us from using the name. But I had already suspected we would have to give this name up, which is why I had the naming contest that led Greg Sands to suggest Netscape for the product name of the beta release—I felt we could easily change the name of the company to Netscape if necessary.

From a practical standpoint, a change would mean a new logo and a top-to-bottom revision of corporate identity. This might not sound like a big deal for a company just approaching its first hundred employees, but the crucial formation of recognition in the marketplace starts early, and from within. In other words, in a variation on the formula I mentioned earlier in this chapter, what a company thinks of itself is often how it ends up being thought of by consumers. At this point, we thought of ourselves almost unconsciously as Mosaic Communications. But all of our lawyers warned us that from the sound of quotes from Smarr and Colbeth in the press, a name change was exactly what they were going to demand.

What Marc and I thought of as our inalienable right, Barr thought of as a bargaining chip. "If you give them this," he said, "they might be a lot easier to deal with on the other stuff." We held off making any decision until we knew exactly what the university's beef was.

On Halloween, John Doerr, Barr, another lawyer named Bob Gunderson, and I flew to Chicago for a November 1 meeting with Colbeth and two of the university's lawyers. Barr had been to a Rolling Stones concert at the Oakland Coliseum the night before and was still in an upbeat mood. My state of mind was a darker, "I Can't Get No Satisfaction" mode. Obviously, it was important that we meet with the other side's lawyers to try solving the problem before the stakes went higher. But I was irked at the idea of having to go to them. It was as if we were acknowledging, if only geographically, that they were the aggrieved party. At least we'd settled on Chicago instead of Urbana-Champaign, but that was hardly neutral territory.

The meeting might result in a workable settlement, but if it didn't, we had planned a strategy of aggressive defense. There was no way to be sure if the university planned to file an intellectual property lawsuit against us. It would be terrible publicity for them to be suing their own graduates, but they might prefer, we thought, to stymie us than to appear noble. At this point, no doubt, the university was under pressure from Spyglass, and probably some of the companies that had licensed Mosaic through them. We had to operate on the worst-case assumption that they'd sue, which would mean we'd be going into a court of law, and when litigation occurs you can never predict what the outcome will be. One thing was clear, however: If we ended up with a jury trial in the state of Illinois, the odds were against us. So before leaving, we prepared our own lawsuit—specifically a declaratory judgment action. It didn't accuse the university or NCSA of doing anything wrong, but simply demanded that they examine our code to allow the court to determine whether it infringed on their intellectual property—something they should have wanted to do in any event if their intentions had been pure. We had someone from Brobeck, Phleger and Harrison ready to file the suit at the courthouse in San Jose if things went badly in the meeting. The important thing, therefore, was that we had to get the suit filed quickly, in case they had a similar plan. The time and date of filing is what determines where a suit is tried, not when the suit is actually served. We had the advantage of two time zones, meaning that when the clerk was closing up in Chicago, we still had a couple of hours in San Jose. What we had to do was keep the meeting going until four P.M. Central time. Each of us had a cellular phone and the number of the car phone of our contact. Short of a meteor strike on that block of downtown Chicago, one of us would reach our man in San Jose if the meeting ended without something close to a settlement.

We sat down with Colbeth, Marcia Rotunda, the university's counsel, and Phil Crihfield, one of their outside lawyers. From the start, things were tense, and it was clear to me we had made the trip for nothing. Their idea, I suppose, was that we were there to surrender, agree to their terms, and generally scuff around saying how sorry we were about everything. Rotunda seemed to have psyched herself up for a full-on confrontation. She was indignant, personally affronted at what this gang of Wild West California rustlers was attempting to steal from her university. She really looked as if she might leap over the table and start choking us. Barr knew after a couple of minutes that while she was part of the problem, she was definitely not part of the solution. As politely as possible, Barr steered the conversation away from her and toward Colbeth and Crihfield. At that point, it didn't seem to matter very much. When Barr, with an engineer's expertise and a lawyer's clarity, carefully explained how our forensic software specialist had determined that our code didn't infringe on the university's, Crihfield shook his head emphatically.

"We don't care about that," he said. "Those guys stole our trade secrets."

For just a second, Barr looked astonished, and I thought he might lose his legalistic cool.

"But Phil," he said, "there aren't any trade secrets to steal. This is a university."

That was the heart of the matter, and I waited to see what the answer to that would be.

"You are intrinsically in violation of our intellectual property because of the information in the heads of those who worked for and left the university," came the response.

The idea that students couldn't take knowledge from a university smacked of indentured servitude. We all knew this was going nowhere. These lawyers had been sent to make demands and accept our surrender, nothing else. Among the demands, to no one's surprise, was that we drop the name Mosaic.

We kept glancing at the clock on the wall of the room we were meeting in. Three-thirty, three thirty-five. I felt the way one of my former students might have felt waiting for class to end before being asked a question to which they didn't know the answer. Then the question actually was asked. Colbeth put it to us point blank: Are you going to agree to a license to Mosaic? He was really upset, because the word was out that Enhanced NCSA Mosaic, his only hope for a future, was grossly inferior.

Playing for time, we danced around the question, trying to put off saying no as long as possible. Three forty-five. Suddenly Colbeth jumped up and stormed out of the room. Crihfield and Rotunda, seeming as surprised as we were, stood up, gave us a last scowl, and followed him out.

I was furious at how the meeting had gone, and at the position I found myself in. How dare these bastards throw bogus demands in the way of a legitimate business that had in every way behaved legally, one that had as its partners and stockholders graduates of the university? I can't remember how we got out of the room, or how we got out onto the street, but there we were, four Californians shivering in light raincoats on a cold, windy corner in Chicago, frantically punching the buttons on our cellular telephones, trying to get a call through to a lawyer waiting outside the courthouse in the warm sun of San Jose. We had to assume that the university lawyers had been watching the clock, too, and that the abrupt ending could have been contrived to let them get to their court clerk in time.

Nobody could make a connection, and finally one of us, Barr, I think, pumped a handful of change into a public phone and shouted into the receiver, "Do it!" And the suit was filed.

By law, we now had forty days to serve the lawsuit or abandon it.

Missile armed.

PART FOUR

RUN TO DAYLIGHT
Spring/Summer 1995

15 Breakaway

C hanging the name of the company wasn't a major setback—after all, what's in a name?—but we had built a company identity, both publicly and among ourselves, so a change from Mosaic Communications—a name that by now had a substantial history—might have led to what amounted to an identity crisis. That didn't happen, which, I think, is a tribute to how much everyone believed in what they were doing. But as soon as it was clear that the University of Illinois was going to demand we call ourselves something to distance our company from NCSA Mosaic, which they'd trademarked, I had decided to cede the point before the issue was even officially raised. Once we'd made up our minds, we moved fast to make change.

Since we had called our browser software Mosaic Netscape, it was a logical step simply to drop the first word and use Netscape for the company name. I'm making this sound far less difficult than it was. Logical steps aren't always easy to take. There was a lot of anguish and anger involved, especially for the core employees who'd been associated with Mosaic since the beginning. But in the end, a company gives meaning to its name, not the other way around. It can be called anything—Smuckers, for instance, or Apple or Amazon—as long as it delivers. We went back to the San Francisco corporate identity firm of Landor Associates to design a new logo. For a brief period, we thought that by calling the company by the shorthand we used for e-mail—MCom—we might save the original logo, a circled *M* formed by the negative space between mosaic pieces of different sizes. But that had a generic feel to it that didn't satisfy anyone. (The world is so crowded with "dot coms" today that MCom would have become even more indistinguishable.) Hoping to hold on to some continuity, however, we tried hard to come up with an uncopyrighted name starting with *M*. Nothing worked. Which, after brainstorming and soul-searching, brought us to Netscape. Once that was decided, Landor came up with the now-well-known *N* against the backdrop of a starry sky, striding over a curved horizon. It was the first of the set of N logos they showed, and Marc didn't immediately like it, but I did. Even

Landor said it would become "tired" after a few years. In fact, it was a huge improvement over the earlier logo. The comet light-show that indicates up- and downloading on the Internet was the result of an online contest for the best idea. It has even entered the jargon of the Internet, as in "My computer is still cometizing."

On Friday, November 11, with the change a fait accompli, I used our usual all-hands meeting to announce the new name. Stepping up onto the stairs near my office, I explained briefly what we had to do and why. As I expected, the reaction, especially among the original Mosaic group, was angry. A collective groan went up at the news. Their goal may have been to kill Mosaic, but they'd been attached to that name for a long time, and they didn't like taking a hit from the university, even if it was largely symbolic. I tried to soften the blow by telling everyone that nobody had liked the name Silicon Graphics at first, either, but very quickly we got used to it. I explained that we owned the name Netscape and that we would establish it as the reference soon enough, while everyone would forget the name Mosaic.

The next day I sent an e-mail to everyone further describing exactly why the name was changed and the status of our legal situation. On the subject line of the e-mail address I wrote, "Netscape Communications Corporation."

Recently, the University asked us to change our name and stop using "Mosaic" in our company name. We thought about fighting them, but decided we should choose our battles carefully. We want no association with the prototype program written by our team when they were students. By changing our company name, we are eliminating one justification they have to fight us. Thus, Netscape Communications Corporation is our new name, and I encourage you to completely expunge the word "Mosaic" from your professional vocabulary.

So much for that. Barr told me months later that once we agreed to back off on the name and trademark, he could see ways to solve our problems. But at that point, it looked as if we were a long way from a deal. For the next month, I thought about very little else. And with everything hanging on the outcome, we certainly didn't bring in any money.

I did not mention to anyone that we had filed, but not served, a lawsuit for declaratory relief against Spyglass and the University of Illinois. I really wanted to tell the troops because they would then know that I was not capitulating to unreasonable demands from the university. But telling them would have increased the chances that the press would learn of the filing, which we were trying to avoid. The strategy we'd settled on was to hold off on serving the lawsuit until the time was up and we had to serve or lose our filing date, which would enable the university to sue us in Illinois. Bob Gunderson was worried that if we came right out and told the university lawyers we'd filed, they'd feel we'd thrown down the gauntlet and a prolonged confrontation in court might then be inevitable. "Once we serve this," he said, "things could get very serious." The following forty days were the most stressful period of my life, and real business development came to a standstill.

Moreover, I had still not convinced Barksdale to join as CEO, and I was worried that he would not join with this thing unsettled. I had gotten him to join the Board of Directors, however. I was on the phone with him often, and he agreed that it would give us a bad image to be in a public legal dispute with the university—we should try to settle the dispute. But he was busy with his AT&T/McCaw merger.

Gunderson wanted to do things subtly, dropping hints that would cause Phil Crihfield to check the court records. When he found our suit on file, he wouldn't have to let us know he knew, and we wouldn't have had to challenge him openly. He could move quickly toward a settlement while making it look as if this was the university's preferred solution. This way no one would lose face, but the suit would have the stimulating effect we intended it to have. In the meantime, we had to hope that no reporter would turn up the suit on a routine search through courthouse records and headline it in the business pages before the university could find out on their own. In fact, for all the noise that had been in the press up to that point, it is a miracle that the *San Jose Mercury* did not have someone routinely checking the courthouse filings, because it was easily discoverable. I lived for the next few days in total fear that this would happen.

I went along with this plan with little enthusiasm. If Crihfield and Rotunda were paying attention and managed to unearth the suit in a matter of days, or a week or two, then the strategy would probably work. But with every day that passed we came closer to disaster. The burn rate was not easily stopped, and we needed to close deals to re-start our cash flow. But that wasn't even the main problem. Until we could get this thing settled, we couldn't move ahead freely to sign up the customers who would give us the kind of market share I knew was crucial. As the clock kept ticking and we could detect no movement from the other side, it began to dawn on me that maybe we were playing chess while the university lawyers were playing checkers. Gunderson kept saying to me, "I can't understand this guy. I'm throwing him all these hints. All he has to do is have someone go to the San Jose courthouse and they'll find the filing." It was pos-sible, of course, that Gunderson didn't really understand the rules of checkers.

If I hadn't been so worried about the lingering effect of bad press, I would have insisted that we just go ahead and serve the damn thing. The newspapers and business magazines would have jumped on it, with unpredictable results, but we might have saved time and a hell of a lot of legal fees. I had a top litigator and a top intellectual property expert on retainer, and those fees were piling up—not the kind of drain you figure into a business plan. (In fact, this was preventing us from finalizing a solid business plan at all.) We had hired more people than I'd expected, especially in customer support, based in part on antici-pated business now on hold. This would lead to the company's first layoffs in December, not an unusual rite of passage in ambitious start-ups, which often outrun reality, but a very unhappy one nevertheless, especially coming during the holiday season.

At some point, we would do another round of funding by raising corporate money, but that couldn't happen as long as there was a legal dispute with the University of Illinois that we would have to disclose. In fact, one corporate investor in Chicago, the top man at the Tribune Company—very sharp on computer stuff and someone I really wanted with us—decided he couldn't work with us because his first loyalty was to the university. I could cover the growing financial gap for a while, but not forever. If we got into a true legal battle, it would be catastrophic for the company. In fact, we'd probably face Chapter 13. By this time I'd invested nine or ten months of my life and $5 million of a decidedly finite personal fortune in the company. If this all came to an aborted end, I wasn't about to let myself, Marc, and all the others be the only ones who ended up suffering.

Frankly, part of me wanted to slander the university in the press, making them look like the biggest dirtballs around. I'm not sure that, left to their own devices, the top people at Illinois, or even Smarr, would have behaved the way they were behaving, but they'd drifted into a kind of fantasy land. Some people lower down in the organization had convinced the university to license its software with the idea that it could build a big, Silicon Valley–type company and perhaps plant the seeds of yet another "next Silicon Valley" in Urbana-Champaign. What they didn't understand was that the real place had been around a long time—a concentration of talent and money that inevitably attracted more talent and money, adding constantly to its powerful gravitational pull. Had I decided to start my company in Urbana-Champaign, Illinois, I doubt I could have gotten Jim Barksdale to hire on, or been able to tap into a vein of seasoned managers and executives like Tom Paquin and Mike Homer. A special kind of symbiosis exists in any region where a critical mass of a given business develops, and it doesn't reach that point quickly or simply because a dedicated group of boosters work hard to make it happen. For years, people and companies have tried to shift the center of publishing out of New York, and they have never succeeded. Likewise for movies in Los Angeles. The same applies to the hegemony of Silicon Valley in technology. Other major companies are headquartered elsewhere, of course, but whether it's Route 128 near Boston or the heavily hyped "Silicon Alley" in Manhattan, alternative sites for a new tech mecca never seem to take on the aura and power of the real thing. Such centers of certain businesses—Detroit, Hollywood, Manhattan, to name three—are there, to a certain extent, simply because they're there, self-energizing and self-sustaining breeder reactors of talent. In late summer 1998, even Microsoft announced plans to build a major new facility in Silicon Valley—an area about as filled with hostiles for the Redmond firm as the Little Big Horn was for Custer.

What really infuriated me was the difference between the ideal way a university ought to act and what some officials at the University of Illinois were actually doing. This is a famous and powerful school, responsible for all sorts of great computer technology. The university had never profited from any of what they'd done—which is as it should be for a nonprofit organization, after all—and I think they saw this as their chance for a real home run. I don't know how closely Larry Smarr was involved in the controversy, but I know he could have brought it to an end quickly if he'd done the right and rational thing at the right time. He ought to have said, "Look, this just isn't kosher. These young men were my students, and I'm not going to let them walk away from this university feeling like they can't take the knowledge they acquired and make use of it." Instead, he let a couple of lawyers argue that we were intrinsically violating the intellectual property of the university by taking away knowledge. Students taking away knowledge, of all things!

Smarr lacked clarity on two key points. He failed to realize the importance of my being a businessman who had created one highly successful start-up in SGI and had a good shot at creating another. And he seemed unable to recognize what truly remarkable talents his own students were. As an academic, he certainly should have been able to see that. If he'd understood those two things, Smarr would have seen that there was a lot more to be gained by taking credit for Netscape than by taking credit for Spyglass. All he had to do was call me and say, "Hey, Clark, this is terrific. If there's anything I can do, let me know. We really encourage our guys to go out and make this thing commercial, because we're never going to be able to do that here." He would have been on our board of advisers, the university would have had a sizable block of stock, and Marc and the others would have started feeling better about the place. Instead, he made Spyglass—a company with absolutely no involvement in the creation or implementation of Mosaic—the master licensee of their creation, and he did this after we started our company! Who knows where Larry's logic went off? Maybe he thought he really could make a business there. Maybe he'd begun to think that he deserved credit for Mosaic. He's a smart guy, and I'd always thought of him as a good guy. But something or someone caused him to lose sight of the logical and ethical resolution.

*　　*　　*

On November 7, after we had filed but not served the lawsuit, I made one more attempt to defuse the situation in a three-page letter written directly to Chancellor Aiken.

Dear Chancellor Aiken:

This is a final attempt to establish a dialog between you and me as heads of our respective organizations. The behavior of the University and its agents [I hated even using the word Spyglass], by threatening litigation with Mosaic Communications and impugning our integrity to our customers, has interfered with the lawful business activities of our company. Please set aside some time to read this letter yourself, as your response is required to avoid what will imminently become a legal dispute that will develop into a media circus that neither of us can control.

As Chairman and Founder of Silicon Graphics, I was personally responsible for supporting your institution and NCSA with in excess of a million dollars of donated equipment. I have no desire to do anything other than express support and respect for your organization, but the business objectives of NCSA articulated by your attorneys at our meeting last Tuesday create a serious conflict of interest for the University.

I then went on to review in detail the original purpose of NCSA, pointing out that the majority of its funding had been provided by the National Science Foundation. I added a capsule history of what Marc, Eric, and Rob McCool had done in creating Mosaic, emphasizing that "from the beginning this was a 'skunk works' project, unassigned by faculty or staff of NCSA." I went over my meeting with Marc in California, our brainstorming sessions, and the ultimate decision to build a better Mosaic. I continued:

Within five days of the original idea, our company was founded. We recruited programmers from the University of Illinois, the University of Kansas, the University of California at Berkeley, General Magic, Lucid, Oracle, Sun Microsystems, and Silicon Graphics.

Around the beginning of June, the team began the design and im-
plementation of a client-server system. It always has been and al-
ways will be an independently developed system. We issued strict
rules about not referring to NCSA Mosaic source code on the Net,
and told former NCSA people to destroy any copies of NCSA Mo-
saic they had in their possession on leaving the University. Along
the way we hired three other alumni of the University of Illinois—
all former NCSA workers who had moved to California before we
formed the company. Later, Rob McCool's brother, Mike McCool,
also asked for a job at the company and was hired. All these people
have significant ownership stakes in the company.

I went on to describe the process through which we'd come to name
the company Mosaic Communications (after discovering that another
California company had our original choice, Electric Media). Though
expressing surprise that NCSA or the university would try to keep us
from using this name, I let him know that we were changing our name
"as quickly as practicable."

Then I got to the real meat:

According to Ms. Marcia Rotunda of the University in our No-
vember 1 meeting, NCSA is a "business" entity of the University,
and NCSA views that Marc and I were aiming to disable the busi-
ness objectives of NCSA by targeting its employees for recruitment.
This was the first time a University representative has said anything
like this. I have never considered NCSA to be a business, and I
believe the University has an inherent conflict if it intends to op-
erate NCSA as a business. If I had known NCSA was a business,
I would never have donated Silicon Graphics equipment. I have
always viewed NCSA as part of a public university supported with
the public funds from the National Science Foundation and other
government agencies.

The University has claimed rights to the creations of these stu-
dents and staff member and has chosen to commercialize these cre-
ations. These students have not disputed the University's claim, nor
have they yet asked that the University share the royalties it derives

from their creations. [This was a reference to our lawyers' view that the students were entitled to 50 percent of the royalties derived from Mosaic, a right that has not yet been exercised.]

We have been informed by your outside attorney that the University considers these former students, staff member, and our company to "inherently be in violation of the University's intellectual property rights." But we have honored the intellectual property rights of the University and all third parties. Moreover, our claims are easy to verify by examination, as we have offered to the University many times. At one point you recommended pursuing a third-party examination of our source code to verify our claims.

The University alumni who formed this company are angry that the university where they were educated is now trying to prevent them from working in areas directly related to their education unless they are willing to pay a "tax." This is the very word used by the University's designated business agent, Mr. Colbeth of Spyglass, in referring to the way our company should view a license to NCSA Mosaic.

I realize the University's relationship with Spyglass is constraining, but if you establish that we are not in violation of the University's intellectual property, the University can be free of this dispute even if Spyglass chooses to continue it. The University has the power to establish this by proceeding with a third-party comparison of the programs in dispute.

Your response to my letter of October 3 in which you agreed to proceed with an external examination conveyed the attitude I would expect from such a respectable institution as the University of Illinois. But I am baffled by the trend of our relationship since that letter. The alumni of your institution who founded our company are indebted for the education they have received, but they are confident in their rights to do what they are doing, and I am equally confident in backing them in these rights.

A university is a center of reason, and I am a reasonable man. You and I have the responsibility and authority to resolve this. Doing so can yield a fruitful relationship that we can all enjoy. Not doing so will yield nothing. I respectfully request that the two

of us meet immediately and resolve this dispute without further resort to the legal system.
Sincerely,
James H. Clark
Chairman and CEO
Mosaic Communications

By now I realized that, despite my reference to his authority, the Chancellor was no longer in control of this decision. Unfortunately for the university, it had ceded the authority in this situation to Colbeth, who desperately wanted to stop us from putting our browser into the market against his. Spyglass had nothing to gain from an amicable settlement, and everything to lose. My letter had no effect, and it seemed inevitable that we'd end up in court. Meanwhile, as the lawyers traded calls and memos, time kept passing. Every exchange seemed to take three or four days, with Spyglass always dragging their feet, because they were smart enough to know that our business was in limbo. The software development group at Netscape kept working hard toward the release of 1.0, despite their growing anger at the impasse, but they still did not know about the lawsuit. The business side was stuck, unable to get crucial deals closed. MCI lawyers were monitoring everything, "looking over our shoulders," as Barr put it. Since they were our only source of revenue so far, we couldn't very well object. Netscape was like an accident victim paralyzed from the neck down. Our brain was working overtime, but all for nothing.

In mid-November, in a story on a cooperative alliance between Mosaic Communications and First Data Corp., a credit card processor, to facilitate Internet purchases using cards, *The Wall Street Journal* mentioned for the first time our name change "under pressure from the University of Illinois." After the article reported on our release of Mosaic Netscape, it added, "The university responded by raising the specter of legal action to enforce its trademark rights." Nothing was mentioned about intellectual property, but legal action was still legal action, capable of casting a shadow of doubt.

I felt like a caged lion, watching our momentum vanish, unable to concentrate on the real work of carrying our message to potential paying customers and corporate investors. Like most entrepreneurs, I revel in forward motion, the faster the better, and detest running in place. Not the least of the results of this situation was that I was driving everyone crazy, and bringing my secretary, D'Anne, to the brink of tears on a more or less regular basis. But Barr and Gunderson kept grinding away at the problem, looking for concessions that would satisfy the other side without hurting us further. We lived in constant fear that the press would come upon the filing, which would have the same effect as serving it. But what we'd originally assumed, that the university lawyers would search the San Jose court records (as we'd searched the Chicago records the day after our ill-fated meeting), didn't happen. I couldn't wait any longer.

"Let's get this over with," I told the lawyers. "Let's find out what it will take to buy them off." I can't describe how crazy this made me, but they had us in a bind and we had to get out of it. So I offered the university sixty thousand shares of stock. They turned it down. They were obviously dragging their feet, working us over, putting more and more terms and conditions on the table. They got so nitpicking and ridiculous that they even demanded that we stop using our mascot Mozilla. Early on in this mess, the engineers had T-shirts made up that showed Mozilla (in the shape of Godzilla) crushing the NCSA building under its feet, and someone at the university must have seen someone wearing one at a conference. I was already facing growing unrest among Marc and the original programmers over what they considered the university's extortion, so I didn't even mention this last demand. Mozilla would have stomped on me if I had.

The entire month of November passed with offers and counteroffers moving back and forth at what seemed to me a glacial pace. I spent hours on the phone with Barr Thanksgiving afternoon. What he remembers most about the conversation was the Eric Clapton CDs he could hear playing in the background. I was doing everything I could to relax, and not having much luck at it.

The fortieth day arrived, and it appeared that we had to serve the lawsuit. If we had not, there was always the chance that the university really did know about our lawsuit on file, and with its expiration, they could have filed one, causing us to have to fight theirs in Illinois. Paranoia reigned supreme in those days, with endless speculation about whether they knew about our lawsuit on file. We served the suit. Then we waited for the public battle to begin, and I felt the company was lost.

Barr sent a note to Crihfield, their outside attorney, trying to mention the suit casually, as if he surely must know about it already. As we'd feared, the Chicago lawyer blew up, and we waited tensely to see what the response would be after he reported to his clients.

I'd like to have been able to eavesdrop on the conversations that followed. University officials had three choices. They could go on protecting Spyglass, or they could file a suit against us, then take the press and public relations fallout for attempting to sabotage their own graduates. They could dodge our suit by agreeing to examine our code, effectively ending any leverage they had. Or they could come to terms as we had been proposing and let us move on.

I amused myself—not an easy task in those bleak days—by constructing imagined scenarios: "Who in the fuck signed this deal with Spyglass, anyway? We've got to settle this thing, fast. You tell Spyglass we're settling, period, and the hell with them if they don't like it." Until then, the university lawyers kept insisting that Spyglass had to be involved in any settlement. Suddenly everyone was ready to talk, eager to find a way out of an impasse that had blocked our progress for precious weeks. In effect, somehow Colbeth was taken out of the mix. Surprise, surprise! Barr was told by the lawyers on the other side not to worry about Spyglass; they'd take care of that.

Sometimes things really do end with a whimper. Within two weeks, on the twenty-third of December, we had a deal. Part of the agreement stipulated that none of the parties could get into the details of the settlement, hence, at this point, I can't describe the final terms. I can say, however, that had the university accepted earlier terms I had offered, they would have been far better off in the long run: They would have had money, support, endowed chairs, and most of all, a set of alumni that viewed their alma mater with respect rather than contempt. And they would have helped enable the success of Netscape, instead of its mortal enemy, Microsoft, who within two weeks of our settlement was given a license to Mosaic that required no, I repeat, *no*, per-copy royalties!

Incredibly, right up to the end, Crihfield was insisting that we give up Mozilla, like the Wicked Witch skywriting on her broom over Oz,

"Surrender Dorothy." I told Barr absolutely not. They were being downright stupid, and I had to show the original troops they had won something. Knowing that this would actually be a deal-breaker, Barr told him to forget it: "We're hangin' tough on the reptile, Phil." And then it was over.

Marc and his group were resentful at the thought of compromising with the university when they hadn't done anything wrong, and I didn't blame them. They would have resisted if I'd given them a chance. But we were burning around $1 million a month by this time, and a lot of that was my money. Unfairly, the boys tended to blame Barr, who had done a terrific job. They didn't realize that if we'd dug in and held out on principle, we'd probably have ended up with nothing. Later, when Barr signed an e-mail to Marc "The Man Who Saved Mozilla," the response came back addressed to "The Man Who Almost Lost Mozilla."

On many late nights I would tell Barr, "Someday, Robert, I'm going to write a book about all this, so people will know what we went through." Now I have. What Barr did, in a hundred small steps, was huge.

Accordingly, *The Wall Street Journal* announced in its Christmas Eve issue that Netscape Communications and the University of Illinois had settled a dispute about intellectual property. It was a quiet day of last-minute shopping and early business closings, so I doubt very many people even noticed the story. My wife, Nancy, and I and some of our friends were already in the clear waters off Cabo San Lucas on our boat *Spes Nostra*. It was a great Christmas present to end a truly harrowing, unbelievable year, and we were free at last. Now I had to get Barksdale signed up.

16 Magnetars and Momentum

In aerobatics is a maneuver called the Lomcevak, named after a Czech who once used it to win the unlimited category World Aerobatic competition. The pilot pulls from level flight up into a forty-five-degree climb, rolls over to knife-edge flight, the wings vertical and only the lift of the fuselage and the rudder keeping the plane on the 45. Then, with full power still applied, a fast push of the stick to the left front corner swaps the tail with the nose and the plane is momentarily flying backward. The plane continues tumbling end over end two or three times, tossing the pilot around a bit. When the tumbling stops, the pilot doesn't know which end is up, but in fact is usually in an inverted spin. That's the way I felt as the year ended in 1994.

Barksdale had still not agreed to join, the University of Illinois had finally settled my lawsuit but it cost a lot of precious time and money, the university and Spyglass had given to Microsoft what they would not give us (a license without a per-copy royalty), we had just laid off about twenty employees out of a hundred and twenty, and thanks to our inability to close deals and raise financing during the dispute, we had just over a million dollars left in our bank account. But in the coming days, Barksdale agreed to join, we suddenly began to get calls from corporate customers who wanted a license to use Netscape Navigator, and the press effused about our first real product. Just eight months after incorporation, we were finally a real company with real products and real revenues. The cash flow turned positive that month and we never looked back.

By the early spring of 1995, the mind-bending pace of Netscape time had us all in its grip. Alexander Pope once wrote, " 'Tis with our judgments as our watches, none go just alike, yet each believes his own." Everyone at the company felt that our watches were going at a pace far faster than those in the outside world, with our judgments set on fast-forward, too. The headlong rush that started nine months earlier had been blocked by NCSA, but they hadn't brought us to a stop on all fronts. While the lawsuit loomed, the programmers never stopped grinding out code. And while Microsoft would soon play its obstructive games with our development process on Navigator 2.0, sales and marketing didn't miss a step. In fact, at the end of a mild Northern California winter, business was growing so fast that keeping up with demand, not creating it, had become the problem. With around four hundred employees we had by this time outgrown our old Castro Street offices and had moved to a larger—though still anonymous—space on East Middlefield Road. In January, February, and March, the frightening cash-burn rate of the previous fall had been extinguished as sales increased dramatically. These weren't letters of intent, handshake promises to do business with us somewhere down the road, or deposits on future development, but what Mike Homer called "real revenues—you know, the kind that come when people actually pay you for your product."

The press had been fascinated by the company since its earliest days, anointing Marc "the next Bill Gates," and portraying me as a benign Svengali, or a highly magnetic mogul (a silly characterization). But at some point, I think, when there was a possibility that the confrontation with the University of Illinois might prove fatal to the company, journalists backed off. Between the burst of excited coverage that came with the beta release in October and the announcement of the settlement at the end of December, reporters remained interested but seemed wary. After all, no one wanted to tout a company as the second coming if it was never going to arrive. Back a few wrong horses in business journalism and your editor starts assigning you to cover Rust Belt stockholder meetings.

Once the threat of our untimely demise was lifted, press interest doubled, as if the settlement released a pent-up curiosity, like hydro-electric power generated by water held back by a dam. Rosanne Siino's magical mystery tours (though "magical mystical" might be more descriptive) were conducted for reporters on an almost daily basis. As winter segued into spring, visiting journalists walking in at our new offices saw a frantically active beehive of cubicles, already as wildly individualized as they had been on Castro Street, filled with pale young people driven by a heady combination of elation, anxiety, optimism, too little sleep, too much coffee, and an abundance of sheer excitement. Programmers were still sleeping under their desks, but now there were more desks. I think it must have been hard for any reporter to walk out of the Netscape offices onto the quiet streets of Mountain View without that hum in the brain that signals something big happening.

Not everyone got it, though. I think some reporters from the East Coast simply couldn't imagine, even in 1995, that anything momentous, or even worthy, could come out of: (1) an undistinguished suburban town in Northern California; (2) an office suite with the style of Bedlam; (3) a bunch of kids in shorts and T-shirts and crazy haircuts; (4) a company less than a year old that—to anyone reasonably skeptical—just might be selling the infamous silicon snake oil. After all, we were trying to make money on the Internet, and everyone knew that the Internet was "free." Even today, the huge importance of what happened in those antic offices isn't understood by everyone, including those who pay special attention to the history of technology. For instance, in a special issue of *Newsweek* published in the winter of 1995 devoted to "How an Explosion of Discoveries Changed Our Lives in the 20th Century," the editors laid out a timeline of significant inventions. Though the World Wide Web got its rightful place in 1990 (the only entry for that year), Mosaic and Netscape—which democratized and energized the Web—don't show up at all. The experts did, at least, acknowledge the first computer, ENIAC, and the bikini, two great breakthroughs invented in 1946.

But we had as much buzz as we could handle, and since buzz begets buzz, coverage accelerated along with business and revenue (and became a factor in a cause-and-effect dynamic). The effect of the rising tide of enthusiastic coverage was to ratchet up Netscape time even higher, and push us into the future faster than anyone anticipated. Like the sweet-smelling racing fuel pumped into competition cars and motorcycles, excitement is high-octane stuff.

The arrival of a veteran CEO added yet another attraction for reporters, guaranteeing even more press from January on. A kind of uncritical critical mass had built up that made Netscape radiate waves of increasing intensity, through computer and business publications and into the popular press. (It was this spillover that brought such unlikely celebrity treatments as Marc's appearance in *People* magazine, and eventually on the cover of *Time* with his bare feet.) In recent years, astronomers have identified rare celestial objects called magnetars, a variety of neutron star that produces bursts of magnetic radiation so powerful they can enter the earth's atmosphere from twenty thousand light-years away and strip atoms of their electrons. In 1995, in the cosmos of cyberspace, Netscape had become a magnetar. It was great fun to be on it, watching so many people squinting at its glare.

We had always understood that the Web and the Internet were global phenomena, and that awareness shaped our strategies; a lot of my travel during the previous nine months had been to Europe and Asia. I'd evangelized the Web at publishing houses, telecommunication companies, advertising agencies, and major banks, as well as to possible distributing partners who would resell our products. Wherever I went, people seemed to love hearing the Netscape story. As 1995 began, we were opening up offices almost everywhere I'd been. Eventually, we would have twenty-eight in Europe and thirteen in Asia. In January, with the university settlement behind us, I was onstage in Tokyo with twelve major, competing Japanese companies announcing that all of them were licensing Netscape Navigator. To lead our global operations, during the university turmoil I'd hired Todd Rulon-Miller as vice president in charge of international sales; Todd had previously worked as the sales executive with Next, the company Steve Jobs would sell to Apple. Todd then hired Didier Benchimol to head up European sales, and each was putting together a network of agents the CIA might envy. As anyone who has ever worked in Hollywood can testify, no one wants to give you money until someone else has. But once the first few people get on board, everybody else lines up. Well, Silicon Valley isn't Hollywood (not exactly), and Marc and I weren't Spielberg and Lucas, but the same rule seemed to apply. Once we had Navigator 1.0 plus two server products for communication and commerce on the market, and companies such as MCI and AT&T as customers, interest snowballed. Not long after he arrived, Barksdale laughed, saying, "This is the kind of business everyone dreams of—double the number of people answering the phone and the revenues double." The prevailing mood changed dramatically from "We're doomed" to "More feet on the street!" Things were so hectic that by May of 1995, when we recruited Lorna Bender from PeopleSoft to help expand our international operation, Rulon-Miller told her he wanted ninety distributors signed up in ninety days. And he wasn't kidding. (That goal proved too ambitious, but the actual number during the next three months ended up being a still-astonishing sixty.)

I was feeling great by this time. Most real entrepreneurs are restless by nature. If they weren't, they'd find themselves nice corporate corner offices and settle in for the long haul (even though today that long haul tends to be a lot shorter). They're not satisfied with the way things are, and their imaginations usually race ahead of the actual rate of change. At Silicon Graphics, I would have liked to move a lot faster, but aside from the endemic resistance to going in new directions, there were natural constraints. SGI was a manufacturing business, and when you're building things, you can only move so fast. The fastest-growing manufacturing company in history is Compaq, yet it took them five years to get to $1 billion in revenues. It took SGI four years to reach $40 million in revenues. In my working life, I'd never been able to find a process that echoed the velocity of my time spent in aerobatic planes and on motorcycles. Now I was moving at a speed that was unprecedented and exhilarating. Making software is almost friction-free. All you need is good computers and terrific brains. You're not held back by the manufacturing process, and though software can be boxed, shrink-wrapped, and put on retail shelves, we were much more interested in distributing over the Internet, thus accelerating past another braking point. Write the code, debug it, upload it: simplicity itself, almost like magic. I had gone from the speed of sound to the speed of light. Luckily for me, Marc Andreessen was totally comfortable with the idea of fast, faster, fastest. It was he who showed me what we could do if we revved the process higher and higher. He and I were perfectly matched, the only difference being that Marc may not have known quite as well as I that we were having the time of our lives.

Netscape was so hot that from the beginning of February I began traveling extensively again, in the U.S. and abroad, giving speeches and talks to audiences of potential customers. Though airline travel is rarely much fun, and spending the major part of my time away from home wasn't something I looked forward to, I really liked this part of the job. In fact, I felt like one of the itinerant Pentecostal preachers I'd seen in Texas when I was a kid, part showman and part shaman. I had a great message, and if I wasn't necessarily delivering my sermons to the converted, at least there was a tremendous interest in what I had to say. What I was describing was a true paradigm shift, and, in the form of Netscape's products, I felt as if I were offering the keys to an amazing new kingdom. The curiosity of my listeners was enormous. What is happening with the Web and the Internet? What does it mean for our business? How did Netscape come into being, and what is its strategy? How can you make money on the Internet? And then, sometimes, the really big question: Where is the world going? Since I'd already had my awakening on the road to Damascus, I wasn't shy about providing an answer. I won't repeat it here, because so much of what I said is already taken for granted.

To have any chance at success, a high-tech start-up needs the malleability of an amoeba. It has to change shape constantly, wrapping around new ideas and new possibilities until they're absorbed into its structure. Knowing that continuous shifting to be a virtue rather than a vice, I felt completely free to push the process by making claims about what we were going to do before I had the commitment of those at the company who would actually have to back those claims up. A start-up always has to be larger than life. It has to project the image that it's bigger than it actually is, not to fool investors or customers, but to create an outline to grow into. If marketing runs ahead, pushing the boundaries, motivated people will work their asses off to fill in behind those big ideas. I remember when one of those big ideas was brought up at a planning meeting. One of the programmers—I honestly can't recall who it was—shouted angrily, "That's just marketing bullshit!" To which Marc, who already had great business instincts, responded, "It's supposed to be marketing bullshit!"

The key factor, however, is that though marketing can lead a start-up (or an established company), it can never be the start-up. With some famous flameouts like 3DO and General Magic, big ideas and big promises were followed by very small accomplishments, a flaw that proved fatal to both. In a marketing age, you don't have to shut up, but you finally do have to put up.

One of the reasons I could spread the word on Netscape with such confidence was that the Web, strengthening us as we strengthened it, was proving to be a formidable ally. When Marc and I formed the company, the NCSA Mosaic browser had about a million users. When we introduced the Netscape beta, there were twice that, and the Web was the fifth largest source of the Internet's traffic. By mid-summer 1995, the number of users—most of them by now Netscape Navigator users—was around 10 million, both private and corporate, and the Web was the biggest single carrier of Internet information. Imagine that kind of growth in an older form like magazines or newspapers. If you can, you've got a more powerful imagination than I.

There was another reason for our optimism. The Internet could only improve as the telecommunications companies awoke and replaced or consumed the smaller Internet Service Providers (ISPs) that had proliferated like gerbils. After all, the phone and cable companies owned the digital infrastructure and they could meld it with other forms of telecommunications, such as telephone and television. To make a comparison with the early days of television, all this growth was happening while the Web was still in its black-and-white, hand puppets and fifteen-minute newscast stage. Netscape made possible all sorts of visual sophistication, but surfing the Web in the spring of 1995 was like watching the Brooklyn Dodgers on a grainy eleven-inch screen in the spring of 1952. If millions were already using the Web in this relatively primitive form, what would the numbers be when content caught up with the technology, and technology provided more bandwidth? Interestingly, we were already catching hell from old Internet hands for making things so inviting—"pleasurable," as *Wired* put it—that the Net was jamming up and slowing down. My answer was that increased bandwidth would come as soon as telecommunication companies realized this was a commercial medium people were willing to pay for, just as they got used to paying for cable television.

The academics and researchers who for so long had controlled the Internet with government funding resented this crass commercialization, believing that it would destroy a resource that rightfully belonged to them. They didn't seem to realize that it was precisely because the government was funding it that it *appeared* to be free. By mid-1995, the government began to transfer the operation of the Internet "backbone" to private industry. Even the government can only afford so much (before a taxpayer revolt), but an industry driven by profits and competition can afford as much as a market will pay. The father of the Ethernet, Bob Metcalf, who had become a widely read author after leaving academia, was openly prognosticating the collapse of the Internet because of all this new traffic, saying he would "eat his words" if it didn't happen by a certain time. A man of his word, he later literally ate a copy of the article in which those words were printed. This is funny now, but I had to live with a certain amount of ridicule for believing and preaching that the Internet and the Web are the future of all communications and electronic commerce.

Increasingly, as our programmers worked on new products, it became clear to all of us that the Web had the potential to become a kind of virtual operating system, providing users with much of what any established OS—Windows, for instance—could offer. To help facilitate this leap, Netscape had licensed Java, a new computer language developed by a group of people led by Bill Joy, the legendary technology visionary at Sun Microsystems. Although I had competed fiercely with Sun while at SGI, at John Doerr's encouragement, Bill and I had met at the restaurant Il Fornaio in Palo Alto in the fall of 1994 to discuss the new language they had developed. I was so impressed with what Bill told me that I asked Marc to meet with him, knowing that Marc had to agree. Afterward, Marc told me and others that Java was as revolutionary as the Web itself, and by integrating it into Navigator 2.0 we strengthened our position as a provider of a whole new kind of computing platform. If successful, there could be a new class of network-based applications that would be platform-independent—that is, the applications would work on the PC, UNIX workstations, or Apple computers with equal ease and without modification. What this mostly meant to software developers was that they would no longer be dependent upon Microsoft for the Applications Programming Interfaces (APIs) that are essential for the development of applications software. This independence would disable Microsoft's control and well-known behavior of withholding APIs for Windows from companies competing with them. (A fact that Netscape became acutely aware of in the next few months, but more about that in a later chapter.)

Even though we had an impressive positive cash flow early in 1995, we decided to finish up the Series C financing, the round that seeks investment from corporations. The previous fall, when our situation was far less robust, I had approached Frank Quatrone, the managing partner in charge of investment banking for Morgan Stanley in San

Francisco. I discussed our rudimentary business plan with him and asked him to help us put together a private placement. This would resemble the red herring that preceded a public offering, but it wouldn't be as official, being for private investors. The memorandum simply was meant to give corporate investors a feel for the company and a few financial projections. I went to Morgan Stanley because they had taken Silicon Graphics public, and I really liked Dick Fisher, the chairman of Morgan Stanley, because he had taken genuine interest in Silicon Graphics when it was going public back in 1986. It was rather unusual for a start-up to hire an investment bank at this stage, but I was already so caught up in the NCSA dispute that I wanted the task of writing the offering document off my back, and I didn't have people in the company who knew much about how to do it.

The real curse of the Tower of Babel isn't that humanity has invented so many different languages, but that one language can be subdivided into so many exclusive dialects. Lawyers speak legalese ("the party of the first part," etc.), doctors speak medical jargon, scientists communicate in a Sanskrit of arcane symbols, programmers think in the code of C++ or Java, and so forth. The result of these demi-glossaries, besides general incomprehension, is that people who speak one professional dialect, or none at all, have to hire translators if they want to be understood by people who speak another. Investment bankers have their corner of the Tower, and they know how to write a document in the language and the form that the investment community wants to see, with lawyers scripting the jargon that ensures that the company stays out of trouble. Morgan Stanley sent people to look at the company, interview the management team, and read what we had written, then translate the information into the dialect spoken by the tribe that manages money.

The bankers opened the third round of discussions in late 1994. In keeping with my initial notion that the browser would be a fundamental tool for the publishing and telecom industries, I had Morgan Stanley line up companies in those businesses, such as Knight-Ridder, Hearst, TCI, Times-Mirror, MCI, and the Tribune Company. Then, as a result of the possible lawsuit, large investors grew cautious, and the process slowed to a halt. As I mentioned before, the tech-savvy president of the Chicago-based Tribune Company, naturally very uncomfortable about being caught in a controversy between the University of Illinois and Netscape, dropped out entirely. (Loyalty did not serve his financial interests, because the companies that invested realized a fifty-to-one return in a matter of months.)

When January came and Barksdale arrived to round out management, we had turned the corner financially, and charged ahead both with staffing and revenues. By February he decided to close Series C, finishing off what I'd started the previous autumn. This was no longer financially necessary because of the growth in revenues, but we did it out of a sense of commitment to the firms that had been saying they would invest when the dispute was resolved. With outside corporate investments added to what both I and Kleiner Perkins had put in, Netscape now had a market value of around $150 million—not a bad amount for a small company, but in view of what would happen a few months later, a pittance.

I could reel off all the companies we signed up as customers, licensees, and partners of one sort or another. The sheer length of the list would be impressive, as would many of the names. But the roster would be long and not particularly interesting (though to us at the time, of course, each new piece of business was tremendously exciting). So I'll just say that, as I'd been described as spreading the contagion of entrepreneurial excitement to the programmers in Urbana-Champaign, Netscape was spreading the contagion of the Internet to the world's corporations.

With money coming in, we were able to bring in new people again at all levels. In April, we hired Peter Currie as chief administrative officer. Peter had been Barksdale's chief financial officer at McCaw Cellular Communications, and before that he worked for Morgan Stanley. In May, Roberta Katz, also from McCaw, joined Netscape as general counsel. Heading toward an eventual two thousand employees, we entered a new period where I began to see people whose faces I didn't recognize. Which meant, I figured in a rather melancholy moment, that there must be some young programmers who passed me in the hall and wondered who that tall, older guy with the smile on his face was. Since Barksdale's arrival, I'd only gone to a couple of the Friday all-hands meetings—he and Marc had made a smooth connection, and there was no reason for me to be there. My place at the center of things was already fading, like a cheap color snapshot on a sunny wall. The trouble with speed is that *everything* happens fast; you look forward to getting to a certain point, then when you get there you can't slow things down. With a kind of psychological Doppler effect, the future approaches with life at a high pitch, then fades into the past with a low, minor note.

At the end of the first quarter we released Navigator 1.1. This wasn't a new product, just an upgrade, but it indicated that we were prepared to constantly improve on what we had done, an important perception in a business where even the really new stuff always verges on obsolescence. According to Marc's relentless production schedule, we were due to come out with 2.0 in early summer. As we added programmers, we were able to begin developing new products, and as we discovered unexpected directions, other new products kind of dictated themselves.

One of the great revelations that comes with the introduction of any new technology is that the users, and hence the market, quickly take on a highly creative role in how the products of that technology are used. Put simply, the market tells you where your market is, and you'd damn well better listen. As I've said, had the printing press been employed exclusively to print the Bible, Gutenberg's original use for it, no communication revolution could have occurred. The quality of a measure of how good a product is—and how smart a company is—can be seen in how quickly both can adapt to new and unplanned-for events. One of the most glaring errors companies make is to build a product, possibly a really good product, discover no one really wants it, then, rather than make a fast turn, put all their efforts into convincing people that they ought to want it. (This may work with some kinds of products, like *Sports Illustrated*, which lost money for years before becoming hugely profitable, or the sitcom *Seinfeld*, which wasn't an instant hit. But with computer hardware and software there's just no time to dither. An elementary product like Microsoft DOS got a break because IBM, at the time the uncontested alpha company in a small market, adopted it.) Economics and business are about how people interact with the material world; there's just so much anyone can do to influence these interactions, no matter what advertising agencies tell their clients. When children stop wanting Cabbage Patch dolls and start wanting Beanie Babies, there's no sense telling them they're wrong. When people begin buying oversized sport utility vehicles because they feel safer in them, there's not much point talking to them about how much more gasoline they're going to be using, or that a small electric car makes more sense if they're just driving around town. Whether it seems logical to a start-up company with a vision or not, the market drives the market.

As has often been the case in the development of information technology, initial visions have tended to bracket the end result, falling to one side or the other of the real need rather than making a direct hit on the first salvo. We had followed a two-pronged strategy that straddled the market up until the end of 1994, but as the phones began to ring from corporate customers, we geared up our corporate sales efforts. What I had instinctively thought was a key part of the future, namely consumer services on the Internet, was de-emphasized because there was no clear way to make money in this arena. On the other hand, customers were clearly willing to buy software to make their employees and departments more efficient.

This was the only real strategy change the company ever made, despite the opinions of all the armchair CEOs who, brilliantly looking back in time, pen in hand, are so quick to criticize us. And it was a mistake. All of our portal-focused activities, such as working with advertising agencies to adapt the "rate-card" concept to an online form, weren't yielding revenues, so we disbanded the "content" group; Bill Foss, Jeff Treuhaft, Kathy Clark, and the others in this gangly gang had to find new jobs within the company. No longer was anyone assigned the task of showing publishers and content companies how they should think of the World Wide Web. We made our Web site, the most heavily trafficked place on the planet, a tool for promoting Netscape products. By February of 1995, the company was so focused on software sales that even Marc would dismiss my suggestion that we try to hire Jerry Yang and David Filo, who as graduate students operated Yahoo! out of Stanford. (Not Stanford again! What does Stanford know that some other universities can't see?) It's unlikely that Yang and Filo would have joined us, however, and even if they had, Barksdale agrees that it is doubtful that we would have done the proper job at that time to make the search-directory–cum–portal business the success that they did, because we didn't think the opportunity was there. This was when the solar system was still forming in Internet time.

We were outright seduced by the amount of revenues rolling in from companies wanting a site license to Netscape Navigator. Seduction is exactly the right word, because as revenues increased on the browser, so grew our dependence on browser revenues. We knew this was dangerous. But revenues are like an addictive drug—once you get used to a certain amount, it's hard to cut back. We began to sell our servers, but in the beginning many companies couldn't see paying for them because freeware servers did almost as good a job, and their price was pretty compelling. So we put large groups to work on adding features to the server and other products for companies.

Now, you have to realize that the browser is a very valuable piece of software. Especially if you own it. Anyplace you go on the Web, any information you access, anything you buy, when you do it, what you spent—anything related to the Internet—goes through it. Owning this Web viewport gives you lots of potential for abuse, in spades if no one else owns one. We knew this, but as a good corporate Web citizen, we were determined not to abuse this power. We were spending over half of our R&D dollars on this one piece of software, so if we couldn't charge for it, we had to find some other way to pay for our costs. So many people were willing to pay for it that we naturally took the path of charging. We gave away pointers from the Netscape home page free of charge, enabling Yahoo! and others to establish brands that would eventually rival Netscape's. We were creating the market, and the market needed the ability to easily find things. I didn't always really agree, but my policy, learned after many years of butting heads with Ed McCracken, was to not interfere, although a few times I "screamed and hollered" at Barksdale, who felt our future was not in our Web site, but in our software, a familiar domain for him since he had been a salesman for IBM and the CIO of Federal Express. Why consider other sources of revenue—we were exploding with revenues! I didn't make a big issue out of it, because who could complain about the skyrocket we were on? But two years hence (an eon in Internet time), after Microsoft decided the only way they could win was to engage in bullying tactics, and after the word *portal* became a household name, with Yahoo! soaring in stock price, Netscape would begin to see the value in the Web site and start the process of regaining lost ground in that area.

Don't get the wrong impression—I think no one could have done a better job of managing all of this than Jim Barksdale, especially not me. (And no other general has ever fought a battle against such overwhelming odds as those presented by Bill Gates.) Likewise, my admiration for Marc is evident from these writings. In the beginning, there was no way to know that Microsoft would behave illegally. No one could predict how this universe would evolve.

As springtime rolled around, we were on a roll. We had just finished the first quarter with over $7 million in revenues, and as April ended, our growth rate appeared to accelerate. We were still a private company, so no one but insiders knew what was happening. The press, especially from the East Coast, were still laughing about our folly, questioning our sanity, sure that the Internet was uncontrollable and the closest one could get to anarchy, although Barksdale had brought a modicum of respectability to the company. Like the preacher played by Steve Martin in the movie *Leap of Faith* (actually filmed in my hometown of Plainview), I continued to preach the gospel, assuring the unsaved that the Internet was their salvation. But we needed something else to get the world's attention. More marketing bullshit!

For a tiny little company with modest but exploding revenues, what was the biggest marketing event of all?

In the early days of May, I'm pretty sure I was the only person at Netscape who harbored any thoughts about an initial public offering. There shouldn't have been any reason to think about such a move. After all, the company was just a little over one year old, with only one quarter of revenues, and no profits. But I had begun thinking about the possibility of going public because of its timing as a marketing event, not because of my well-known impatience; the move was entirely in keeping with the character of the company. Tempo, as much as technology, was what Netscape was all about. Our product cycle was only six months, and the products we brought out were famous for their speed. Inside the company, in the press, and (from the beta download on) in the marketplace, we had created the kind of momentum few start-ups have been capable of. And despite a couple of serious speed bumps and a roadblock or two, we'd managed to maintain that momentum. At Silicon Graphics we had worked against the resistance of a new and unknown market, like hacking through virgin forest. We pioneered 3-D graphics, then found ourselves all dressed up with no place to go. Sometimes that's the cost attached to new ideas. When the automobile was invented in 1895, there wasn't a great public clamoring for cars; roads were bad, and people weren't particularly dissatisfied with horses, which had provided adequate transportation for thousands of years. Except for a relative handful of oddball enthusiasts, the horseless carriage was a tough sell, and a long, long time would pass before we ended up with bumper-to-bumper rush hours on the Santa Monica Freeway and the Long Island Expressway. Though this comparison may be a stretch, a somewhat similar situation faced SGI. We had breakthrough technology, but it took a while for people to understand its applications. I remember potential customers telling me, "This is fantastic, sure, but what can we do with it?" No one said, "Hey, this is cool. Let's make a dinosaur movie!" So it wasn't until its fourth year that SGI made $40 million.

At Netscape, we entered a market waiting to explode and looking for something, or someone, to light the fuse. The World Wide Web had been around since 1990, and it already had a number of dedicated users. Millions more were ready to use the Web if only someone would make it easy. Andreessen and Bina had already built and demonstrated a prototype browser. So there was no in-built friction, no resistance, once we produced the vehicle. To switch metaphors from one transportation revolution to another, it's as if an entire global network of railroad tracks had been laid down five years before the invention of the first steam locomotive. When we showed up with our mightier-than-Mosaic browser, the only friction we encountered was artificially created. Other than that, the only limit to our momentum was our own ability to think fast and work hard with real urgency, first out-racing NCSA Mosaic, then stealing a march on Microsoft. It was this powerful urgency that gave the company its character, and it was that character that before long revved up the entire industry.

There are friends and associates of mine who suspect to this day that the idea of going public after so little time came up because I wanted to build the sailing yacht of my dreams. After all, to paraphrase a line from *Barron's* advertisements, IPOs are what turn money into wealth. The suspicions of these cynical friends may well have been confirmed when, in late September of 1998, the 155-foot, aluminum-hulled, computer-controlled *Hyperion* was lowered (slowly and very expensively) into the murky waters of the Rhine-Meuse delta of Amsterdam. And I won't deny that I might have daydreamed of building such a boat. But I already had a boat, and not enough time to spend on it. The truth is, the idea of the IPO came—at least in part—as the result of misreading of signals by Spyglass, and my reaction to that misreading. I'd made the fairly unusual move of hiring Morgan Stanley to help with our corporate financing round, and the investment bankers—well known as the advance guard for many successful public offerings—had shopped the company around for Series C financing in much the same way they might before a public offering. This didn't go unnoticed.

It's often been said about Silicon Valley that "the Valley has ears." The bigger truth is that the entire high-tech business has ears, and those ears are especially fine-tuned when you're listening for the sounds of a competitor sneaking up on you through the tall grass. So Spyglass made the obvious deduction: Netscape's going public. Which led them to an obvious conclusion: Well, shit, we ought to go public. They had some revenues (they must have reasoned), and a deal with Microsoft that had more or less automatically granted them the status of players. They were selling a slightly improved version of the original Mosaic, and in large part because of Marc and Netscape, Mosaic had enjoyed a lot of press attention. And there was a lot of interest in the Internet. Coincidentally, Wall Street was pumped up with optimism and the steady flow of cash into mutual funds. If ever there was a time for what Alan Greenspan would later called "irrational exuberance," the spring of 1995 was it.

But there were limits. When I began hearing rumors that the investment bank Alex Brown was planning to take Spyglass public, I was astonished. Even the boldest (or most self-deluded) companies traditionally waited until they had a full year of revenues and some significant positive cash flow. I couldn't believe that a company we had already left far behind technologically was going to go public before us. Of course, I wasn't about to do nothing. IPOs are thought of mainly as a way to create capital value, and sometimes they can create spectacular amounts. But going public can also be a marketing coup. All at once, as if out of nowhere, a company has a public image; it's part of the daily chorus line of hot stocks. Naturally there's a risk. An IPO that falls flat, or even does okay when the market expected something big, can make a company wish it had stayed in the shelter of privacy. Going public successfully is a question of doing as much as possible to manage a process that has its own set of natural laws and is subject to forces that can be understood but not entirely controlled. Luck matters, but you don't dare depend on luck.

One of my instructors in aerobatic flying is a former three-time national champion named Patty Wagstaff. During my first flight with her, I hung on as she put my plane through a 360-degree turn that had imbedded in it four 360-degree rolls, one for each 90 degrees of the turn. She repeated with rolls in the opposite direction, then repeated with three inside rolls per complete turn before I told her I was going to get sick. It was like being in a washing machine. Watching from the ground, someone might have thought there was a kind of jazz-riff spontaneity about the flight. But what impressed me in the cockpit was how absolutely precise Patty was; she was like a surgeon, using her aircraft as a scalpel to operate on the sky. Tremendous physical forces were at work, forces that could be predicted only up to a point. But she had reached a level of skill that let her transform a high-risk activity into a (relatively) low-risk activity. Similarly, no one can eliminate the unexpected elements from the drawn-out process of offering stock to the public, but it can and should be done with as much precision as you can bring to bear.

The rumor that Spyglass was readying an IPO was confirmed when I got a phone call from Lorna Meyer at Alex Brown asking if their taking Spyglass public would make it hard for Netscape to work with them. Alex Brown had been the bankers for SGI along with Morgan Stanley, and I knew the company well. In fact, Mayo Shattuck, who was by this time the president of the bank, had traveled with me while I was out on the road pitching SGI to investors for its public offering eight years earlier. I knew him well, and I knew the bank well, and my experience with both had been good. I told her Spyglass was not well liked at Netscape, using the nicest words I could muster, but I did notice a trace of venom on the phone when I hung up. She said she would inform them, but evidently one of the East Coast bankers was all over the deal and desperate for a notch in his belt. After all, Spyglass had been anointed by the University of Illinois, and they had the real Mosaic plus a deal with Microsoft. Mayo was on vacation, so the executive committee decided to be the investment bankers for Spyglass, thinking we were much further away from an IPO. Who knows, maybe they misunderstood the expression "No conflict, no interest." But at least I now knew definitely that Spyglass was in the hunt.

In my mind, the idea of going public as soon as we could was now clearly the right move. It wasn't so much a question of "Can we do this?" as "How can we not?" Spyglass may have started me thinking about an IPO, but now my approach became proactive, not reactive. Once I'd come to that point, I wanted to move as fast as possible. We'd done everything else at unprecedented speed, so why should this be any different? But just because I had become convinced that we had to go for it, there was no guarantee that the rest of the board of directors would agree. We still had a small board—besides me, there was Marc, John Doerr, Jim Barksdale, and John Warnock, chairman and CEO of Adobe, the desktop publishing software company, who had joined a few weeks before. So I wasn't faced with a long, drawn-out lobbying job in order to move toward a decision. The main person to convince was Barksdale, as he would make the final decision.

I figured the scorecard this way: Marc, having nothing to lose and quite a lot to gain, wouldn't care one way or another. His main concerns were technology, not money. John Doerr, a venture capitalist to his core, would like the idea as a marketing event, and it would establish the company's credibility. It would also place a market value on the stock Kleiner Perkins owned. Doerr's formula for going public was simple: that the management team be complete, which ours now was, and that management be able to predict eight quarters of performance exceeding investor expectations, which we thought we could do. John Warnock, new to the board and enormously enthusiastic about the company, would probably go with the majority. Jim Barksdale, however, was someone who, I knew, was against going public for a few perfectly good reasons. First, he had just left a public corporation, and hadn't had much time to enjoy the pleasure of not having to answer to thousands of stockholders, or publish all the company's financial business, or live and die in three-month increments—what a CEO I know calls being "drawn and quartered." Second, Jim had come from Federal Express, McCaw, and AT&T; to him, Netscape must have seemed very small, relatively unproven, and far from ready for the prime-time exposure of Wall Street. And finally—perhaps most important for Jim—the publicity an offering would generate, both during the run-up and after D-Day, publicity I considered good marketing, would instantly make us much more interesting to Microsoft. They were already more interested in what we were doing than we liked, and they were obviously capable of tightening the thumbscrews whenever they thought it necessary. I knew Jim hoped to have more time, more revenues, and a more secure market share before taking on the enemy in open combat. As long as we weren't public, we could operate as guerrillas. After an IPO, it would be all tank battles, artillery barrages, and scorched earth.

I understood Barksdale's reluctance. Had circumstances been different I might have felt the same way. The old cliché that there's no free lunch certainly applies to going public. You can raise enough money to take your company to the next stage of competition, but you also create a daily report card in the form of the share price; it takes superhuman management not to start making decisions with that report card in mind—to think long term rather than in ninety-day bursts. But nothing about Netscape time resembled any business experience I'd lived through, or even heard about. The rule book was being rewritten and we were rewriting it. Others were already playing by those new rules, and we had to play by them, too.

In order to strengthen my case for the IPO, I asked Frank Quatrone from Morgan Stanley and Larry Sonsini, of the law firm Wilson Sonsini, our corporate counsel, for their opinions. This was stacking the deck, since I was pretty sure what their responses would be. Investment bankers make their money dealing in public companies, not in private business, and their commissions on a successful IPO can be huge. So it wasn't any surprise that Frank was very positive about the idea of going public. Sonsini, in good lawyerly style, went through a list of pros and cons, saying that ultimately, it depended on whether Barksdale wanted the scrutiny of a public company, because he would be on the line. But I knew that corporate law firms also make their big money doing public lawyering for public companies. It was pretty clear that Larry wasn't going to discourage me, even though the pros and cons more or less balanced each other out. So, thus far, it was three in favor of the IPO, none opposed.

I asked Quatrone to come to our board meeting early in June. Sonsini was already attending the meeting, acting as secretary. I had discussed the IPO possibility with Barksdale, but he had been less than enthusiastic. I figured that if I was going to bring up the proposal that we go public, it would look better—and serve as a reassurance—if a trusted counselor talked us through the concept. I like to think that everyone in the boardroom had some regard for my instincts, but I wanted to show that this idea wasn't simply the result of waking up one morning with a gut feeling.

After the board had completed its regular quarterly business, including a report from Jim Barksdale indicating that we had ended the quarter with $22 million in revenues, I told the board that I had asked Frank and Larry to join us. I asked each to summarize his view of the pros and cons of our going public at this early stage. An eloquent silence followed Frank's input, and Larry Sonsini came in to lay out his analysis, his voice as smooth as a baby's skin and as soothing as its mother's lullaby. As he spoke, I tried to read Barksdale's face, but at best all I could deduce was a kind of genial skepticism. Jim was too much of a gentleman to jump up and tell me I was crazy, but for all I knew at that point he may have thought this was a completely insane proposal. In the end, we had hired him to run the company, and this would be his decision. As the meeting adjourned, he smiled rather cryptically and said, "Okay. Let me think about it."

Over the course of the next couple weeks, he thought about it, and I talked about it. I held conversations with members of the board and confirmed that I'd been right in my original judgment of how they felt. The more I talked about the IPO, the more crucial it seemed to me, and with my usual missionary zeal I probably raised the level of enthusiasm several notches, and with it the sense of urgency. So it was up to Barksdale, and for that reason I decided not to lobby him. This was the biggest decision he would have to make during his half year at Netscape, and I didn't want him to feel any more pressure than the future of the company already brought to bear. Frankly, I was counting on his natural competitiveness, which is what attracted him to Netscape in the first place.

In mid-June, we reconvened the board by telephone. "So, what do you think?" I asked Barksdale once the other members had announced they were on the line. After a momentary pause, during which I could imagine Jim, with his feet up on his desk, shrugging amiably. "Okay," he said. "Let's do it." As soon as I hung up the phone, Peter Currie called Frank Quatrone at Morgan Stanley and told him to get his people to work on a prospectus.

We were off, and not a minute too soon. A few days earlier, Spyglass—which had obviously begun to learn a few things about speed—had put 2 million shares on the market at $17 per share, and at the end of the day those shares were selling for over $21. Once again, I couldn't believe it. We had a product far better and ten times faster than theirs, and they had . . . a contract with Microsoft. (They also had other customers, but I don't think that aspect of the business impressed the Street.) If Spyglass could score a successful IPO, we had to get our asses in gear. Usually, it takes eight to twelve weeks to get the prospectus done, file the necessary documents, take care of all the details, and go through Security

Exchange Commission reviews that mark the transition from private to public. This is another process we had to shift into Netscape time. Since we were already in mid-June, the soonest we could get to our IPO would be sometime in August. This came up at our first meeting with Morgan Stanley, since something close to a deep-seated superstition holds that the dog days of August, when any broker worth his or her exorbitant commissions is sautéing on the sand at Southampton or Martha's Vineyard, is a bad time for an IPO. But Netscape had already disproved plenty of shibboleths, so we all concluded that we might just as well go ahead. We believed that what we were doing had the power to revolutionize everything from publishing and banking to communication and commerce, and the press had decided we were right. So we had to take the chance that investors wouldn't miss the opportunity to buy in just because the temperature was 94 degrees in the shade. There were definitely going to be buyers for this stock; we were too high-profile by this time for there not to be. Would there be a lot of buyers, willing to pay top dollar? Sometimes fate lurks in the arbitrariness of process, and there's no point trying to evade it. Move on, straight ahead, and damn the torpedoes.

News travels fast along the investment banking grapevine. Far too late, I got a call from Mayo Shattuck. He told me he'd been out of town when the decision was made at Alex Brown to take on Spyglass, or he would have called then and talked to me personally about it. A good lesson, I guess, not to be out of town when serious decisions are made. I told him that if he had called, I would have given him a simple choice: Netscape or Spyglass. But since they'd now taken one of our main competitors public, it was out of the question. How could they possibly represent two direct competitors, especially where such bad blood was involved?

Typically, though, a company going public has more than one underwriter. It's a matter of increasing the resources allocated to the effort, and institutional coverage for the placement of the stock. More feet on the street again. Shortly, I got a call from Bill Hambrecht of Hambrecht & Quist. He and I had been on a board together and I had always thought highly of him. He asked me to consider them for the so-called right-hand-side of the prospectus. H&Q had been a high-profile, boutique investment bank and venture capital outfit until one of their companies, on whose board Bill sat, had shipped bricks instead of disk drives to a warehouse at the end of a quarter—a bad thing to do unless you are in the brick business. The discovery by accountants, then investors, had resulted in lawsuits, and Bill's name had been sullied as a result, even though he had no knowledge of the deed. Such is the nature of being a public company—a lieutenant does something wrong, and the general gets crucified. Their investment banking business had not really recovered, so they needed a high-profile deal to become a major player again. (Bill had stepped away from running the company, leaving the job to none other than Daniel Case, Steve [AOL] Case's brother.) So I asked Peter Currie to consider letting them come in along with Morgan Stanley.

After quite a lot of discussion, the price of the stock—always a crapshoot decision—was settled at $15 per share (after the road show, the price became $28), and the number of shares to be issued at 3.5 million (over and above what employees and earlier investors already owned). Was the price so high that buyers would be put off? Was it so low that we'd end up leaving too much money on the table? There's only just so much that experience can tell you, since markets and moods can change dramatically from one day to the next. You and your bankers make a calculated guess, and it's far more guess than calculation.

From this point on, our situation resembled a thriller movie cliché: The terrorist's time bomb is set to explode in six minutes, and the bright red digital clock fills the screen, its seconds counting down remorselessly while some hero in an impeccable Italian jacket tries to hack into the computer program that can disarm the weapon. For us, the six minutes was six weeks, but the countdown was no less frantic.

A road show had to be organized quickly. This amounts to something very much like a political campaign, during which stockbrokers, bankers, analysts, mutual fund managers, and other institutional investors get a chance to hear about the company directly from the management team that runs it. Though in one sense it might seem that any savvy money manager ought to be able to get whatever information he needs from the prospectus and a few intelligently placed phone calls, road shows play a tremendously important part in raising the level of interest and reassurance in the investment community. In the end, the act of investing money in a new company—even other people's money—is extremely personal. It's the nature of prospectuses to be schizophrenic, on the one hand sounding attractive, which is why we hire professionals at investment banks to write them, and on the other hand sounding like if you put your money here you'll lose it all, which results from hiring lawyers to make sure the company doesn't get sued. It's miraculous that any company passes this IPO test, a testimony that everyone tosses the cautious jargon of the lawyers to the wind. Which makes it more important to potential investors to lay eyes on the principal players on whom they're being asked to place some very big bets. Road shows take on even more importance in high tech, where profits may be slim or none, and products may be untested and incompletely understood.

This has led to a certain amount of consternation in Silicon Valley and other centers of technologic innovation. While there are some company founders and entrepreneurs who have a sense of style and a wardrobe that extends beyond Gap T-shirts and Dockers—Oracle's Larry Ellison in his *Playboy* magazine "best-dressed" getup and Adobe's John Warnock (crocodile loafers!) come to mind—many are true nerds who spent their college years in a state of defiant sloth and have worked too hard since then to bother with the trappings of sartorial civilization.

This disregard for such things as neckties, dress shirts, and suits has long appealed to reporters (not always particularly well dressed themselves), but it's courting disaster to take a typical computer genius and drop him, unreconstructed, into the midst of an Armani-ed army of sleek investment types, then let him squirm and mumble his story. Even where numbers count for a lot, style counts for something. As a result, a highly profitable side business has sprung up in the past ten years for coaches and consultants who put smart young shamblers through a crash course in how to speak, how to dress, and how to impress. I once heard of a college football coach who admonished his players, "When you get into the end zone, try to look like you've been there before." This is essentially the message these style gurus hammer home: "When you're sitting in a room with people whose wristwatches cost more than a Honda Civic, try to look as if you belong there."

In an article in *Forbes ASAP*, George Gilder assumed this was a problem we had to deal with before sending Marc off on our road show:

> As Wall Street began pouring money on any rival company with an Internet product, the stock market became a Netscape imperative. This posed a problem for Clark. There would be no difficulty attracting a frenzy of interest. The question was, Where would they hide Andreessen during the road show?

As he does about half the time, Gilder got it wrong. It was true that Marc hadn't had a spare minute to do any image polishing, but upgrading his wardrobe was a small enough matter. I didn't see any need to push Marc beyond the khakis-and-moccasins style most young engineers favor for a Saturday dinner in Palo Alto. A few neckties and dress shirts and a jacket or two was all the upgrading he needed. When Marc started talking about the Web, and about what Netscape was doing to open it up to millions of users, he was so impressive he might be wearing a sweatshirt and jeans for all it mattered. A young engineer with nothing much to sell might make a good impression with enough theatrical tutoring, but I was sure the smart money would see that Andreessen was the genuine article, whether or not he'd remembered to put his socks on that morning.

CEOs, who are usually professional managers, can be counted upon to make up any style points lost by their technology colleagues. Barksdale, his impressive résumé and evangelical passion for Netscape's future backed up with dark, well-tailored suits, impressive ties, and a gold signet ring, wore what amounted to material reassurance. Jim could be every bit as zealous an advocate as I. I had heard him give pep talks to new employees, telling them that Microsoft was trying to lead customers back into the cave, whereas Netscape was committed to keeping them in the sunlight. He could be as passionate as he was smart and determined, and there was nobody better to excite investors.

Which leads me to a significant moment in my eventful time with the company. As the preparations for the road show were quickly assembled—the schedules, the visual and printed materials, all the paraphernalia of promise that makes up the presentation—it became obvious that Barksdale wasn't going to ask me to be part of the team.

I could have insisted; I was, after all, the chairman and largest individual stockholder. But I had already been out on the stump for the company for several months, and to some extent had prepared the way for Marc, Jim, and chief administrative officer Peter Currie, who did the road show reinforced by a changing cast of bankers.

In fact, those trips had been the indirect result of my turning over the day-to-day operating reins to Barksdale. In the couple of staff meetings I'd gone to since January, it was clear to me that Jim and I had different styles—not conflicting, but different. I tend to get worked up about things, a little more anxious. Jim's style is calmer, less openly demanding, and less mercurial, although he could scorch someone's eyebrows if he's angered. I could see at those meetings soon after Jim arrived that my presence was confusing to everybody; I'd been the boss, now he was, and an awful lot of people were looking at me when they should have been looking at him. In order to make it obvious where everyday leadership, control, and authority belonged, I had to get out of the way. Barksdale and Andreessen were both completely capable of keeping everyone focused on what the business was, and how it was going. By design, I had made myself redundant.

Yet when the moment finally came for me to back away, to let others do something on which the future of the company hinged, I had to accept that my relationship with the company I'd cofounded and poured myself into was changed. I'm going to use a comparison that I hope won't sound patronizing, since Jim Barksdale is older and wiser and a better manager than I'll ever be, and Marc had taught me more than I ever taught him. But the experience of relinquishing my place in the scheme of things at Netscape, even though it was just what I wanted to happen, was like teaching a kid to ride a bicycle. You run along, your hand on the back of the seat to steady the wobbling, letting the kid know you're there until the bike speeds up. Then, in a transition both symbolic and real, you let go and drop back as he goes on, not knowing yet that he's riding on his own. The mixture of emotions is well known to any parent who has ever gone through this rite of passage: pride that another level of independence has been reached, and a twinge of sadness that you aren't needed as much as you were just a few minutes before. Now the pieces were in place, the schedule was what I'd hoped it would be, and the team was ready to take off.

All I could do was wait to see what happened. I couldn't help thinking of Gregory Peck in *12 O'Clock High*, the grounded squadron commander forced to sit at headquarters and listen to the radio transmissions of his air group's bombing mission over Germany.

But all that is way too dramatic. I'd always tried hard to avoid interfering with Marc and his group, and, with only a few exceptions, I'd been able to hire business and marketing people who didn't need a lot of managing. Marc had set the technology goals and I had set the business goals. Then I'd tried to grease the skids, pay the bills, and fight the fights I was best equipped to fight. Netscape wasn't a one-man company, and it wasn't a cult of personality; it was a culture of formidable effort by—at this point—hundreds of people. To find myself for the moment not in the thick of it wasn't upsetting, or even unsettling.

So off they went, no longer Marc and Clark, but Marc and Bark. I stayed fairly close to the company during the next few weeks, getting calls about where they were and how it was going. They were in New York, their days full of campaigning in wood-paneled conference rooms with views of the Verrazano Narrows Bridge, laying out a new map of the world being assembled in a bunch of unglamorous cubicles three thousand miles away. Then they were in Chicago. Then Dallas. After that, I got phone calls from Europe. From everything I heard, it sounded as if the show was getting rave reviews. Because of the press attention and several appearances on national magazine covers, Marc had a celebrity status that was only enhanced by the fact that he was probably one of the youngest people who had ever stood before the Medici of major money and talked them through a brilliant concept. Barksdale, though well known from his highly successful corporate positions, still must have been something of a shock to people accustomed to earnest entreaties for their trust (and cash). Jim was charming and confident, there to offer a great opportunity, not ask for largesse. Sometimes he ran the normally sobered gatherings with investment bankers like a preacher at a Southern tent revival meeting, telling the attendees to take seats down in the front row. "It's just like church," he'd drawl. "Come on down front and be saved."

The response was enthusiastic. So many of the institutional investors got religion, in fact, that the bankers quickly increased the amount of common stock to 5 million shares and pushed the price up to $28 per share. Eventually another 750,000 shares would be added in what's called the "green shoe option," which doesn't mean, as I first thought with SGI, taking money out of a spare shoe, but refers to the first time this was done by the Green Shoe Company when it went public. We were being described as the fastest-growing software company in history. Rosanne Siino had to set up special phone lines just to deal with hundreds of calls every day about the IPO. Temps were hired to field inquiries about how to get in on the offering. I had figured on a lot of excitement, but not this much this soon.

Amazingly, nothing seemed any different about the scene in our Mountain View offices. The relentless pressure to get Navigator 2.0 ready for release didn't let up. Barksdale had worried that the anticipation of going public—with its potential for an end-of-the-rainbow payoff—would create a diversion. But if you had leaned into any office or cubicle—other than the area occupied by Rosanne Siino and her hyperactive phone crew—you'd never have known anything was going on that hadn't been going on since we first turned on the computers just over a year before. More people, same pressure. Mathematician Paul Erdos once said that "a mathematician is a machine for turning coffee into theorems." The software equivalent might be that a programmer is a machine for turning Coke into code. Our "machines" were still working at full-on capacity.

It was a strange and wonderful time. The road show was going well, serious investors were investing seriously, and, for a brief, becalmed period, I didn't have much to do. Since we were in the "quiet time" mandated by the SEC prior to a public offering, I couldn't even talk to the press, something I'd grown accustomed to doing. Two men I trusted were out carrying the banner of our company, while a lot of other people were still chained to their oars, making and marketing our products. Through the cloudy mornings and brilliantly sunny afternoons, I could only wait to see how things would turn out. Since that first cup of coffee with Marc at the Cafe Verona in what now seemed another epoch, when I decided to hitch my wagon to his star and he decided to hitch his to mine, I had ridden waves of elation, anxiety, vexation, anger, and hope. Now everything focused on anticipation, which, for someone impatient and inclined to action, someone geared for life at Netscape time, was a highly unnatural state.

Time, at once the most measured and mysterious of all man's inventions, seemed to drag from day to day. Then, suddenly, it had flashed past. The "Mafia convention" scramble for pay phones I described in the first chapter took place at the truck stop outside of Baltimore. Then the show closed, the tent was struck, and the preacher and the prophet came home. Marc and Jim went back to work as if nothing had changed, but of course that was just an illusion. We were on the brink.

Which brings this story full circle. In an Internet minute, we found ourselves at August 9, 1995, D-Day, with me trying to have a normal day while knowing that my life would never be the same again; with Marc, as usual, sleeping late; with Barksdale steadfastly discouraging thoughts of the Big Score; and with my secretary (and Netscape stockholder), D'Anne, giving in to the entirely human impulse to shout "Show me the money!" by putting up her electronic stock price scorekeeper.

By the end of the day, what a score it had kept. The numbers ticked off by D'Anne's insubordinate display told an astonishing story, about Netscape, about the Internet, and about how business was going to work from that point onward. The amazement of even those who are rarely amazed was reflected the next day in the *New York Times* article I referred to in Chapter 1:

WITH INTERNET CACHET, NOT PROFIT, A NEW STOCK IS WALL ST.'S DARLING

A 15-month-old-company that has never made a dime of profit had one of the most stunning debuts in Wall Street history yesterday as investors rushed to pour their money into cyberspace.

The Netscape Communications Corporation became the latest—and hottest—company in the Internet business to list shares on the nation's stock exchanges. Shares of Netscape, which had been priced at $28 before trading began at 11 A.M., opened far higher—at $71. The shares soon surged to as high as $74.75. By noon, money managers at big mutual funds and other institutional investors fortunate enough to be in on the ground floor could have cashed in a profit of more than 150 percent and gone to lunch. . . . The company's cofounder and chairman, who holds 9.7 million shares, ended up holding a stake valued at a half-billion dollars.

It was the best opening day for a stock in Wall Street history for an issue of its size. The overall dollar value of the one-day gain in the stock was $173.9 million. And the total market value of Netscape, including the shares held previously by management and venture capital firms, grew to $2.2 billion. That makes Netscape instantly bigger than some well-established software companies like Broderbund Software Inc.

But even more significantly, the surge was a sign of how the rush to commercialize the global computing web known as the Internet has created an investor frenzy not seen in the technology industry since the early days of the personal computer more than a decade ago.

In other words, we'd hit it out of the park. In an equally awestruck piece, *The Wall Street Journal* added the details that at the end of the day, Jim Barksdale's shares were worth $244.7 million, John Doerr's and Kleiner Perkins's were worth $256.3 million, and Marc Andreessen's were worth $58.3 million. What neither article mentioned, a detail about which I was enormously proud, was the many, many people at the company who had spent more than a year at the hardest work they'd ever done, or even imagined, and ended the day with wealth they deserved but had never dreamed of.

Stock options are only as good as the stock price, of course, and stock prices ultimately depend on how well a company does. We'd have to make a profit, not just revenues, to be as rich as the newspapers claimed. So there was only a comparative blink of an eye to bask in our blaze of glory. We had Navigator 3.4 and 5.0 to finish and dozens of new products still to come, and the full fury of Microsoft to confront. In other words, we had miles and miles to go before "We're doomed!" could be retired. But for one precious day we could put Netscape time on hold.

And make time for one hell of a party.

18 The Best of Enemies

Certain adversaries are made for each other. They are such perfect antagonists that each is shaped and changed by the existence of the archrival—made better or doomed, sometimes both. Historians love the dramatic connections of such competitors, in part because they offer a lens that seems to put chaotic events in sharp focus. Good guys and bad guys, white hats and black hats, give us an almost novelistic way to understand the clash of opposing forces on which history so often turns. So we inevitably link the names of Achilles and Hector, David and Goliath, Napoleon and Wellington, Grant and Lee, Custer and Sitting Bull, Rommel and Montgomery. Who is the hero and who the villain may depend on your point of view, but the real significance of these larger-than-life enemies is how their conflict gives us the context to judge them and their times. Sometimes the ultimate loser is far nobler than the winner. Who wouldn't prefer Hector, who went out onto the plains of Troy into a fight he knew he couldn't win, to Achilles, half god, half mortal, all bully? Sometimes the winner is clearly on the side of the angels (though probably far less often than we'd like to think). But what matters most is how legendary rivalries define the rivals.

The same kind of defining conflicts dramatize the history of business. Whether the fierce competition between Portuguese and English explorers to discover trade routes to the East, the shadowy conspiracy of Venice and Norman crusaders to sack Christian Constantinople and eliminate a trade rival, the little-known but fierce race between Thomas Edison and the Englishman Joseph Swan to be first to market with the electric light, or the competition between General Motors and Ford to win the hearts, minds, and money of American car buyers, at the core of all these famous struggles is the fact that business, like politics and war, is conflict. Someone once said you could judge a person by the quality of his enemies, and the same can certainly be said about a company. In the world of business, Netscape's archenemy is nothing less than Napoleonic.

We had been involved on three fronts—programming our client and server software, carving out a customer base, and dealing with the threat of a crippling lawsuit. The last of those battles had nothing to do with building a business, but rather with keeping a new business from being destroyed. For months, that action had so preoccupied me and our lawyers, and to one degree or another distracted everyone else in the company, that for a brief moment, when we came out at the other end of the tunnel, we might have been forgiven for thinking we had won a war. In fact, we'd actually just come through a fight that would allow us the dubious honor of confronting a much more famous and formidable foe.

In historical terms, our situation was like that of the Greeks early in World War II. When the Greek army dealt a humiliating defeat to the Italian invaders, the victory only convinced the German general staff that battle-hardened German divisions were needed to defeat Greece, which they brutally proceeded to do. In retrospect, after suffering under a typically harsh German occupation, the Greeks might have wondered if they wouldn't have been better off had the Italians won. Of course, there's no choice: You fight the fight to win, and if the reward is just another fight, well, that's what business is all about. You've got to be competitive; you're there to prevail in a battle with your competitors, and if you don't, you're probably not going to be a very significant company even if you manage to keep the doors open.

Sometimes that essential engine of business that has been called "creative destruction" leaves a lot of wreckage in its wake. The irony is that you're always striving for some kind of security, but you're never really secure—not in the sense that you can consolidate your gains and cling to the comforts of the status quo. Not if you know what's good for you, that is. The only safety in business is to keep growing. Once you stop, you may hold your own for quite a while, but essentially there's no place to go but down. This is probably more true in the technology business, where "quite a while" is not an option, than of any business in history; as I said in the chapter on speed, the status quo is deadly because it ends growth and eliminates the ability to change. The personal computer revolution is less than two decades old, and everything is so new that there simply is no status quo. In a mature, established business—soft drinks, let's say—it's pretty tough to come up with anything that's a lot better than Coca-Cola. But in high tech, people are coming up with better things every day, and there's nothing that can't and won't be dramatically improved upon, or rendered obsolete, in the space of a given year.

No one in American business understands this better than Bill Gates. The fact that his company absolutely dominates its industry, and has the cash and capability to dominate other industries, too, has never slowed him down or cooled his fierce ambition for a minute. Even the biggest soft drink companies can reach a point where the market is pretty much saturated (literally), and then, with huge ad campaigns to keep the product in front of everyone, go on generating dividends for years. But Gates's Microsoft constantly operates as if it's under siege by enemies that threaten its existence. If survival and paranoia are intimately linked, as Intel's Andy Grove has said, then the empire of Microsoft is going to be around for a very long time.

Just look at the company's competitive edge. The core computer today—ninety-seven or so out of every hundred—is the PC, and Microsoft virtually controls the application interfaces to these computers. Turn on your PC, and you're in Gates country; a huge installed base, growing every day. In fact, outside of such famous monopolies as the old Standard Oil, DeBeers, and pre-breakup American Telephone & Telegraph, it's hard to think of a company that has ever had this kind of armor-plated advantage. Success in the software business is, up to a point, self-perpetuating. In a sense, it can run counter to the well-regarded theory that the marketplace will always create and support better products. An operating system need not be the best available as long as enough people use it. The sheer expense of reversing a decision to use a particular system tends to protect that system even when a better one comes along. Not many people I know ever thought Microsoft's DOS for IBM machines and IBM clones was a great operating system, but because the sales and marketing power of IBM had made the PC the dominant machine, especially in business situations, DOS was on the majority of desktops by default.

IBM dominated the industry for years when large mainframe computers were what the business was all about. Then they woke up one morning and realized they'd woefully underestimated the importance of operating system software, and that one of their suppliers, run by a couple of badly dressed geeks from misty, mossy Seattle (of all places), had grown into a monster—all without ever having to build one box. Sometimes you will still hear people say that Bill Gates has benefited from dumb luck, especially early in his career. But what he has had fairly often, I think, was the good luck to run up against some comparatively dumb competition. At a time when most people thought of hardware as the glamour side of the business, Gates and Paul Allen realized that computers are, in themselves, not all that useful. It's the applications and the application programming interfaces, including the operating system, that make the things work. If you can control those, you can—in essence—rule a world increasingly run by and dependent upon computers.

And rule is clearly what Bill Gates is determined to do for as long as he can. He seems constantly afraid that someone is going to slip into his vast, expanding territory, and somehow undermine his business. And even though Microsoft is publicly owned, it's easy to imagine Gates seeing it as "his" business. You've got to give him credit; he's constantly vigilant, constantly out there hustling, constantly doing whatever it takes to stave off and stifle competitors. I've often wondered where Gates gets his insatiable drive. It's easy to work out the pop psychology of somebody like me, a man who grew up poor and not at all likely to succeed. Let the Jim Clarks of the world get any kind of advantage, you just about have to use a tire iron to make us let go. Gates, however, grew up in a well-to-do, upper-class professional family, a family not inclined to preach the fine points of ferocity. But, hell, Caligula came from one of the best families in Rome, and look how he turned out.

By any standards, but certainly by the measure of what he has accomplished, Gates is a brilliant businessman. As the competition got smarter, he's always stayed a jump or two ahead. (Well, almost always.) He's also utterly ruthless, which is not necessarily a criticism. Generally, I think those good folk who deplore ruthless behavior don't understand how well it works in business. The great founding fathers of American commerce were, almost to a man, merciless to those who tried to take even a few dollars out of their overflowing coffers. Emperors with any sense know that empires rise as long as they can rise, and then they fall. Extending the first phase and putting off the later phase indefinitely is every emperor's duty, and second nature to the most successful ones. To be tolerant toward any potential usurper is—according to the Successful Emperor's Rule Book—the worst kind of dereliction. Up to a point, Emperor Gates is a classic example of a Machiavellian prince.

In 1984, when Apple introduced the Macintosh system with the mouse and graphic point-and-click features we now take for granted, free-market logic might have dictated that Microsoft, with its user-unfriendly DOS, would be left in the dust. Except for the fact that they already owned the operating system on millions of computers, and few chief information officers or purchasing managers had the guts, or the budgets, to throw out hundreds or thousands of perfectly usable machines in order to make life better for the work force. (In those days, only the rarest top executive had the knowledge or the inclination to use a computer; while they might demand the absolute best and most expensive desk chair, they didn't care about whether one operating system was better than another.)

In the car rental business, when a better car comes along, Hertz or Avis can add that model to an existing fleet as attrition allows, eventually ending up with an entirely revamped line in a given category. This is because, basically, all cars are essentially the same, and a customer who can drive a Ford Escort can just as easily drive a Nissan Sentra—the accelerator is to the right of the brake, the car turns to the right when the steering wheel is turned to the right, etc. With computers, things aren't so simple. Anyone who works in a modern office has experienced the nightmares of incompatibility, even between ostensibly compatible computers, or between one system and another made by the same manufacturer. Microsoft purposely makes successive releases of its Office product in such a way that files saved with the newer version are unreadable by the older, even if the file doesn't use any features of the new release. The new release cannot stand on its own merits, so it brings the mayhem of incompatibility in any organization that might have both releases in use, eventually forcing the organization to upgrade everyone. More money for Microsoft! (This is in the best interests of consumers?) Whether this makes sense, or will someday be viewed as a kind of late-twentieth-century form of idiocy, is beside the point here. The fact is, when a company expands and needs new machines, or decides to purchase new, faster machines, the odds are overwhelming that the new equipment will come equipped with the same operating architecture and applications as the old ones. Since Apple chose for such a long time to keep its system proprietary— if you wanted the Macintosh system, you had to buy a Macintosh— and IBM and its clones owned a far greater market share, Microsoft had time to play catch-up with Windows. Eventually they introduced a product roughly similar to the Mac. Good enough, as they say, for government work—or for the vast installed base of users who had long suffered with DOS.

So though Microsoft can't kick back and coast—no company ever can in this business—it has a captive audience for its periodic upgrades, and can charge relatively high prices without worrying about a better product coming in at a better price. Inertia is always on the side of the entrenched technology. Most of the time, people stick to what they've learned and what they know. Tell consumers that Brand X is actually better than Brand A, even a lot better, and they'll still stay with Brand A if that's what they're comfortable using, especially if effort is required to change. Maybe electric cars will someday make more sense than the traditional internal combustion automobile. But in order to get substantial numbers of consumers to change from what they've known all their lives to an entirely new approach, electric cars will have to make more sense by a factor of ten. Given that powerful tendency to stick with the familiar, it's hard to imagine anyone dislodging Microsoft from their home turf. They simply own the market.

Could they ever lose it? Absolutely—if they went to sleep for five or ten years, which they won't. Microsoft doesn't go to sleep for five or ten minutes. Even without Bill Gates, the company owns the computer industry for the foreseeable future. Too many people all over the world have invested time and effort in learning how to use a computer, how to use applications, whether word processing or spreadsheets—all those investments by all those millions of employees are investments in Microsoft, and they'll pay dividends to the Redmond giant for a long time to come. By 1994, 80 percent of all personal computers were using Microsoft's operating system. With Gates at the helm, someone whose word is treated as gospel and whose determination to rule is boundless, Microsoft could only be threatened on territory it hadn't yet bothered to conquer. Or hadn't yet discovered. Enter the Internet, and Netscape.

Returning to the spring of 1995, we had won a major battle and were, for the moment, in the clear. But though I'd been totally distracted by the immediate threat, I'd never forgotten about our true competitor. Microsoft wasn't interested yet in our promising piece of turf, but was bound to notice quickly enough when we proved there was money to be made and a new market to be gobbled up. The eight-hundred-pound gorilla in the business had its sights set on other possibilities, a break for us. Microsoft's main technology visionary, Nathan Myhrvold, was fascinated, as I had been, with interactivity, both in television and linked computers within a company. The Microsoft Network, the company's own online service, was formed in 1994, and effectively absorbed a lot of the creative energy that might have gone into figuring out ways to use the Internet. They spent all of 1994 and most of 1995 trying to make a dying concept live, giving us a chance to build a foundation. In September 1993, Myhrvold, a mathematician with a Ph.D. from Princeton who had worked with Stephen Hawking at Cambridge, wrote a somewhat apocalyptic memo called "Road Kill on the Information Highway," in which he predicted a dire future for anyone who didn't exploit the possible connections between computers and the information highway. (Interestingly, his paper had a lot of ideas from the keynote speech I had given at the Special Interest Group for Graphics [SIGGRAPH] the previous summer.) But he imagined many connections to many individual points. As writer Ken Auletta wrote in *The New Yorker* in the spring of 1997: "What is striking today is that Myhrvold (and Microsoft) failed to envision how the Internet, particularly the World Wide Web, would provide just that sort of synergy. In fact, the Internet was not mentioned in Myhrvold's 'roadkill' discourse; his 'information highway' was defined not as a single universe (the Internet) but as a series of separate planets, with each, Myhrvold hoped, reliant on Microsoft software."

I can't gloat about this misreading of the future. In the fall of 1993, I had no more understanding of the potential of the Net than Myhrvold and Gates. Had I not met Marc Andreessen, as a result of Bill

Foss introducing me to Mosaic on my last day at SGI, I would have stayed clueless a lot longer. In fact, Myhrvold's myopia wouldn't be important to talk about at all if it weren't for the fact that Microsoft now claims to have been actively interested in the Net since the early spring of 1994, before Marc and I had formed Mosaic Communications. As I mentioned earlier, it's true that at a corporate retreat in April of that year, according to Microsoft memos quoted in the Justice Department brief, Gates gave orders that more attention must be paid to the Net, but I suspect he meant—in classic Gates style—it was something that Microsoft should keep an eye on. The idea of an open network with unlimited access wasn't on his mind. If it was on the minds of people several rungs down on the corporate ladder, that wouldn't have mattered unless Gates, or at least someone as highly placed as Myhrvold, had caught the enthusiasm. Nothing major happens that Gates doesn't sign off on. I think it's pretty funny that Microsoft executives have such a sharp recollection of that retreat, especially in light of this report in *The New York Times* early in September of 1998:

> WASHINGTON, SEPT. 1—In a court document made public today, the Justice Department accused top executives of the Microsoft Corporation, including its chairman, William H. Gates, of "an astonishing lack of recall" when they were questioned under oath for the Government's antitrust suit against the software giant.
>
> That assertion, plus several pieces of new evidence to support the Government's case, were submitted to Federal District Court here as part of the Justice Department's response to Microsoft's request that the case be dismissed.
>
> "Executives who are stated to be the authors of documents claim not to remember writing them," Government lawyers wrote. "Executives who are the stated recipients of documents claim not to remember receiving them. And both authors and recipients claim not to know what the documents mean."

I understood that Microsoft was a formidable competitor for Netscape, since it couldn't miss such a brave new world for too long. The fact that Gates and his planners couldn't possibly see us as significant competitors didn't mean we were going entirely unnoticed, however. But the longer we flew under the radar, the better. We were simply thought of as such a small fish that Microsoft could gobble us up, spit us out, or ignore us entirely. In fact, after our mid-October download, Gates sent an internal e-mail called "Sea Change Brings Opportunity," in which he talked about ways Microsoft could take advantage of new developments in the Information Age. But, according to Auletta's *New Yorker* article, "Gates did not, however, cite the Internet as a 'sea change.' In fact, in three single-spaced pages he mentioned the Internet twice, and then only in passing, when speaking of the growth, first, of private corporate networks (intranets), and then of 'public networks (including Internet and online services).' "

In September 1994, about a month before our beta download, Paul Koontz, our VP of marketing, was approached by Brad Silverberg, who ran the Windows 95 program at Microsoft. We had gotten so much attention that they were interested in talking to us about potentially licensing our product. Brad indicated to Paul that they might be interested in paying as much as $1 million dollars for a paid-up license to the software. My reaction to Koontz, laced with expletives here deleted, was "I'm not even remotely interested in doing anything with Microsoft, even discussions." I said I would reconsider if he could name one company, just one, that had successfully licensed anything to Microsoft and had become a serious player in the software market. That is the most telling thing about dealing with Microsoft—any software "partner" who licenses to them is eliminated. Later, in my videotaped deposition related to the Department of Justice antitrust case against Microsoft, I would be asked why I did not consider this offer seriously. My response to the lawyer was "You must not be a businessman." (I felt the judge wouldn't appreciate the Eddie Murphy diction, so I stuck with my Texas drawl.) It elicited laughter in the courtroom. I had already spent about $5 million of my own money in developing Netscape, so why would I license our crown jewels to the most powerful company on the planet for only $1 million? In fact, why would I license to them for any price? I wanted to build a big company, not sell out to the Evil Empire.

This response was based not just on my longstanding antipathy for

Microsoft and its imperial ways, but on the strong instinct that what was being offered was pixie dust, not fertilizer to help us grow. It might make us look good for a while and bring in some positive press attention (bearing in mind that back then not many business reporters had misgivings about Microsoft's divine right to dominate), but when that passed, would we be better off? When dealing with empires, small principalities have usually paid the price of independence in order not to be crushed. In some rare cases, the tail may end up wagging the dog—as Microsoft itself did with IBM—but not often. Small companies that ally themselves with Emperor Gates often find immediate advantages turn out to be stalking horses for Microsoft's ever-aggressive tactics. (Consider Rob Glaser, a former Microsoft employee, and founder and CEO of Real Networks, who licensed technology to Microsoft but was in court testifying against them a few years later. Or Sun, which licensed Java to Microsoft only to have to sue them later for violating the agreement.) The company has stated its policy of dealing with small fry in almost laughably benign terms: Embrace and extend. At Netscape, Mike Homer accurately restated this as "Embrace and pretend." Spyglass, which ultimately provided the basic Mosaic software for Internet Explorer, has learned this lesson dramatically. Over the years, it collected a total of $13 million from Microsoft. Not bad, you might think. But in December 1995, when Microsoft announced it would give away the browser free, the move effectively killed off a number of minor Internet software companies and dried up what was left of the licensing revenues Mosaic depended upon. In 1997, Spyglass declared a loss of $9.7 million, and at this writing is scrambling for survival. So much for the advantages of cozying up to the Bash Brothers of Redmond.

Most important, to license our fast, feature-rich browser to Microsoft would be to give up any advantage we already had in the growing browser market. Once Microsoft planners saw the possibilities of Mosaic Netscape (later Netscape Navigator), they weren't likely to remain casual about the Internet. You don't sell your stealth fighters to your most implacable foe just to make a little money. We were developing software ten times the speed of anything anyone else had, so the only chance we had against Microsoft was the element of surprise. It's the only chance any start-up has against a company whose chairman seems obsessed with crushing all opposition.

Unfortunately (I suppose), Paul Koontz relayed my response to Silverberg verbatim, expletives intact. Whether it made its way all the way up the line to redden the Great Man's ear, I don't know. But for however many people at Microsoft who heard it, the remark must have drawn a line in the sand. They were accustomed to having people play ball with them; after all, it was their ball. The deadly battle between Netscape and Microsoft today didn't arise because I said something impolitic, but because we dared to challenge them by getting one big idea they hadn't thought of. Put yourself on the wrong side of Microsoft, however, and they have ways to make you pay.

After the beta release and the extraordinary response that came with it, I was involved almost full time with the NCSA troubles. Thinking about our eventual "High Noon" confrontations with Microsoft was a luxury I'd had to put off. A few days after our settlement with NCSA, Ram Shiram, the head of one of our sales groups, stuck his head into my office. He had heard from a couple of friends at Microsoft that their company was about to sign a licensing deal for Mosaic with Spyglass. As far as Ram was concerned, this spelled disaster. He knew as well as I the downside of dealing with Microsoft, but he felt that not dealing with them was even worse. If Spyglass got the business, Ram was sure the press would anoint them the browser company of choice. "Look," he said urgently, "we can't let them sign with Spyglass. We really need to license our stuff to them."

Against my better instincts, I agreed to call Brad Silverberg at the end of December 1994. I hadn't changed my ideas about Microsoft, or about our need to protect a competitive advantage. But I felt increasing concern about money, the spending of it coupled with not making it. And the lawsuit with the University of Illinois had left me weakened, as if I'd just gotten over a terrible case of the flu. That might have pushed me in the direction of a deal that would have been a huge mistake. I was, frankly, exhausted and completely strung out. On December 29, I also sent an e-mail to another Microsoft executive, Dan Rosen, suggesting that the two companies could help each other. (This e-mail would surface years later when Microsoft lawyers offered it as evidence that we had, in some way, invited their later hungry attention.) Luckily for us (in retrospect), neither Silverberg nor Rosen was in the mood to forgive me for my plain-spoken response earlier in the year.

When Silverberg answered his phone, I tried to make the conversation friendly. I generally say what's on my mind without a lot of small talk, but sometimes there's nothing like old-fashioned hypocrisy to grease the skids of business.

"I'm wondering," I said, "whether you'd consider going with Netscape instead of Spyglass." Taking a cautious step forward, I reminded him that he'd been interested in licensing our software a few months before.

He immediately reminded me of my message to Microsoft at the time. Verbatim. I was caught off-guard. When you offer hypocrisy, usually you can expect hypocrisy in return. To get past an awkward moment, cut to the chase, and sweeten the deal all at once, I said that Microsoft could have an equity position and a seat on the board. I was opening the door a crack, confident that I could keep Microsoft's share of stock small enough to prevent any future meddling. Well, somewhat confident. Microsoft could run a school on the Trojan-horse strategy.

Surprisingly, considering what they might have gained at that moment, Silverberg turned me down, saying they were already way down the road with Spyglass. With that, dripping with sarcasm, he slammed the door. By going with Spyglass and throwing down the gauntlet, he prepared the ground for one of the key corporate conflicts of the Information Age. He may even have started a process that will eventually erode the indisputable dominance of Microsoft.

After that, as if on cue, our fortunes improved dramatically. We successfully resolved the University of Illinois situation, and in February 1995, at last, Jim Barksdale joined Netscape. I don't think anyone, even Barksdale himself, knew how relieved I was to see him walk through the front door. A month before, during my Christmas vacation, I had called him and said that it really was time for him to come down. I'd had some good moments as temporary CEO; as I've mentioned, there's a lot to be said for the joy of unilateral decision-making. But along with the exhausting emotional roller coaster of the NCSA problem, I'd had to deal with the December financial crunch and the layoffs it precipitated as well as the daily business of helping guide sales and marketing. Because I had told Barksdale he was going to run the company without interference, I hadn't wanted to make any more major decisions than absolutely necessary. Nothing would be worse than having him feel I was handing him a situation set in stone in which his influence was minimal. Since he'd been on our board for a few months, I'd kept him informed about everything that was happening, so he was able to step into his office, take off his jacket, and get right to it.

As Barksdale doubled the size of the sales staff, then doubled it again, sales followed suit. We had turned the corner financially, and now the business side of Netscape began to catch up with the software development. Was Microsoft watching? No doubt about it; like Big Brother—and they were, even then, headed toward being the most highly valued company in the world in terms of capitalization—they're always watching. But we were still small game, a hundred employees or so, and couldn't have seemed worth worrying much about. Microsoft's cash reserves let them buy any company that annoys them, and their dominance lets them cripple any interloper they can't buy. So it takes more than we were doing then to set off the alarm bells in Redmond.

Nevertheless, they had hardly forgotten us. We had released Communicator 1.0 in mid-December, our first official post-beta product, and we were gaining momentum every day—not just signing customers, but discovering directions for previously unimagined growth. Kipp Hickman put it perfectly when he said, "Every week I turned over a rock and found a new business."

By early March 1995, we had reached a point in development of our 2.0 release where we needed from Microsoft the application programming interfaces (APIs) to enable our software to dial up Internet Service Providers from Windows 95–equipped computers—the phone book APIs. Our 1.0 release had been compatible with Windows 3.1, but now we had to gear up for Microsoft's release of a major upgrade. We could go on writing software, but without the APIs we couldn't completely implement and debug our Windows 95 version. This sort of cooperation was no big deal. Even in a fiercely competitive industry, a certain awareness of mutual benefit prevails. A lack of standardization has long tormented computer consumers, but Apple's disastrous failure to let its operating system migrate to other platforms taught everyone that at some point, cooperation and competition have to coexist. Imagine a roughly parallel situation from the early days of color television: NBC refuses to allow CBS programs to run on the sets made by its parent company RCA, because the companies are locked in competition to see which will establish the standard for color broadcasting. This didn't happen, of course, because no one who wanted to watch Walter Cronkite would have bought RCA sets.

But something different was at work in the mid-nineties. One morning in March, the engineer working on the dial-up part of Navigator came into my office with an annoyed look on his normally unemotional face. "They're dragging their feet about giving us the dial-up APIs." It was obvious who "they" were. So here was Microsoft, beginning to lean on us, fully prepared to wall off Netscape from 90 percent of the world's computers, and thus keep nine out of ten computer users from having access to the Next Great Thing.

In recent years, Microsoft's public relations efforts have portrayed the software giant as just another hard-working company doing what it must to stay alive. Well, hard working they are. But their tactics are something else. Tough business tactics are one thing, but exclusionary and other anti-competitive actions, especially when practiced by monopolies, can be illegal. We were able to win by making a better, faster browser, not by simply making it impossible for them to do business. This isn't to imply that Marc, Bark, and Clark are saints. I don't doubt, given absolute power, we might be capable of all sorts of low blows and eye-gouging. The nicest people can become despots, I suppose. But we didn't have that kind of power, and, to be honest, I think all of us, and everyone else at Netscape, really liked the idea of winning because we built a better mousetrap.

Doing things better, however, has almost never been the way Microsoft has come out ahead, because it has almost never started out with a superior product. You can get into a race with Microsoft, which is tough enough even when all things are equal. But they're never equal, because Microsoft controls the track, and they make sure there's gravel and maybe some oil in your lane. Sometimes Microsoft lets it appear as if a race is going on, at least in some area that doesn't matter much to them. But ultimately they can decide who wins and who loses. They'll even invest just enough money in their tottering rival Apple to keep it alive, so that there will at least be the illusion that they still have competition. If Apple, which has had a comeback success with such appealing products as the iMac computer, returns to contender status, the long knives will come out again.

When our engineers made a routine request for the phone book APIs, they were told that the APIs weren't ready yet. Yet we had heard that other customers of Microsoft already had the APIs that we needed, so they appeared to be lying. This had a distinctly extortionist smell to it as far as I was concerned. They had something we needed, and they were holding out until we gave them something they wanted. I was sure it was just a matter of time before we'd find out what that was.

The impasse dragged on through the spring, an echo of the kind of delay we'd been through the previous autumn. The delay, over many months, was a huge problem in a six-month product cycle. It's hard enough to keep to that kind of schedule when the barriers are internal— racing against the clock, hiring and motivating talent, making the right decisions quickly—without what amounted to an ambush stopping our forward progress. For me, the difference this time was that I had turned over to Barksdale responsibility for all day-to-day operations, as I'd promised I would, so I could enjoy the sheer luxury of not knowing on a daily basis what Microsoft was putting us through. Not that I didn't care—I still had everything riding on our start-up's success, and I had a lot more than money invested in it. But my work now mostly involved traveling, often to Europe and Asia, talking to prospective customers and helping salespeople close deals. In other words, Web evangelism, with the gospel according to Netscape. How we dealt with Microsoft was no longer my call, which, given my growing personal dislike for their style, was probably just as well. So I was able to keep my distance. In terms of energy and emotion, the NCSA standoff had just about eaten me alive; this time I could do what I had to do without being sidetracked or sucked dry.

On June 21, 1995, Marc, Barksdale, and Mike Homer met with a delegation from Redmond. Gates didn't come, but there can't be any doubt that he was calling the shots. Microsoft was now prepared to give us the APIs we needed, and they wanted plenty in return—a seat on the board and an equity position. They were ready to make an investment, of course—cash was something Microsoft had plenty of— but everyone at the meeting knew the figure wasn't going to be a measly few percent. No actual number was mentioned, but accounting rules dictate keeping the number below 20 percent to avoid consolidating our losses with their profits, so I assumed they wanted about 19.99 percent.

Even though, at a earlier desperate moment, I'd given Microsoft a chance to get its claws into Netscape, that was a voluntary move on my part. Whether it was wise or not, I had done it in an effort to induce them to license our browser. This was fundamentally different. Where the former negotiation had been about business, and a standard sales incentive—"I want you to sign on the dotted line, and here's what I'm willing to do in order to make that happen"—this was about the exercise of power and control. For us, having Microsoft as a customer wasn't a life-or-death matter. And, frankly, when Silverberg turned me down and signed a deal with Spyglass, I suspect he thought that would be the end of us. But once they knew we were in the game, they figured they could delay us just as we were bringing products to the market they most coveted, on Windows 95. Most of our browser customers, whether private individuals or businesses, were using Microsoft operating systems and applications, so Microsoft had us over a barrel. There was no question of a voluntary offer anymore; all that would do now was our capitulation.

When Mike Homer stepped out of the meeting and told me about their demands, I said, "If that isn't illegal, it sure as hell ought to be. I'm going to try to get the Department of Justice to stop this." I went back to my office, picked up the phone, and called Gary Reback, the now-well-known Microsoft nemesis. Reback is a lawyer with Wilson Sonsini, and is to Bill Gates's imperial designs what a Doberman pinscher is to a burglar's ankle. He is sometimes strident, which can undercut his effectiveness on occasion, but he knows how to get people's attention. And that began a process that took the next two years but led to the landmark lawsuit against Microsoft.

I don't claim to be a great visionary, just a scientist with a good nose for business opportunities. But I do credit myself for being someone who understood, when most others still saw Microsoft as a hero of the Information Age, that its steamroller tactics were stifling innovation and killing free-market competition. For us, this was just the beginning. Soon enough, Netscape would be the target of powerful and subversive attempts by Microsoft to stop our growth and take away our air. Today, only a few years later, many others have noticed that they're getting short of air, too, and people are fighting back. But it may be that my phone call to Reback, and the lawsuit that resulted, could be, with a little luck, the beginning of the end for a monolithic company that is able to exert phenomenal control over one of America's most important industries.

Jim Barksdale shared my antagonism for Microsoft. I think he'd have preferred to be eaten by piranhas than to have Microsoft sit on our board and own a piece of the company. So, in the face of their demands, he said, in his courtly, Southern way, "Thanks, but no thanks. We don't think we can have you as an investor, since we're probably going to end up competing with you."

Weeks later, near the end of June 1995, Microsoft finally gave us the phone book APIs for Windows 95. We missed the release date of Netscape 2.0 for Windows 95 and Microsoft did not have to share any glory on its introduction; it took us a few weeks afterward to get the release out. No explanation was ever given for the delay, or the eventual change, other than the phony implication that the application hadn't been ready before and now it was. I wondered if word of our meeting with Reback, or even some prescient sense that Netscape might not be inclined to roll over and play dead, had got back to Redmond. So someone had decided that, once we'd turned down their equity bid, they'd given us enough trouble for the time being and to get trouble in return wasn't worth it.

In pointing to a future of competition, Barksdale had stated what I had long known: Netscape and Microsoft were going to be enemies on the Hector and Achilles scale (though I think I prefer the outcome of the David and Goliath match). But at that moment, the competition hadn't really begun. With Navigator 1.0, we had introduced a major Internet product, while Microsoft was still determined to make their proprietary Microsoft Network the dominant gateway, a proprietary online service like America Online and Compuserve. They'd spent a small fortune to get the rights to the Rolling Stones' "Start Me Up" to help launch Windows 95, but they hadn't yet developed anything that improved upon the Mosaic they'd licensed from Spyglass—or made any attempt to bundle Internet software with all the other bells and whistles of their new operating system.

For us, as for so many other companies, Microsoft casts a huge, intimidating shadow. But the sheer size of its market penetration—by the end of the next year, 1996, the installed base of Windows 95 would be around 65 million users—presented a major opportunity. On this rare occasion we had a chance to use their advantage to our advantage. So in late 1995, we went to many of the biggest PC manufacturers and suggested that they add Navigator to the operating system they were installing in their computers, as an added feature for their customers. This was akin to a company with a global positioning navigational system approaching Ford, GM, and Chrysler and offering their product as an appealing extra to help boost sales. We would continue to offer our browser online, of course, as well as supplying corporate clients, but with pre-installed browsers in popular-brand PCs, we could expand our market share to people who might not normally buy Internet software or be able to download it.

This seemed to us at Netscape a natural and mutually advantageous way to put our product into wider circulation than just the base of Net-savvy people who were using it so far. Most of the PC companies were eager to embrace this idea, but as usual, Microsoft heard of our overtures. Suddenly the enthusiasm faded, and we sensed fear on the part of those PC vendors who had previously been confident. Several companies told us that they could not tell us why because they were under nondisclosure, but they were prohibited from putting our browser on the computers they shipped. They said that only under a CID (Civil Investigative Demand), the Department of Justice's term for a subpoena, could they tell us. By using this term, we knew that they, too, believed Microsoft was breaking the law. It was this experience, finding the door blocked to a legitimate and innovative sales approach, that finally led us, early in 1996, to send a letter to the Justice Department, the effects of which are still being felt. Recently, of course, it became apparent why these PC vendors were afraid, as it is now a matter of public record revealed in the antitrust case against Microsoft. In calling their bluff, Compaq put Netscape Navigator on the desktop of several computers they shipped. Microsoft officially canceled Compaq's Windows 95 license! Microsoft's behavior paid off, and Compaq agreed to stop installing Netscape. They had no choice; they had no other source for Windows. (A good definition of a monopoly.)

One of the PC vendors told us that Microsoft threatened to charge an extra three dollars per copy of Windows 95 if Navigator was bundled with the operating system. In a sense, they were demanding a license fee for *our* software! When you're talking about hundreds of thousands of units, three dollars was certainly enough to make ours an offer computer companies definitely could refuse. After all, Netscape might have been a terrific thing to provide to computer buyers, but adding some discretionary value wouldn't be worth creating bad blood with the giant that absolutely controlled the software without which their machines would be about as desirable as old black-and-white televisions. The quality of our product was completely irrelevant; no computer company dared touch it. (In a similar move, Microsoft later told content suppliers that if they dealt with Netscape, they wouldn't be given a spot on the screen of Windows.) This wasn't hard-nosed competition, just old-fashioned coercion.

As another example, I had a business acquaintance at a company that did a lot of business with Microsoft. (His name is withheld to protect his job.) This person was one of a number of people I knew, or knew of, increasingly disenchanted by Microsoft's heavy-handed dealings with allies as well as competitors. We met in my office around this time on Netscape business, and he told me about witnessing Gates—one of the world-class tantrum-throwers in the business—launch into a tirade when the subject of Netscape came up.

"I've never seen him so upset," he said. "He was ranting and raving, red in the face, shouting, 'I'm going to give away everything free that Netscape tries to sell! I'm going to take away their air!'" (A variation on this last quote has been attributed by *The New York Times* to "a senior Microsoft official," in the same way the newspaper used to attribute Henry Kissinger's deep background quotes to "a highly placed official at the State Department." Though I cannot be sure it was Gates, I trust my informer's report.)

Obviously, Gates had got the message that we were a possible problem, and had heard that we weren't playing by the rules he lays out. Whether or not Microsoft executives remember it that way (for the sake of court testimony) today, the remote chance that we might become a problem must have occurred to Gates. So at that point, I think he figured, "Well, we either have to get in on this, or we have to throw some blocks in their way."

I'm not someone who calls out for government intervention the second I find myself in a street fight. Especially when it comes to the Internet, with its freewheeling, free-market, thoroughly satisfying boom-town dynamic, I'd like the government to keep its distance. I also don't have a reputation as a whiner. Business is tough, and there are winners and losers. I fervently believe that anyone who manages to get legitimate business leverage and doesn't use it to make life harder for competitors is an idiot. If someone gets the edge on me and I'm not good enough to blunt that edge, more power to them. Sun routinely kicked SGI's butt, yet I admire and like Bill Joy and Scott McNealy. But when it's a monopoly that is leveraged, the rules change, and the game is fixed. With the end result pretty much guaranteed, the winner doesn't have to work hard anymore, just make enough improvements to give consumers a reason to buy new products and upgrades. This was the way, in Detroit's days of absolute hegemony and peak arrogance, that General Motors used to change chrome grills and tail fins instead of engineering substantially better cars.

Like most monopolies, Microsoft has done some good things. (Shakespeare has shown us that even villains have some redeeming qualities.) With its vast market share and ever-aggressive marketing, the company—now the richest in the world—has been largely responsible for a massive growth of computing technology around the world. That's the good news.

The bad news, however, is that as Microsoft sets out to crush any company whose small piece of territory Gates covets, fewer innovative start-ups will risk confronting them. As a result Microsoft, always more of an imitator than an innovator, will have less reason to do anything new. The battle between Netscape and Microsoft, and the fact that in 1999 our company has essentially moved out of its original core business of selling browser software, serves as a discouraging cautionary tale to anyone who thinks they can do something better than Microsoft. If Netscape had to cede territory originally taken with brilliant work but indefensible against overwhelming odds, who is going to try again? Getting a jump on Microsoft with a great product, hard work, and great timing, as we once did, is now seen as a temporary and therefore meaningless advantage; with what is by now an installed base of 95 percent of all computers on the planet, they can push anyone out of the way whenever they want.

What does this mean for the future? The great paradigm shifts once brought about by imaginative companies such as Apple will only happen in the distant outbacks that Microsoft has somehow overlooked (as they'd overlooked the Internet until we got their attention). And those little bits of back country are getting fewer and fewer. Microsoft's advertising copy asks, "Where do you want to go today?" When it comes to their own territorial ambitions, the answer seems to be "Almost everywhere." They're going after AOL, they're going after the airlines reservation systems and the travel industry, they're going after Disney. Only because they're a monopoly in such a crucial industry can they be so massively ambitious.

Since our fateful beta release in October 1994, Netscape has represented the last outpost of possibility in a world where Microsoft calls all the shots. We came along and caught hold of a new paradigm, a new distribution approach for software and an entirely new way for people to do business. Because of that I believe the world is a better place, just as our idealistic young programmers thought it would be. But we were just a wedge in between Microsoft's ubiquitous operating system and the newly developing networked applications. If they are allowed to drive us out of this business through the power of their monopoly, what chance does any young company with a great idea have in the future? I'm convinced that if Microsoft is allowed to go on leveraging their advantage to the full extent they're capable of, they'll be able to keep anyone from competing with them ever again. When Microsoft stalled on that essential dial-up API, they not only delayed us, which in itself might have proved fatal, but even more important, they distracted us. Causing management to waste four months dealing with this issue meant we couldn't deal with the other issues of growing a business and inventing newer things for the consumer. It's nothing for Gates to assemble a group of people whose sole task is to keep a small company preoccupied. But for a company with no cash and a staff of fifty or one hundred, using manpower that way is a nightmare. If we'd been up against Microsoft instead of the University of Illinois in the Mosaic dispute, we'd never have been able to survive.

It was our good luck that by the time Microsoft launched its attack on us, we were strong enough to fight back. And significant enough to get the Justice Department to pay attention to our concerns—eventually. More and more start-ups today have only one goal: not to change the world, or to make something new and exciting happen, but to be bought by Microsoft as soon as possible. What this means is that what has become a business monopoly has also become a technological, even a cultural monopoly: Smart young entrepreneurs won't want to do things the elegant, interesting way, but merely the Microsoft way. In addition to this stifling effect, there is another specter lurking in the natural hierarchy of the Internet. Browsers enable applications, and applications enable services; if Microsoft owns the browser as well as the operating system, there will be no Yahoo!, no Infoseek, no Excite, just Bill standing at the gate, pointing out where he wants us to go. Microsoft will be the one and only "portal."

Even today, when so much more is known about how Microsoft does business, people still make the argument that its power to move into so many markets is good for the consumer. There was a time, when its share of the operating system market was being built, that consumers no doubt benefited. But consider that originally, the operating system DOS cost IBM and other PC computer vendors about $5—back when they had a choice. Now, years later, with no significant competition, the price is $125. What has been added to justify that kind of price rise? Initially, Windows 3.1, then Windows 95, and now Windows 98 were laid over DOS. Admittedly, Microsoft had to spend a lot of money initially to create Windows—or, rather, to figure out how to copy what Apple had already done; they simply didn't know how to build graphic user interfaces. When they finally got something half-assed good, the installed base of DOS dictated that Microsoft could essentially take over, and at that point the price went up hugely. It's hard to say how much Windows would cost if there were a truly competitive product on the market, but I know it wouldn't be anything like $125. I suspect the price in a truly competitive market would be about $10. (If the browser can be given away free with a staff of a thousand people working on it, maybe the OS price should be closer to the original $3.)

A monopoly, by definition, got that way by eliminating competition. When Gates said, in the fall of 1994, that he hoped no one except operating system vendors would make money on browsers, because everyone who has operating systems (now let's see, who could that be?) would probably embed them, it was clear even then that his intention was to intimidate us. Of course, it's a natural urge to want to take out your opponents. I did that at Silicon Graphics every chance I got. But in a healthy business environment, you have to be better than the others to prevail, whether it's in design, production, or marketing. A monopoly, however, can beat the competition without having to try particularly hard.

I believe that the world has a more or less uniform distribution of smart people. Sometimes, as in the Athens of Pericles or the Florence of Michelangelo, one place will seem to have an unusual number at one time, but that's usually because conditions are such that talent gets a chance to flourish. In any event, Microsoft doesn't have a corner on brains any more than Netscape does. What Microsoft has is $10 billion in cash, accumulated as a result of their vise grip on the operating system market, and increasingly the applications market. So when Bill Gates wants to give something away—as long as it's not one of his core products—he can damn well afford to do it. But Microsoft didn't become the world's richest company by giving things away; when freebies start flowing out of Redmond, you can be sure there's a reason. And the reason the decision was made to give away their Internet browser, Microsoft Internet Explorer, was starkly simple: to put Netscape out of business. With billions in cash, it's not hard to hand out free prizes. But our core business in the early days was the browser, and there was no way we could give it away free. It stands to reason that if someone offers a person a new refrigerator as a gift, they'll usually take it, even if they could actually buy a better one. "Free" is always a compelling price, whatever the product.

But when you're dealing with a monopoly, nothing is ever really free. Internet Explorer costs nothing now; it was embedded in Windows 98 (with the tacit consent of a Justice Department knee-deep in depositions). But if Microsoft comes to dominate the browser market totally, then the price of Windows is going to rise to reflect the "added value" of what they've been giving away. Maybe the price will go up to $200, or even $250. Meanwhile, the commodity hardware prices are dropping. So more and more of the total cost of a computer is the operating system, which has no replication cost. Microsoft, able to resist price and profitability cuts that competition forces on Compaq, Dell, Gateway, IBM, and other computer manufacturers, represents the floor in pricing, the one element that keeps PCs from ever dropping below a certain point. Leaving aside the damage a relentless monopoly does to innovation, the idea that one company's control of an entire industry can make life better for consumers just doesn't wash. It's like thinking that life under a totalitarian regime would be better because things are so much simpler. When it comes to prices, there's Moore's Law, and there's Bill's Law, and they go in opposite directions.

Those in the technology business who fight the good fight against Microsoft's conquest of the known world have long understood the nature of the enemy. Since I began writing this book, that voracious nature is becoming public, through the efforts of people such as Scott McNealy at Sun Microsystems and Jim Barksdale (and others who prefer not to be mentioned out of fear of retribution from Microsoft). The dominance of the operating system market didn't worry the majority of computer users, mostly because as Microsoft's prices went up, overall computer prices fell more rapidly, masking the problem. But the Internet, which promises the heady freedom of a kind of productive anarchy, is seen as a new medium worth guarding. Thus, the war between Netscape and Microsoft, a battle for choice, has been the dramatic event that brought out the truth, and finally made the government take a hard look. I'm writing this chapter before the actual conclusion of the lawsuit against Microsoft brought by the federal government and several states' attorneys general. So maybe, by the time this book is in print, the hegemony of the Redmond giant may not be as dangerous as it is today. But whether the case is won or lost, sooner or later (and by this time, later is too late), something has to be done about Microsoft.

Naturally, I have an idea. Or, as the Department of Justice would call it, the "remedy." I suggest the following plan not to save Netscape, whose destiny is already determined by AOL, but because the future of America's phenomenally powerful technology engine is at stake. The time has come—is, in fact, long past due—to break up Microsoft. The single company that now has its tentacles in so many aspects of business life ought to be split into three parts: an office applications company, an online services company, and Windows Inc. The office applications company—let's call it MicroOffice—would be kept out of the markets of the other two companies. It could create and sell office applications, and maybe even Internet browsers, but it would be prohibited from offering Internet services. The services company, MicroOnline (let's say), would be able to get into such online services as airline reservations, health care, banking, financial services, and so forth. And Windows Inc. would continue in the operating systems business, with regulation controlling its prices, regulation prohibiting preferential deals with anyone whatsoever, and regulation to keep it out of the MicroOffice and the MicroOnline markets. But it would be able to concentrate on making the operating system better than the competitors that would inevitably spring up, or be revived, as a result of a leveled playing field. And it could incorporate a browser if it wants—it just couldn't charge more for it unless given permission by the regulators. The point would be to divide the company into layers that already exist, but to keep the layers from helping one another out.

As nasty as the resulting regulatory bureaucracy sounds, I think this is the only way to open up the market for continued innovation. With each of these three separate companies having to function without the vanguard of Microsoft's monopoly power, innovation, lower prices on other operating systems, and financial incentives to license to other platforms would make sense. You can bet that the MicroOffice company would then support the Macintosh OS and UNIX with the Office suite, and Steve Jobs wouldn't have to bribe them. Why? Because it would be in their economic interest to do so. The services company could offer the browser and would be a serious competitor in the portal business—MSN already is. None of the companies would be likely to amass billions in cash, and the Windows company couldn't support its weaker siblings by giving away the browser or services to put competitors out of business.

Breaking up Microsoft wouldn't mean hard times for the resulting companies, or the sorry sight of Bill Gates on the dole. Look at how well the fragments of AT&T and AT&T itself have done in the years after its breakup. The collective market capitalization of these companies is far greater than it would have been on its own. And who could imagine that we would have cellular phones on the Internet if AT&T had not been broken up? The only reason the Internet happened at all was because there was a competitive market between telecommunications companies to lease spare capacity in the increasingly digital phone system. What it would mean is that each of the three new companies (or four, or ten) would have to make it on merit, not monopoly. The move would limit power, but profits would not necessarily be affected. In fact, Chairman Bill would probably end up even richer than he is now, as he'd be the biggest shareholder of all three.

As big and powerful as it is today, Microsoft is not invulnerable. No empire lasts forever, however overarching its reach at its zenith. The Visigoths are always lurking, bless their pagan hearts. For all the money it spends on R&D and high-priced programming talent, the company has always had a hard time creating new products. Elegant simplicity has never been a Microsoft strength, so their software gorges itself on memory and is as crash-prone as a Suzuki Samurai. At this moment in time, they are struggling to debug Windows NT 5.0, which, since the program has 40 million lines of code (80 percent of which are new), is likely to carry a baggage of problems. Coincident with this struggle, a free operating system called Linux is being downloaded from the Internet (the Netscape paradigm strikes again!) by millions of users. It works well, doesn't react to other software like antibodies to invading viruses, crashes far less often than Windows, and people can't get their hands on it soon enough. Windows never has inspired the kind of cult devotion that Macintosh enjoys (even though that cult is ever smaller); people use it, some of them admire it, but nobody really loves it. Too cloying in its cute little critters, too clunky in its operation, too fragile by far. Windows actually engenders a cult of aversion. So if a good system comes along that works well and costs nothing—and doesn't need to beg for shelf space in retail stores—the presumptive reign of Windows could begin to disintegrate. And, given the speed of Internet-based commerce and communication, this process could accelerate with phenomenal speed.

But if you're holding your breath waiting for this to happen, you're going to die. Linux doesn't have the world's most popular applications, such as Microsoft Office, so it will not be successful. Microsoft is big, tough, durable, ruthless, and not tormented by the niceties of ethical behavior. It will fight to survive, to use Malcolm X's ominous phrase, by whatever means necessary. At this point, its vast installed base is like a hilltop fortress. No attacking force can even reach the base of the walls. Netscape, with a phenomenal new weapon—the Information Age–equivalent of Medieval cannons suddenly able to breach stone ramparts—had the best chance in recent times to break Microsoft's hold on its empire. Now the company finds itself being acquired because it was so weakened by Microsoft's assault. The Justice Department seems, at last, to have realized the breadth and depth of the unfairness. Let's hope it has the skill to make its case against such a formidable foe. The problem is, the DOJ's case against Microsoft is centered on specific unfair business practices. It doesn't address the possibility of a breakup, as the case against the old AT&T monopoly did. Justice may be hoping to proceed against Microsoft in small steps, in which case it has drastically underestimated its opponent. So if, by the time you read this, the process of breaking up Microsoft isn't yet under way, as my mom used to say, "You're in for a heap of trouble."

On August 9, 1995, two things happened that had never happened before. A small company making its first offering of common stock saw its share price end the day up more than 100 percent. And the employees of Netscape Communications left work, en masse, at five in the afternoon.

The phenomenon of our Wall Street rocket shot was not the end of the Netscape story. Far from it. In most respects, in fact, the amazing success of the offering didn't change anything about what we had to do, and when and how we had to do it. The work of speeding products to market, capturing market share and consolidating those gains, signing up distributors and forging strategic alliances, imagining new directions and figuring out ways to move down unmapped roads—all these challenges remained just as formidable as ever. Plus, now that we had shifted dramatically from the category of intriguing possibility to the biggest story the Internet had yet produced, the baleful eye of Lord Sauron was fixed on us with an intensity we hadn't felt before. We would find our story easier to tell to customers and prospective partners from this point on now that we had a brand with both brains and brawn behind it, but everything else would be just as hard as it had been so far.

All that could wait, however. For a precious few hours, we had earned a break. A $2.2 billion market value bought us a little non–Netscape time time. A lot of us had made a tremendous amount of money that day—or rather, we were worth a lot of money on paper—and there was no way to try keeping a lid on the high that welled up as the market closed in New York and everybody did the math. My worth, theoretically at least, had jumped by a factor of sixty or so, which made me feel just fine. Marc's had gone up almost infinitely. And a lot of cubicles now housed millionaires. Netscape had suddenly gone from being a multimillion-dollar company to a multibillion-dollar company. The battle wasn't over, and never would be, but on that day we could revel in the fact that we'd definitely taken the high ground.

No one could have predicted the frenzy that drove our stock so high. But Barksdale and I had figured, from the response to the road show, that the company would probably end the day with a pretty impressive market capitalization. We knew, too, that the shares held by the employees were going to be worth at least the initial price we and our bankers had given them. So we had a party arranged to let everyone celebrate a year and a half of hard work and one day that none of us would ever forget.

Starting just before five in the afternoon, people who would usually work until midnight or later pushed back from their computers, or put down their telephone handsets, leaned back with a collective sigh that combined relief and disbelief, and headed for the door. All morning, since the stock had finally begun trading, an air of barely suppressed jubilation had filled the building, like the exultant mood in a school on the last day of the spring term. Many of our mostly young staff had no doubt called their parents to announce that the kid did all right (and would not be asking for money ever again). Rosanne's staff had fielded countless calls from reporters all over the country, swarming to the biggest story to come out of Silicon Valley in a long time. TV mobile units had arrived as if by magic, and carefully coiffed correspondents were taking their turn taping segments for the evening news with the Netscape offices as a backdrop. For the moment, it was all over.

But for the shouting. So everyone poured out into the parking lot, into cars that many would soon be trading in for something better, and headed for the Palace, a club a few miles south in downtown Sunnyvale that had once been a movie house. With a stage and a dance floor downstairs, and private dining rooms upstairs, the Palace was a suitably theatrical setting to celebrate what had been a day of high drama. We had reserved the club from five until eight, when the moderate heat of Sunnyvale's Wednesday-night fever would push us aside, no matter how much money we were worth.

Though Jim Barksdale was running the company, my position of paterfamilias designated me the natural master of ceremonies for the party. It was a role I was glad to play. As I stood on the stage, I had a feeling of tremendous pride. I couldn't, and wouldn't, claim credit for what had been done over the course of the past fifteen months that resulted in Wall Street's resounding response. Marc and Eric had the vision, and their original Mosaic crew, augmented by recruits such as Lou Montulli and Jamie Zawinski, had shared that vision and made it a reality. My engineer-managers from SGI, Tom Paquin, Michael Toy, Kipp Hickman, and others, had been able to make a mind meld with their younger colleagues and expand our horizons. Barksdale had arrived just in time (though sooner would have been even better), fitting in seamlessly and ramping up our sales effort. Jim, however, adamantly refused to take credit for the success of the day: "I didn't do anything but be amazed," he told me. When he spoke, it was to congratulate everyone in the room on the astonishing growth of the company and to recognize their work.

One of the great things about our booming IPO was that so many deserving people actually got what they deserved. I'm not being falsely modest here; I had some specific victories at crucial points along the way, and I savored them.

But at that moment, I had the pleasure of knowing that whatever else others had done, none of this could have happened without me. This feeling, of having been absolutely essential to something extraordinary, is the kind of pleasure that doesn't come often in life. Perhaps great concert soloists and opera stars feel it all the time, or Cy Young pitchers. But in business, it's rare and hence doubly delightful. Of course, Netscape couldn't have happened without Marc, either, but if I hadn't recognized the special quality of that subdued, sleepy kid at our first meeting, who knows what he and all the others excitedly milling around on the dance floor would be doing?

One by one, I called the original Mosaic team up onto the stage. Despite the occasion, they were dressed in the same shorts or jeans and T-shirts they wore on any day at the office. Only Marc, with dark Bermudas and a blue sports shirt, and I, in a jacket with a dress shirt open at the neck, offered a nod to ceremony. Some of the programmers were wearing old T-shirts that Aleks Totic had handed out at the signing party back in Illinois. These relics had the original NCSA Mosaic globe logo from which "NCSA" had been conspicuously omitted. After they had signed the letter of agreement to come to work for the company, each had autographed everyone else's shirt. Now here they were, pulled out of cluttered bottom drawers, a reminder of what a short time ago this whole wild ride had started.

Next up were the core group of SGI engineers, the Valley veterans who had managed to bring experience and some kind of order without ever squelching the enthusiasm. When the "founding fathers" were all onstage, I poured myself a glass of champagne and offered a toast. I have no idea what I said, and I doubt that anyone on the stage remembers, either (and frankly, I'm not about to ask now). I'm sure I tried to be funny, and maybe I even succeeded. This wasn't the day, and these weren't the surroundings, for a ringing oration about what we had all done for mankind, how we'd won one for the Gipper, etc. I doubt that I could have adequately told them how I really felt. Triumph, vindication, phenomenal good fortune, and an almost dizzying amazement all blended into the purest kind of satisfaction. It's a feeling we don't tap into very often in life.

That satisfaction wasn't just over what we had accomplished. It was also over being on the good side of fate. This feels especially fine when, not too long before, you've been on the bad side. To quote an eloquently existential bumper sticker: Shit Happens. Some people try to wish it away, or simply forget about it. Others use it as fertilizer. I like to think I'm in the latter category. When I left Silicon Graphics, I felt that I had been pushed out of a company I helped create. I won't go over the whole ordeal yet again, but once out of there, I could have gone in a couple of directions. Though I didn't have the amount of money I should have, I had enough to sail off to Bali and live well without doing anything else. Retiring at fifty is hardly unprecedented in Silicon Valley. Had I been the kind of person inclined to be content with my lot, I might have been happy enough to drop out. But what happened, and the way it happened, pushed me the other way, on an intercept vector with the future at the Cafe Verona. My particular encounter with the shit happening helped me grow another company, and another life.

After the toasts and speeches, we spent the next couple of hours just having a good time. The preceding year of intense work had been punctuated by spontaneous venting, everything from the episode of the remote-control model cars to surprisingly fierce roller-hockey games in the parking lot. The year definitely had not been all work and no play. But aside from my small party the previous Fourth of July, we hadn't had a lot of official social gatherings. With almost four hundred employees, we could now generate a kind of celebratory critical mass. In the back of everyone's mind during this party must have been the gloomy thought that tomorrow we'd all be back at our work again. An IPO is an incident, and a milestone, but it's not the end of anything. In high tech, as in life, you don't get to hang around for long on the slopes of Mount Olympus.

Eight o'clock came, and it was time for us to leave the Palace (a bunch of Cinderellas, four hours early). As everyone drifted out onto the sidewalk in front of the club, I was shocked to see that it was still light, in the way I'd been surprised as a little kid when leaving a Saturday movie matinee. I wondered, for a moment, if some of the people at the party, at the end of one of the most amazing days of their lives, would drift back to work. But I really didn't want to know.

"When we issued Netscape stock, we should have handed out seat belts and neck braces." That is how Jim Barksdale has described what has happened on the market since our IPO. August 9, 1995, served as a microcosm of the months and years that have passed since. At some point during the day, the share price reached close to three times its initial $28 valuation. By the end of the trading session in New York, gravity—if not sanity—exerted some force, and shares ended off a bit, but still at more than twice their value. For the rest of the year the stock price spiraled steadily upward, like a hawk on a desert thermal, until, on December 5, it hit $171—my greatest day as a paper billionaire. (Since shares that expensive tend not to sell as well as shares under $100, Netscape split the stock 2-for-1 in February 1996. A split increases everyone's number of shares, of course, but adds nothing to the cash value of their investment.)

How annoying for stockholders (and paper billionaires) that the old adage "What goes up must come down" is, at least here on earth, so invariably true. On December 7, two days after the stock peaked, Microsoft held its "Pearl Harbor" press conference to announce its Internet strategy (promising far more, of course, than they were anywhere near being able to deliver). Partly in response to this declaration of total war, and partly because of the effects of gravity, Netscape stock fell sharply. Over the next couple months it worked its way back up, then in February began to fall again. Only brokers, mutual fund managers, and obsessive-compulsive investors pay attention to the daily up-or-down ticks of a stock, and in high-tech investing, those who watch closely are subject to nosebleeds and queasy stomachs. About a year after the IPO, factoring in the split, the stock was still at a very profitable $86. As I write this epilogue, on a mid-October day in 1998, the price (again accounting for the split) is $40.50. Marc, Barksdale, and I, and most of the other people with stock options, have sold some stock over the years, starting in early 1996, but are still heavily invested.

Like the stock price, the fortunes of the company have risen, fallen, and risen again. We began to show profits in September of 1995, and those profits rose quickly and spectacularly, going from $3.6 million in the first quarter of 1996 to $5.8 million in the second (on revenues of $55 million and $75 million respectively). By June of 1996, with 38 million users, Navigator was the most popular PC application in the world. But Microsoft had been shocked fully awake by the IPO, and by the realization that we had grabbed at least 80 percent of the browser market share (as compared to Microsoft's 5 percent or so). As a Merrill Lynch analyst said to *Web Week* in August of 1996, "Microsoft never takes a pit stop. Those guys up there never have to refill for gas. I don't think they ever sleep, in fact."

Well, we had caught them napping, but not for long. Microsoft struck back on all fronts. The Redmond giant's ferocity would have been laudable, even by those of us on the receiving end, had its methods not been so questionable. In January of 1998, Netscape reported an $88 million loss for the last quarter of 1997, and for the first time since the cash-crunch of December 1994, we had to cancel some engineering projects and announce layoffs. Our share of the browser market had declined as Microsoft's rose.

In response, the company has reverted to the guerrilla tactics that had served us well in the beginning, avoiding pitched battles (if possible) and maximizing mobility and surprise. We posted the code for the browser on the Web, giving the inner workings of our machine away. Rather than give Microsoft a stationary target, the decision was made to shift the core business from browsers to software for corporate networks, applications for Internet commerce, and a new Netscape Netsite Division under the leadership of Apple veteran (and longtime Microsoft fighter) Mike Homer. This puts us in the kind of Internet publishing and commercial service business I had originally thought would be the most logical way to make money on the Internet.

These have been smart moves that have put Netscape back on track, but they serve as illustrations of how Microsoft's stranglehold on the operating system market severely influences the actions of even the most vigorous competitors. As I come near the end of this story, the Justice Department's case against Microsoft is moving forward. The first name on the government's witness list was Jim Barksdale, who testified brilliantly and came back to a hero's welcome in Mountain View. As I mentioned, the case is narrow in focus; even if the government wins, there's still a long way to go before the company's overwhelming monopoly power will be seriously threatened. But the government's case will probably turn on the question of whether Microsoft is illegally tying products, which means forcing consumers to buy things they don't want in order to get what they need, or bundling, which is the addition of products in one "suite" for efficiency. This last isn't necessarily against the law, though Microsoft has used it to stifle us.

By the time this book is published, whether Microsoft has won or lost will no longer matter as much as it once might have. In mid-November of 1998, as the trial progressed along its tortuous path, Netscape and America Online, with Sun Microsystems involved for its Java software, announced that Netscape would be merged into AOL. The deal was a stock-for-stock transaction, with Netscape shareholders receiving just under half a share of AOL for each share of Netscape. The transaction was valued at $4.2 billion. Had the company still been primarily a builder of browsers, it might not have been so appealing to AOL. As a growing portal company, however, with its 9 million–member Netcenter growing in the same dramatic, exponential way we had seen when we released the beta and 1.0 versions of Navigator, Netscape gives AOL a tremendous added reach combined with the ease of use that has been a hallmark of the company's products since the original rewriting of Mosaic. Not entirely coincidentally, I think, in mid-December of 1998, about a month after the deal for Netscape was announced, Standard & Poors revealed that it would add AOL to its list of five hundred key companies, replacing a venerable company from an earlier time, F. W. Woolworth.

For the industry as a whole, and for consumers, the convergence of AOL, Netscape, and Sun's Java is a major plus. Each element represents a leading edge in communications and technology, and the three together offers the most formidable challenge to Microsoft since Netscape first came on the scene. Not surprisingly, the lawyers defending Microsoft in the Justice Department suit pointed to the merger as proof that competition is alive and well in the industry. This is partly true. In the vibrant, volatile high-technology industry, alliances will inevitably rise up to do battle with the dominant empire, though the odds against these alliances succeeding are steep. But the real meaning of the sale of Netscape to AOL is that Microsoft's huge advantage changes the shape of the industry itself, in the way the gravitational pull of some huge celestial bodies actually warp space and time. Ever since 1997, I've been looking for a company that might buy Netscape, and rumors were so incessant that Jim Barksdale sent out an all-hands e-mail in February of 1998 to discourage speculation about the future of the company and, as he had just before the IPO, urging everyone to concentrate on the business at hand. So for me, seeing the company merged into AOL is neither a surprise nor a disappointment. In all areas of business, we're in a period of mergers. But had the playing field been level for Netscape—had Microsoft not been able to leverage its monopoly in operating systems—there would have been no reason to look for shelter beyond the natural alliances that have always formed on a temporary basis in the high-tech industry. For me, and for many others at the company, the AOL deal is a financial break. I have no doubt that Netscape will retain its identity as an innovative leader in the exploding Internet economy, but, by definition, it cannot be independent. It's hard to know what the future might have held for Netscape in a normal competitive environment, though given its dramatic initial successes, I have no doubt the sky was the limit. As a result of finding itself in a life-and-death struggle far grimmer than it ought to have been, Netscape can't grow on its own in the way it would have. Will this be a bad thing in the long run for the industry, and the consumer? Probably not, but I say that mainly because Marc Andreessen has been named chief technology officer of American Online. With luck, and enlightened management, Marc's imagination will be given greater latitude and a more formidable research and development budget.

So if Microsoft loses in the Justice Department case, it won't matter as much to Netscape as it would have when I began writing this book. But in a way, Justice's victory still will be Netscape's victory. I believe Microsoft has been pulling aces out of its sleeve for years in its sales and marketing practices, long before Mosaic became Netscape. But Bill Gates's fury at what we had accomplished was what made him go too far for the Justice Department to ignore. In his determination to cut off our air, he managed to forget that there's a limit to the number of ways you can strangle your competition.

For Marc Andreessen, the years following the IPO have perhaps been even harder than the year preceding it. His role expanded steadily, as I was sure it would, right up to his promotion to a major position in the newest darling of Standard & Poors. This expansion is by no means a given for a creative engineer central to a start-up's early success. In July 1997, Barksdale made him executive vice president in charge of the company's product development, with a staff of a thousand engineers and managers reporting to him. Marc doesn't have time for programming anymore—one of the costs of leadership. It can be comforting to sit writing code while everything around you is blowing up. But that kind of deep-hacker immersion isn't a luxury Marc can afford. He developed a remarkably close working relationship with Barksdale, and the two spent much of their time thinking ten moves ahead in the exhausting chess game of the Internet business. Leaving this relationship to move into the AOL hierarchy is a natural evolution for Marc, but probably not an easy one. From the very first time we talked, I felt Marc was going to be bigger than any particular technology, and in the last three and a half years he has broadened his awareness of life, leadership, where the future lies, and how Netscape can get there first. A nerd no more, he has even developed a taste for well-tailored Italian suits and Robert Talbott's best shirts. Marc, still in his mid-twenties, will be one of the true leaders of American business in the years to come. Count on it.

The intensity of Netscape time has eased, as it inevitably had to. That doesn't mean a leisurely pace for the more than two thousand people who work at Netscape's several buildings on East Middlefield Road in Mountain View. But now, at least, they can sleep at home, not under their desks, and fifty-hour weeks have pretty much taken the place of twenty-four-hour days. The sprint has become a marathon, no less demanding, but different. Mozilla is no longer a Jolt-spiked, snarling beast, but rather a hard-working, semidomesticated creature who has settled in for the long-term, difficult process of innovating within the constraints of the daily business routines. Netscape has introduced dozens of products since August of 1995 and has expanded through purchases of other companies such as Collabra and strategic partnerships with companies such as Sun Microsystems, Hewlett Packard, and Excite.

On the fiftieth anniversary of the Allied landings on the Normandy beaches, I listened to veterans in their seventies and eighties talk about what it was like to be there on that momentous day. Half a century later, tears still came to their eyes. In their teens and twenties, these men had lived through something so intense that it was hard to imagine what it must have been like for them to come back to the ordinary pleasures and problems of everyday life. There must have been an overwhelming relief at having survived, but it must have been hard to readjust to a life no longer on the edge. Could anything ever re-create that kind of extreme experience? What our small group of original engineers went through can't be compared with war, of course, but it was exhausting and exhilarating in a way none of us had been prepared for. We created Netscape time, then served it; the making of a machine that could kill Mosaic and challenge Microsoft had an emotional power over a highly compressed period of time that made the somewhat more orderly process of building and maintaining a company seem comparatively routine, like a combat veteran's job back in his hometown pharmacy. Success in the post–start-up stage is a matter of holding the line, moving forward through calculated risk, and solving hundreds of small problems every month, instead of coming up with big ideas every day and risking everything. Insanely great becomes sanely great, because if it doesn't, things simply come unglued.

Don't get me wrong, nobody at Netscape today can afford to coast, even after the AOL deal; inspired by the success of the IPO and the phenomenal expansion of the Net powered by our browsers and servers, hundreds of companies have sprung up that compete with us in every area. And Netscape time, aka Internet time, speeds all clocks; nine- and six-month product cycles, once inconceivable, are now the industry standard. All the while, Microsoft never sleeps. Jim Barksdale must sometimes think he's worked in the trenches for a lifetime, not four years. But for the "band of brothers" who were there from Day One and are now millionaire legends, life is more livable, but less vivid. If you start your career on the wild ride of a start-up, you may end up addicted to start-ups forever. I know I am.

Of the original engineers who signed on in Urbana-Champaign, Chris Houck and Jon Mittelhauser have moved on, Aleks Totic and Lou Montulli are on leaves of absence, and Eric Bina, cocreator of Mosaic, is still living in Illinois, less involved with the company than before. Jamie Zawinski, our Berkeley "hair" apparent, works mostly at home now and rarely makes the trip down 101. The McCool twins, Mike and Rob, are still there. Aleks has told me he thinks the breakup of the old gang is "sad but necessary." To me, it's simply inevitable. These were young revolutionaries. They set out to overturn the old order and succeeded beyond their wildest dreams. Now their revolution has become everyone's reality, and it would be pretty close to unnatural for them to stay in one place, dreaming the same dreams.

I don't know, and won't try to guess, how much difference money has made to them. Like lava pushing up in the dome of a volcano, sudden personal wealth changes the shape of things. You can swear that you'll go on living the way you did before you got rich, but it's really impossible. If I had made several million dollars before my twenty-fifth birthday, I wonder how the rest of my life would have gone. Probably, like them, I would have gone right on working. That is, after all, what you're used to doing, and your wealth depends on keeping your stock healthy. But eventually you can sell stock, and with money your options multiply; life gets easier in some ways, but far more complex. I've always been glad that I was able to keep my promise to them that they'd all get rich, but I'm not sure I'd want to trade places. Early success can be a decidedly mixed blessing.

D'Anne Schjerning, my gritty secretary and our reluctant den mother, has retired to an easier life. It's hard to believe that she missed being mistreated by me on a daily basis, but there's no accounting for taste. John Doerr has jumped on the fun-house ride he helped create with more triumphs, financing Amazon.com and @Home, which, with Tom Jermolak as CEO, also doubled its offering price on July 11, 1997, its first day on the stock market. John has become such a fixture in Washington, D.C., called there whenever administration officials want to figure out the new technology, that some of his colleagues joke that someday the Democratic ticket will be "Gore and Doerr in 2004."

Money and fame aside, the greatest beneficiary of Netscape's success was the Web itself. A print advertisement or television commercial in which a company's URL isn't shown has become a rarity, like a hand-written letter. A Web site is a given, not only for companies, publications, television shows, organizations, and retailers, but for long-dead rock stars, UFO cultists, conspiracy theorists, Barney, Beanie Babies, and almost anything and anyone else imaginable. Christmas of 1998 was notable as a time when millions of Americans did their shopping while sitting in front of their computers, and Internet stocks pushed the NASDAQ to record levels. The Internet is now a primary information and publishing medium. Among computer users, many people looking for a new or used car disregard newspaper classifieds and turn first to Web search engines. Plenty of CD and book shoppers wouldn't think of leaving the house to do their browsing. And when the Congress wanted the notorious Starr Report put into circulation quickly, they dumped it onto the Internet before sending it to the government printing office. Before 1995, media forecasters talked about a five-hundred-cable-channel future. Now we're rushing toward a million-Web-site world. If scores of us at Netscape got rich, hundreds of other Internet entrepreneurs, inspired by our example, got just as rich or richer. Jeff Bezos, who realized that the Web was a great place to build a virtual bookstore, is worth billions. Jerry Yang and David Filo, two Stanford twenty-something postgrads, decided to pick through the expanding number of Web sites to list the ones they liked, then went public under the aegis of venture capital firm Sequoia Capital in Palo Alto. Now each owns more than a billion dollars' worth of stock. And so on and on. The amount of wealth generated by the post–

Netscape Web is about the biggest thing since King Leopold of Belgium cornered the African rubber trade. Well, actually a lot bigger.

My own wealth has fluctuated since our public offering. On the tail of an executive jet plane I bought not long after August 9, 1995, I put the identifying number 663MN, representing, in millions, what I was theoretically worth at the end of that day. This wasn't bragging, since, until now, few people knew the number's significance. Rather, it's a kind of talisman, a number that reminds me of one of the luckiest days of my life. I won't claim that having a lot more money hasn't made a difference to me—I really can't stand people who tell that colossal whopper. Being able to build a beautiful boat, give up commercial air travel, buy a couple of nice houses, and fly my own helicopter are considerable pleasures. But so is six hours in front of a computer screen, trying to chase down a bug in the software that will control that sailboat. Can money buy happiness? That's a question almost too tedious, and irrelevant, to answer. It certainly increases your range of possibilities, and if you make the right choices, you ought to be, at the very least, more satisfied with life.

I still work hard, and to my regret money doesn't make me any smarter or more likely to be struck by the lightning of great ideas. But now I can invest in good ideas others have, and get involved in the excitement of start-ups without worrying about losing most of my money if things go wrong. I can also have the satisfaction of knowing that the University of New Orleans, where I was part of the Class of '69, is really glad I went there. Also, as an entrepreneur with a track record of three multibillion-dollar start-ups (including Healtheon, which went public in early 1999), I know that the money I've made is a kind of résumé that commands the close attention of others to whatever I'm doing. The question changes from "Why bet on him?" to "Why bet against him?" In that way, money is a lot more than just money. But whatever my personal fortune may be on any given day, I never find it hard to remind myself that as a boy who grew up poor in Plainview, Texas, all I once hoped for was to be able to support myself. While I can say that Netscape would not have happened without me, I know enough not to give myself unqualified credit. Fate always plays the biggest hand in any game. At the end of the 1998 baseball season, a fan sitting in a luxury box in left field at Busch

Stadium in St. Louis happened to catch Mark McGwire's record-setting seventieth home run, a nine-dollar baseball that sold for $3 million. When friends equated catching the historic ball with winning the lottery, the happy fan said it wasn't the same thing at all. "When I bought my ticket, I bought my ticket to go to a baseball game. I wasn't looking to win a prize or anything like that. Yeah, I was lucky, and you have to be lucky in the lottery, but that's where it diverges greatly. I was in the right place at the right time." To which I say, Amen! Of course, I was hoping to win a prize, but that hope wasn't even possible until I realized that I really was in the right place at the right time.

In this book, I have tried to tell the story of how Netscape happened, as I saw it when it was happening, and as I've remembered it since. Because we unleashed such a digital hyperdrive, many of the things I've described already seem to belong to another era, a far-off, almost quaint period, the time before Netscape time. There's now a saying in the industry that one Internet year is the equivalent of seven calendar years, so it's as if more than twenty years have passed since Marc and I exchanged our first e-mail messages.

I once heard an author interviewed about a memoir she had just published. She said that writers tend to assume their memories are the gilt-edged stock that they've put away so they can live off the dividends. Then, when the time comes to cash in, they find out what they own is actually an acre or two of Florida swampland. In other words, memory is rarely as dependable and valuable as we hope it will be. This is my Netscape story, and I've tried to get it right. What went on was powerful, and the emotions of the unfolding events form such a distorting lens that whether my view is always in perfect focus is a question I can't answer. As any historian knows, every version of an event is to some extent unique. All I can say without any question is this: Being present at the creation of Netscape, being one of the major players in the drama, was something like catching a legendary slugger's legendary home run ball: an experience that can never be repeated. To end by paraphrasing a famous beginning: It was the best of times. It was the fastest of times.